LEARNING INTERVENTION

This book explores what learning intervention means in inclusive classroom settings. It provides educational professionals with the knowledge and skills they require to reflect on, and respond to students' individual learning needs, and enables them to choose, implement and evaluate evidence-based strategies for learning intervention.

Taking an ecological perspective, and placing a capability framework at its core, the book considers how *responsive teaching* and *educational casework* combine to create intricate layers of learning intervention, and recommends tailored teaching and support strategies that can be used to address a wide variety of student learning needs. Learning intervention is thus understood in its broadest sense, and educational professionals are equipped with a range of interactive and adaptive strategies to support student learning. Chapters introduce and unpack numerous frameworks for practice, provide an extension to Response to Intervention models, and bring together key evidence-based ideas in an accessible format.

Effective teaching in response to clearly defined learning needs is central to the achievement of all students. *Learning Intervention* will provide future and current educational professionals with the structures, knowledge, insight and skills they need to respond effectively to each and every student.

Jeanette Berman is Associate Professor of Inclusive Education at the University of New England and Principal Fellow (Associate Professor) in Learning Intervention at Melbourne Graduate School of Education, Australia.

Lorraine Graham is foundation Professor of Learning Intervention at the Melbourne Graduate School of Education, she is a Fellow of the International Academy for Research in Learning Disabilities, Australia.

LEARNING INTERVENTION

Educational Casework and Responsive Teaching for Sustainable Learning

Jeanette Berman and Lorraine Graham

Routledge
Taylor & Francis Group

LONDON AND NEW YORK

First published 2018
by Routledge
2 Park Square, Milton Park, Abingdon, Oxon OX14 4RN

and by Routledge
711 Third Avenue, New York, NY 10017

Routledge is an imprint of the Taylor & Francis Group, an informa business

© 2018 Jeanette Berman and Lorraine Graham

British Library Cataloguing in Publication Data
A catalogue record for this book is available from the British Library

Library of Congress Cataloging-in-Publication Data
Names: Berman, Jeanette, editor. Graham, Lorraine, editor, Hattie, John, editor.
Title: Learning intervention: Educational Casework and Responsive
    Teaching for Sustainable Learning
Description: Abingdon, Oxon ; New York, NY : Routledge is an imprint of
the Taylor & Francis Group, an Informa Business, 2018. | Includes
    bibliographical references.
Identifiers: LCCN 2017056939 (print) | LCCN 2018011156 (ebook) | ISBN
    9780203711675 (eb) | ISBN 9781138560338 (hbk) |
    ISBN 9781138560307 (pbk) | ISBN 9780203711675 (ebk)
Subjects: LCSH: Inclusive education—Environmental aspects. | Effective
    teaching—Environmental aspects.
Classification: LCC LC1200 (ebook) | LCC LC1200 .L39 2018 (print) | DDC
    371.9/046—dc23
LC record available at https://lccn.loc.gov/2017056939

ISBN: 978-1-138-56033-8 (hbk)
ISBN: 978-1-138-56030-7 (pbk)
ISBN: 978-0-203-71167-5 (ebk)

Typeset in Bembo
by Apex CoVantage, LLC

For the generations of teachers and learners in our families, and for our students and colleagues, from whom we continue to learn so much.

CONTENTS

FIGURES

TABLES

FOREWORD

So much more is expected from educators today. Classrooms are now more diverse in this globalised world with the percentage of students with special needs increasing from about 4 per cent 15 years ago to closer to 20 per cent today; the curriculum is more crowded; schools are expected to resolve most of society's problems; and it is less clear what schools are preparing students for. The old model asked teachers to teach 'the norm' and to invite specialist teachers in for students who were deaf, blind, autistic, gifted et al. This does not work – if for no other reason than the costs of making these provisions is prohibitive. The 'special' is becoming the 'norm'.

Jeanette Berman and Lorraine Graham tackle this problem by arguing that we need to focus on learning intervention for all students, and that what works for 'special' students can work for all students (although what works for the norm, may not work for the special). This is a breakthrough in thinking and a book that makes this case.

Berman and Graham argue for responsiveness in teaching that is attuned to the individual needs of students; collaboration among teachers to maximise their impact; assessment as a basis for educational casework; deep awareness of students' learning processes and capabilities, and evidence-based design for learning. They springboard from Response to Intervention to describe a model for teaching all students not just those with special needs. This is a critical aspect of the argument in this book; that layers of learning intervention are linked to classroom learning and aimed towards classroom success. Rich ideas indeed.

This is a 'breakthrough' book asking all teachers to use the powerful interventions that we have learnt from special education are effective for all students. A reversal of over 100 years' thinking! Enjoy this book.

Laureate Professor John Hattie
Melbourne Graduate School of Education
October 2017

ACKNOWLEDGEMENTS

We would like to acknowledge the traditional owners of the lands on which we have worked in putting this book together, the Wurundgeri people of the Kulin Nation. The Melbourne Graduate School of Education continues the long tradition of learning and teaching on this country.

Thanks to our postgraduate students in the Master of Learning Intervention in 2016 and 2017 for their feedback on key frameworks used in this book. We would particularly like to acknowledge the students who came to an additional group feedback session: Jacinta Conway, Sue Erdal, Tricia Christie, Bec McGrath, Ellen Steele, Cheryl Cai Ying Yee, Claire Stubbings, Lauren Maidment and Margot Spence.

Thank you also to Chris Corbel, who travelled with us as we completed our work. His considered responses to our ideas have been greatly valued.

1

INTRODUCTION TO LEARNING INTERVENTION

Everything we do with children acts to intervene in their development and learning. Such action begins with parents using activities of talking, reading or singing to a baby growing inside the womb. As soon as a baby is born people interact and this is the beginning of social interaction as intervention in that person's lifelong learning journey. This activity develops into formal instruction that is provided in education settings.

Some of the people intervening in children's development and learning take this role by virtue of their relationship as parent, grandparent, auntie or uncle, or older brother or sister of a child. Others are professionals, with tertiary education and qualifications and accreditation that have prepared them for formal, strategic intervention in students' lives. The distinction between these two very different, yet similar, roles is highlighted through the definition of intentional teaching (Leggett & Ford, 2013) by which teachers activate and nurture active learning for young children and which is used to distinguish early childhood education from child minding.

In order to ensure that all students have the opportunity to benefit from such intentional responsive teaching education professionals undertake formal *intervention* of varying kinds. In this book we will explore what learning intervention is in formalised educational settings. We show how such intervention needs to be flexible and adaptable in order to respond to the variability of learning needs of individuals or groups of learners. Intervention is not doing things *to* people. It is not coercive, nor is it training. Instead it is about using expertise in child development and learning to provide opportunities for learning that best meet the learning needs of students at any particular time. It is also about using interactive, adaptive strategies that help the learner to make the most of the learning opportunities.

In particular, we will consider two processes of learning intervention, *responsive teaching* and *educational casework,* which have different perspectives: the former has a focus on a classroom of individuals, and the latter a focus on individuals who are members of a class. These processes are examined in detail in the next chapter.

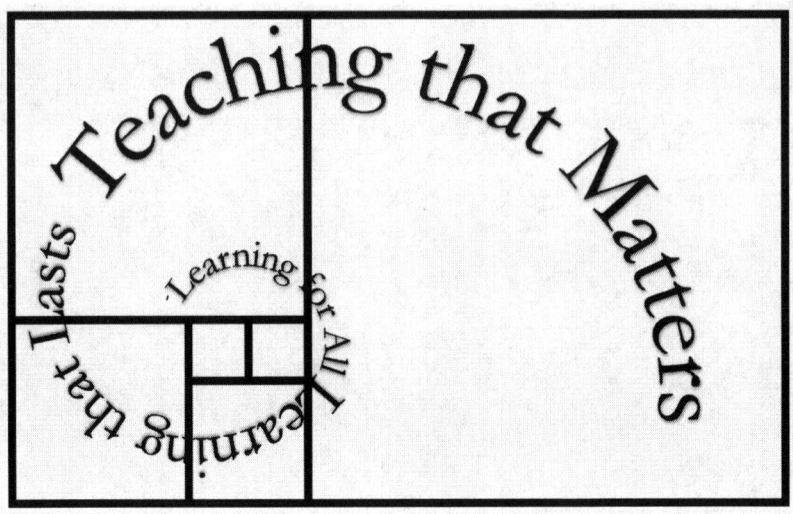

FIGURE 1.1 Sustainable learning

Source: Graham, Berman & Bellert, 2015.

Sustainable learning

Learning intervention supports sustainable learning – learning for all, learning that lasts and teaching that matters (Figure 1.1; Graham, Berman & Bellert, 2015). Learning is holistic, and an important part of the development of learners so they can fully participate in life culturally, physically, psychologically and spiritually – and in connection to community (Royal Australian and New Zealand College of Psychiatrists, n.d.). As far as possible, all of us use the capabilities we develop as children and adolescents to live flourishing lives marked by positive emotions, positive relationships, engagement, meaning and accomplishment (Seligman, 2011). We alter, refine and renew the capabilities throughout our lives to match the contexts within which we are living, working, relating and learning. Sustainable learners are those who are able to continue to learn and adapt throughout their lives by drawing on their capabilities for learning.

Learning for all

As education has become more formal and teaching has developed into a profession, the community responsibility for children's learning has changed somewhat. The natural human interactions of teaching and learning that are embedded in our families and their cultural and social worlds have been transformed into formal education. The role of teaching is now sometimes seen to be exclusive to those who have met the qualification and registration requirements of our society, and learning intervention is implemented with considerable structure and contrivance. This book is about learning intervention within that education system, that responds to the learning needs of all students through the professional activity of not only classroom teachers, but also other professionals with deeper or different expertise who can contribute to strengthening what is happening in teaching and learning in contemporary inclusive schools. There are a number of important considerations in relation to inclusive schools that are presented here as a foundation for considering professional practice in learning intervention.

Groups of learners in schools are increasingly diverse and display a large range of achievement even across what were previously thought to be homogeneous groups of students of the same age. Schools also include students who have disabilities or who experience significant learning difficulties. The enormous variability in the development of humans needs to be recognised and responded to by those who are teaching. The *diversity* of human development and of learning means that not all our students will follow expected patterns or typical rates of learning, and therefore inclusive education systems need to be responsive to the needs of all learners.

In a similar way, curriculum has increasingly recognised that learning is not just about fixed bodies of knowledge and skills. Instead, opportunities to learn have become more diverse and interactive over time, allowing learners to respond actively and authentically to teaching. Whereas once all students were expected to respond in the same way by sitting examinations or listening and then producing short answers or essays in particular formats, we now accept a range of responses that demonstrate learning.

Increasingly, responsibility is being passed to students to manage their own learning and behaviours in classrooms. Teacher-work is less about controlling responses, although the skills of establishing behavioural expectations and maintaining them are still integral to good teaching. Instead, teachers are proactively seeking to increase students' responsibility for their own behaviour and learning.

Learning that lasts

Knowledge and skills taught in schools have changed considerably from the fixed body of knowledge of the early 20th century, due to the explosion of knowledge and the constant, almost overwhelming, access to information that we now encounter. The focus of education has, subsequently, turned towards learning processes and capabilities because these can be used as needed across the curriculum to approach many different types of learning tasks.

The challenge for educational settings is to provide students with the foundation for managing their lives in a dynamic world. As an example, a recent advertisement stated that students currently entering the workforce could expect to have up to 30 jobs in a lifetime. This means an almost constant demand to adapt to new work circumstances and roles. 'Learning that lasts' is learning for life and learning for the future, the demands of which are not yet known. As it is impossible to predict what jobs, careers and pastimes are going to be popular in the future, schools cannot provide opportunities to learn all future knowledge and skills. What can be provided,

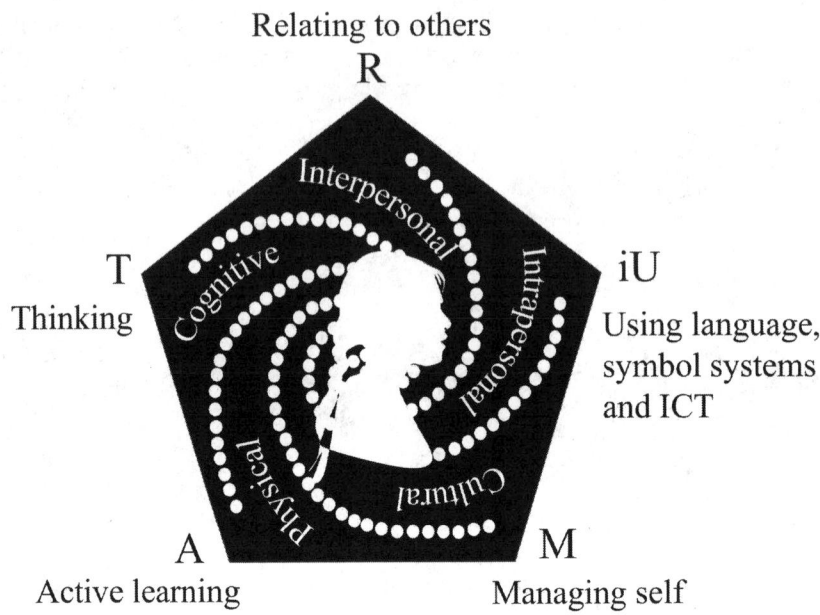

FIGURE 1.2 ATRiUM capabilities and five dimensions of human learners

Source: Adapted from Graham, Berman & Bellert, 2015.

however, is a focus on developing the psychological processes that humans need in order to continue to learn and adapt to whatever the future holds. In this book we are using the ATRiUM model (Figure 1.2; Graham, Berman & Bellert, 2015) of human development and capabilities for learning in our consideration of responsive teaching and educational casework for learning intervention.

Sustainable learning involves all five of the ATRiUM capabilities: active learning, thinking, relating to others, using language, symbol systems and ICT; and managing self; and, draws on the adaptability and flexibility of humans in an increasingly uncertain world.

Teaching that matters

Teachers have the enormous responsibility of contributing to the development of the processes of human functioning for each of their students so that individuals can become successfully intelligent, that is, able to apply analytical capabilities practically, creatively and with wisdom throughout life (Sternberg, 1997; Sternberg & Grigorenko, 2007). When learning is visibly at the centre of everything that goes on in the classroom, teachers and students sustain each other's learning. Learning in the 21st century needs to be not only lifelong, but also 'life-wide', with a focus on the capabilities of individual learners as they engage and interact with their wider world and respond to the demands of new careers, new technologies, cultural shifts, and rapid and unpredictable change.

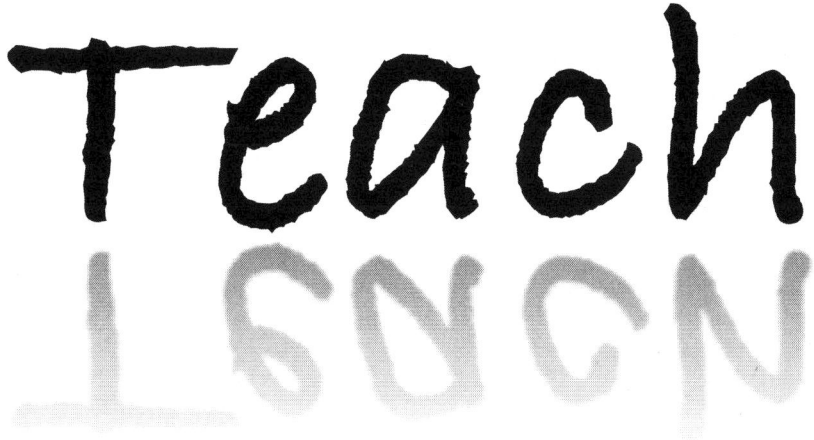

FIGURE 1.3   For many learners, teach does not necessarily mean learn

Inclusion of all learners in a classroom depends on each student's learning needs being met, and on learning happening through effective teaching. Although many learners will achieve academically irrespective of the teaching provided, it is a teacher's intentional activity focused on activating learning that makes a difference for many students; skilful teaching matters enormously to learners who experience any sort of difficulty. The sophisticated responsive work of professional teachers really makes a difference for learners, and it is this type of teaching that is the focus of this book.

There is a meme that shows a reflection of the letters in 'Teach' that can be read as 'Learn', as in Figure 1.3. The calligraphic design, that needs distortion to work, reflects the idea that to teach is to activate learning and that these are two sides of the one activity. This idea of teaching and learning depending on one another is ancient and is evident in a single word meaning both teaching and learning in some languages, for example, 'ako', in Te Reo Māori (language). These calligraphic and linguistic blurrings of 'teach' and 'learn' are significant because until teaching translates into learning, it is not effective teaching.

Instead of these activities reflecting each other, in this book we use the notions of overlap and dependence. Learning can happen independently of teaching. Many students learn irrespective of the teaching they receive, as they have effective learning strategies and have access to opportunities to learn. However, a key issue for learning intervention is that, for many students, learning will not happen unless the teaching responds to their specific learning needs.

Intervention for sustainable learning within families

While our focus in this book is the formal learning intervention undertaken by education professionals, it is important to remember the role of informal learning intervention, particularly within the family. Traditionally teaching to support child development occurred in families and extended family communities, drawing on adults and older children to support the learning of all younger children. Group responsibility is evident in this situation and the child draws on the teaching of a range of people. When one teacher is not immediately available there are others to engage with. Such teaching in everyday life is often incidental rather than deliberately planned, but in many ways it is naturally intentional, as parents and older relatives consciously engage with a view to teaching for everyday learning.

We are social beings and we strive to engage socially and to have influence on others through our interactions. This influence includes sharing new information and new ideas, prompting higher-order thinking as well as activating and facilitating a thirst for new knowledge and skills. This focus on the whole child and on capabilities for life is inherent in the teaching that happens in informal settings, in homes and communities as parents and family members work to strengthen capacities that are needed for life.

Much of the teaching of the capabilities for sustainable learning is grounded in the transmission of family culture, often with parents teaching in ways they have been taught, and using family expectations around behaviour and learning. At the same time, older family members engage in their own lifelong learning journeys, while they become involved in the learning journeys of their children, grandchildren, nieces and nephews. In contrast to previous beliefs, adult humans are not fully mature people who have finished learning. Instead, they continue to learn as they engage with younger family members in teaching and learning exchanges.

All of us experience childhood learning as children, and then again as parents or older relatives. Our children's lives are the second period of time in which we intensively experience child development and practise teaching. Many parents say they wish they knew then (when their children were young) what they know now about child development and learning. But that is never the case, and so it is important to have multiple generations of people supporting the development and learning of young people where possible. Indigenous models of child rearing that explain traditional practices (e.g., Poananga, 2011) emphasise this reliance on multiple generations to support young people's learning.

Families teach children foundation capabilities for what is needed throughout their lives by shaping expectations and providing opportunities for the child to grow as a complex multidimensional (e.g., cultural, cognitive, physical, intrapersonal and interpersonal) being. Families foster the development of skills and knowledge within all of the ATRiUM capabilities (Graham, Berman & Bellert, 2015) described above, so that children become active learners, thinkers, socially related people, competent users of language and symbol systems and ICT, and managers of their lives.

Active learning

Adults who continue to learn actively in everyday life model sustainable learning (Graham, Berman & Bellert, 2015) and lifelong growth mindsets (Dweck, 2006) for their children. Families can establish and nurture expectations around sustainable learning that influence the learning of their children at school. They draw the younger members of the family into learning activities, and perpetually learn together. For such families, this love of learning becomes a key dimension of everyday life, of holiday experiences and the stuff of career pathways. They actively pursue learning opportunities for their children, follow curiosity and interest, and spend leisure time at places that promote learning. Based on an understanding of the impact of experience in social and cultural settings for human development and learning, such strategic travel and physical, musical and social activities are inherent to the family life of sustained learners.

Active learners are people who see and experience the transformation that learning brings. They also know that learning is activated through social and cultural activities, and that this leads to individual learning and growth. Such active learners are also aware of what experiences support their learning, and how to make the most of those experiences.

Thinking

Thinking is the primary tool of transformation and families teach the basics of thinking skills to their children in many ways. These range from everyday modelling of thinking such as 'thinking out loud' and transparent problem solving, to higher-order thinking activities such as cryptic crosswords, board games, discussions around politics and current events, and critiquing literary, creative arts and multimedia experiences. Parents also provide books and are seen to read and discuss what they read and related information. Exploring new ideas and other people's opinions through research on the Internet also provides lots of opportunities for being aware of others' thinking. Parent vocations may provide opportunities for children to have access to higher-order thinking vicariously or by being invited to contribute to work and life problem solving. Similarly, household routines, such as shopping, arranging the home, building houses, looking after pets and planning travel, all provide opportunities for families to engage in collaborative thinking and to expose the thinking that goes into everyday lived experiences.

The most evident strategy that parents use to extend and shape thinking is through their questioning of their children, since thinking is altered through sharing. The use of questioning is also evident in young children who often go through phases of asking many, many questions about how the world works, why things are as they are, or why things aren't different. These questions can be about everyday ideas and concepts, but also about intellectual, philosophical or scientific concepts that are contained in school curricula, arise in response to the content of documentaries or emerge after family experiences.

Some parents are expert at linking their child's new ideas to prior knowledge and experience, and to shaping children's attention and perception. Based on many shared experiences, they know exactly how to draw the past and present together in thinking. They may recall previously discussed information or experiences and connect these to newly introduced information or experiences. Many parents seem to have a built-in sense of their children's current levels of thinking and capacity for new ideas. They are also in the position of being able to reintroduce an idea that was previously not able to be understood, but could be now. A sense of readiness for deeper thinking, and the use of many chances to extend thinking can be inherent in many family conversations.

Relating to others

The first relationships that children engage in are with family members; these are the relationships that will continue for life. It is within these relationships that children learn to give and receive love and care, to take turns, to share, to read and express emotions, to share meaning; all of the things we do together as humans.

A crucial part of these early relationships is the negotiation of teaching–learning roles with family members. These are fluid roles that alter depending on the content of teaching and learning, and who happens to be the more competent other at the time. As children grow they can become the teacher at times, and explore how to behave in both roles. This experience and the expectations for what it is like to act as a learner, and a teacher, transfers into more formalised relationships with teachers in educational settings. In these relationships learners need to be able to seek assistance, to ask questions, to respond to questions, to justify thinking, to take risks in proposing ideas and trying new skills, and to express their emotional needs.

For children who have had experience of successful parent to child interactions that result in learning, the transfer of expectations around relating to others in formal teaching and learning is likely to be effective. However, this can be complicated and many children experience a considerable shift in expectations within relationships when they start school; they need to navigate these expectations in order to be able to relate effectively in this new setting.

The other type of relating to others that is pertinent in formal education settings is that of relating to peers. Since our education system groups learners together by age it is imperative that children can relate to a large group of others of the same age. Skills for this may be taught within families, and further shaped in early childhood settings as children grow and become more conscious and deliberate in their interactions with others. Their capability with language and in managing themselves affects this considerably.

Using language, symbol systems and ICT

Language is used as part of everything families do, and is the target of learning in all early interactions. Families use considerable skills to extend language development by modelling, speaking for their children, asking targeted questions, reading structured language from books, and interpreting word and sentence approximations expertly. They also provide opportunities for children to demonstrate their more proficient vocabulary to other family members in person or on the phone or through video calls. Their single words, strings of words (two words, three words, nine syllables, etc.) and then full sentences are shown off and analysed, demonstrating developing language. Children's responses to instructions are also analysed by the family to demonstrate their level of understanding of language. It is accepted that language development takes many years and that opportunities for learning need to be provided by families and communities to support the long process of development of capability.

Many families and communities use more than one spoken language in their everyday activities and many children develop skills in not only multiple languages, but also in switching languages depending on who is the other partner in conversation. Some children even become translators for their families in contexts that do not rely on the family's primary language.

Capability with reading and writing of our language takes even longer to develop and is a primary target of formal education where it is systematically taught throughout the 13 years of school. Exposure to, and use of, written language varies considerably between families and some children come to school with years of engaging with books and beginning to write letters, words and 'stories', while others have minimal experience.

Other symbol systems that are used by families become available to younger members of the families in the context of shared activities. The number system is used variably in families and is usually coloured by the attitudes and emotional responses to mathematics of parents. Musical literacy is an important part of the lives of many families, but never seen in others. Some children also experience other scientific or vocational symbol systems within their family lives.

Families also vary greatly in their experiences with information communication technology. Many children come to school with considerable skill in using computers as tools for many different activities including learning, while others do not have access, and do not see family members using these for anything other than social connection.

Managing self

Families support and nurture children as they grow and learn, with the aim that the children becoming increasingly independent and self-managing as learners. Families set expectations for appropriate behaviours for the many contexts within which children are expected to engage, from home to other family members' homes, to neighbours' homes and community settings. These behaviours are culturally determined and have considerable expectations around them for different-aged people. Some of the expectations align with those expected in formal education settings while others will be vastly different. Just as children learn to manage the changes of expectations about their behaviour in a range of settings, they need to do this in relation to expectations of more formal education settings. We see behaviour as much more than training; we know that to manage behaviour involves regulation of emotions, being able to read situations successfully and to deal with the emotions generated in order to select appropriate behaviours at any time.

Families also support other aspects of human functioning that we increasingly manage as we grow, including managing the self in relationships, managing negative thinking, managing initiative and risk taking, managing the frustration of failure and related needs for persistence and diligence, and developing planning and organisation skills. A contradictory aspect of this capability of managing self is that it is not only about managing the self, but also about how to share management with others and being able to manage when others are in charge.

Ecological influences on teaching and learning

As we consider the dynamic growth of the five ATRiUM capabilities for learning, we need to acknowledge and make sense of the context within which each learner engages. Social, political, economic and cultural influences (Zubrick, Williams, Silburn & Vimpani, 2000) affect families, communities and schools. A useful way to think about these influences is through the notion of complex ecologies. Bronfenbrenner (1977) provided a foundation for teachers to think about teaching and learning in terms of ecosystems derived from study of geographical, geological, biological and zoological systems in our world. This kind of thinking is applicable to education settings within which humans interact with each other and with their environments. The ecological representation used in this book is shown in Figure 1.4.

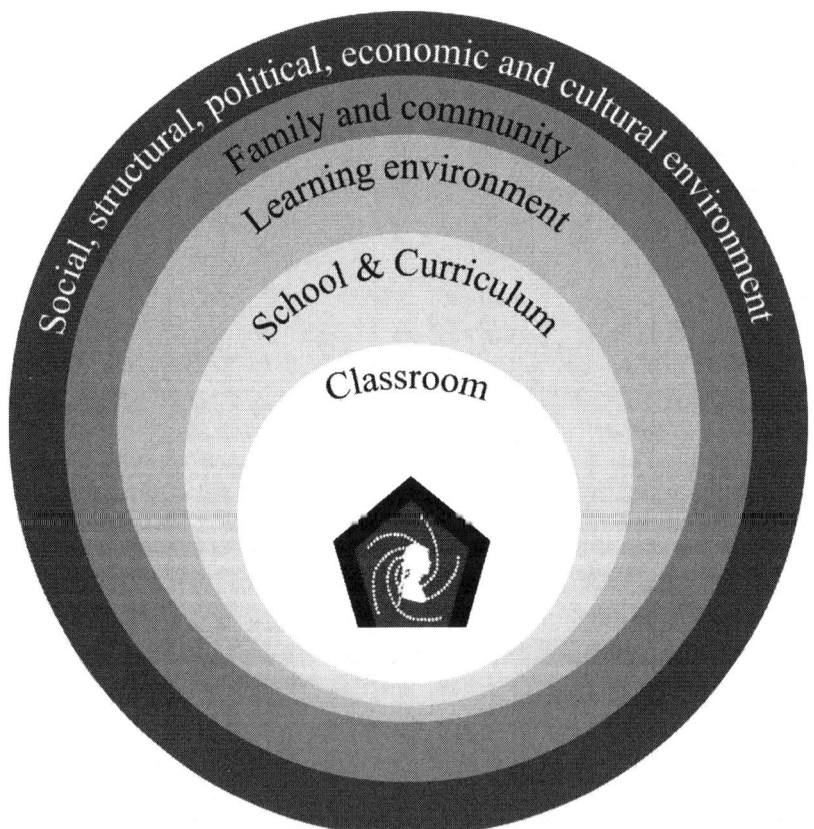

FIGURE 1.4 Ecological influences on learning and teaching

Source: Adapted from Graham, Berman & Bellert, 2015.

The dimensions in this model clearly demonstrate an ecological way of considering students as holistic learners. It conceptualises learners as developing humans, who engage in social and cultural activity to continually grow their capabilities for learning. Learners respond to aspects of learning environments and to influences from family and community.

Another representation of this ecological model is provided from within a research study into factors supporting successful Māori learners from one iwi (tribe) of central northern Aotearoa New Zealand (Figure 1.5). The layers of influence are defined by Māori communities: whānau (family); hapū (subtribal group); iwi (tribe); and local, national and global contexts.

From this study it was determined that successful Māori learners develop strong cultural identities, and emotional resources that allow them to take risks in learning and in life. Many students who are part of involuntary minority groups (such as colonised Indigenous peoples or refugees) find living in their cultural community and the world of schools and classrooms a huge challenge. For example, the five key factors supporting success for Māori young people at school emphasise the importance of family and community influences. These were found to be: a positive sense of Māori identity; a sense of courage and resilience; a sense of place; a sense of two worlds; and being nurtured into succeeding in both worlds by their whānau (family) (Macfarlane, Webber, McRae & Cookson-Cox, 2014). One way responsive teachers take these layers of influence into account is by drawing on evidence from research into influences within learning ecologies, as well as actively seeking insights from families in order to plan the most appropriate teaching for each student's learning journey.

The chronological dimension of learning is central to the Ka Awatea model because ancient worlds are acknowledged as continuing to influence today's world as well as the future world. This temporal dimension helps us to think in terms of

Te Ao Tawhito — Ancient world   Te Ao Hurihuri — Today's world   Te Ao Tūroa — Future world

FIGURE 1.5 Sociocultural model from Ka Awatea

Source: Derived from Macfarlane, Webber, McRae & Cookson-Cox, 2014.

individual learning journeys, as well as journeys for our families, communities, the nation and the world. This theme of the past influencing the present, and thereby the future, is a key dimension in Indigenous ways of seeing, and refers not only to the personal experiences of young learners, but also to generational experiences for communities of learners. For example, many Indigenous learners bring with them generations of family and community responses to colonisation and the accompanying education systems that have profound influences on their active learning in schools (Fitzpatrick & Berman, 2016). In light of this dimension, the history of a country will have an effect on each individual and needs to be acknowledged.

Within individual learning journeys, many students who are the focus of educational casework have had experiences of unsuccessful or frustrated learning, and thus bring with them resistance to being supported by learning intervention. Their previous learning experiences influence their present engagement and affect future success. Additionally, there are often generational experiences of unsuccessful engagement with schools that accompany many students. All life experiences, and how we respond to these experiences (as a group and individually), shape our continuing learning journeys.

Students usually spend 13 years in schools. Add on a few years in early childhood settings and in tertiary education, and this is life for two decades. This experience is central to who we are and who we become throughout life. Successful learning experiences contribute to considerable change in how discouraged learners see themselves. The profound impacts that occur on self-efficacy through success are a core element of effective learning intervention.

In terms of learning that lasts, human development used to be seen as something relevant only to children; after becoming physically mature we were all fully made and somehow complete. Now human development is considered as lifelong; we are still developing throughout the total lifespan based on our experiences with our world. The findings of developmental research over the past century or so have organised considerable evidence about the patterns of human maturation. This research evidence has been analysed in different ways to show trends, and the typical or normal pathways of development, as well as variation across the range of development that is present in the whole population. Research has also explored distinctive patterns that are found in subgroups of the population, such as with individuals who have identified disabilities or who are gifted and talented.

Observations about human development have been gathered in many ways: experiments; child studies; case studies; cross-sectional sampling and correlational research; longitudinal and sequential studies on the whole human, or on tiny strands of development. The data from this research have been gathered through physiological measurements, observations, assessment tasks, reports and self-reports to allow us to anticipate child, adolescent and adult development and predict what developmental pathways generally look like.

Students may have gifts, talents or increased sensitivities (hyper-abilities) or they may have lower than usual ability levels (hypo-abilities). There are many reasons that individuals develop different profiles of strength and weakness, including their genetic make-up, in-utero and birth experiences, general health, opportunities to learn, accident and trauma. It is vital for teachers to have confidence that everyone can learn and deserves the best situations in which to learn and to flourish. The teacher's role is to remove as many barriers as possible so that all students have the best possible opportunities to learn.

Even so, many people's experiences of difficulty learning in school have lifelong implications and may lead to individuals putting in place compensatory strategies throughout their adult lives. Such strategies include employing people to do reading and writing for them, or pairing up with partners or colleagues who have a complementary set of abilities and skills. The lesson from these outcomes is that even though the goal is for every individual in inclusive classrooms to be independently competent in every ATRiUM capability, in reality humans cooperate to make the most of each person's skills and talents. Often the key to this is a high level of self-awareness and the self-management capability to make it possible to set up supportive circumstances.

The need for intervention to have impact across all the contexts within which any learner functions is inherent to the ecological framework and the traditional notion of *transfer* of learning. As well, any learning intervention would also ideally have an impact across time, into the future for the learner. *Maintenance* of performance of particular skills or knowledge is therefore also a key construct in learning intervention. These two notions, derived from special education and behavioural psychology, are inherent in our definition of sustainable learning, which aims for transformation through learning that can be carried across contexts and time within learning journeys. In order to activate sustainable learning, it is the teaching that really matters; teaching that is provided in response to careful consideration of learning needs, with a clear aim of developing capabilities so that all learners become increasingly responsible for their achievement.

From special to inclusive education

The focus of learning intervention is to facilitate the learning of all at an appropriate rate and to accelerate learning for those who are experiencing learning difficulties. Over time the locus of this endeavour has moved from special education to inclusive schools. Learning intervention for students with learning difficulties or disabilities has traditionally been the responsibility of a segregated section of the education system in special education schools or units. Special education is still alive and well in parts of our education system even within systems that present themselves as inclusive. Its viability has been influenced by many factors, however, and is managed differently by different communities.

Special education began with special schools for students with physical or sensory impairments, who were non-ambulatory, blind or deaf, and who could not access teaching in traditional classrooms. These special schools were set up when the system and community response to the mismatch between teaching and learning needs was to provide a different learning setting rather than try to change the current setting. Many early special schools were set up by charities, and were later taken over when it became widely accepted that the education of all students was the responsibility of education systems.

As more families chose to send their children with disabilities to local community schools at the end of the 20th century, the numbers of students in these special schools decreased, making many of them unviable as separate institutions. In some communities there was deliberate restructuring to move special classes into regular schools, or to disband separate settings altogether. This integration or mainstreaming of students previously enrolled in special schools was managed in very different ways. As a result there are, in many communities, no alternatives to local schools. Instead responsive teaching and educational casework by other professionals in these schools respond to student learning needs. However, in larger cities there are still special schools and students may be transported considerable distances to attend these. Families and educational caseworkers often spend considerable time weighing up options for school enrolment before having time to work together to respond to learning needs.

At the same time, increasing numbers of children are being diagnosed with conditions such as Autism Spectrum Conditions (ASCs), and strong lobby groups around these children have advocated for special classes and schools that have become more common in recent years. Such classes have been established on the assumption that there is a different type of effective teaching for children who have ASCs than for other students, and they will be catered for more appropriately in a separate setting.

Most education systems present themselves as being inclusive, yet they continue to have special education as an integral part of that system. Decisions around which school to attend, as well as continued reluctance from many schools to enrol students who are 'special', continue to take up a lot of the time and energy of education professionals. Arguments continue about whether learners should be sorted and separated, and it is not uncommon to hear statements like "inclusion doesn't work". However, since inclusion means catering for the learning needs of all, by definition it *does* work. If it is not working, it is not inclusion. Instead it is mainstreaming; putting students in mainstream education settings without necessarily making appropriate provisions for resourcing or changes to make the setting responsive to the needs of students.

There are a number of students for whom schools 'do not work' and they are often not those with identified disabilities. Rather they are students who have been discouraged by a mismatch between their learning needs and the nature of the teaching provided, or who are dealing with much more important complexities of life that include aspects such as family illness or violence, trauma and abuse, neglect and poverty. All students are influenced by many factors including their family and community, the nature of the learning environment, and how they individually and within their family and peer group respond to their world experiences.

There are many case studies of students who enjoyed a wonderful education in both special education and inclusive education. The shape of education will continue to be influenced by politics and community groups and local decisions about the structure of educational settings. As the nature of education changes it is important to focus on the relationships and interactions between different settings and to take these into account when exploring educational casework and responsive teaching.

In this book we are advocating responsiveness in teaching and in educational casework in order to focus closely on the individual needs of students who are not achieving as well as anticipated, whether it is through inherent developmental characteristics, or influences from other layers of their worlds. Collaboration between classroom teachers and any other professionals who can provide input into managing the most effective learning journeys for all students is essential. There are many ways to integrate classroom expertise with other deeper, or different, expertise in order to ensure the best possible decisions and outcomes for every learner.

To summarise, prior to the impact of inclusive education over the last 30 years in Western countries, 'learning for all' was provided through special education programs. This meant categorising children and placing them in separate educational settings, such as schools for children with sensory impairment, or intellectual disability, or high and complex needs. As inclusion has become the guiding ethos of many countries and education systems, 'learning for all' has changed shape. Instead of trying to design different settings for different groups of students, it is based on the assumption that all learners need different types of teaching at times and can be flexibly grouped together to receive what they need. The goal now is to provide responsive education within all settings to meet the needs of the wide range of learners who are within every community.

Intervention for sustainable learning in inclusive schools

Important assumptions for learning intervention are associated with an inclusive approach to schooling. Instead of reacting to student learning difficulties and classifying learners, then allocating them to alternative specialist programs, we deliberately focus on making learning accessible for all learners and actively remove potential barriers to learning. We strengthen classroom teaching by building in practices that have been shown to be most effective. We increase our focus on individual learning needs and responsiveness to teaching. We strengthen classroom teaching with collaboration through educational casework practice and we provide intervention in overlapping layers to complement classroom teaching.

The focus of intervention in casework can be thought of in a number of different ways. Traditionally, learning intervention has been focused on remediating learners' deficits, with assumptions that once skills and knowledge have been demonstrated in intervention settings they will naturally be transferred to the classroom. Alternatively, students have been placed in other educational settings, special schools or classes, within which the aim has been to meet all their needs. Education systems use a variety of classifications to define deficits to be remediated, and require evidence of significant deficits in order for students to have access to educational casework and intervention. Despite the context of more inclusive education and attempts to be less categorical, education systems still use categories to organise learning intervention for students with special education needs and disabilities (SEND) (Department for Education, 2014) or identified disabilities and named learning difficulties (New Zealand Ministry of Education, 2000).

Behind these categories there is considerable focus on learning needs that are defined in terms of access to learning opportunities. For the purposes of this book, we use the ATRiUM capabilities, within the ecology shown in Figure 1.4, as the framework for defining the focus of learning intervention. Behaviours that support learning are defined in this framework. We centre the ATRiUM capabilities as learning processes, within cycles of teaching, and then position them within learning environments, family and community influences and, lastly, within the wider social, structural, cultural, political and economic context. Although any of these influences can be in need of change, the focus of educational casework is usually on the interactions of the learner with the teacher and with the learning environment. Learning intervention is also explicitly aimed at accelerating learning and development by providing responsive, targeted and intense evidence-based learning opportunities and teaching strategies for learners who have experienced difficulties. Three of the most significant of these learning opportunities and strategies are related to universal effective classroom teaching, prevention and early intervention, and educational casework.

Universal effective classroom teaching

Through effective classroom practices, such as Universal Design for Learning (Meyer, Rose & Gordon, 2014; Rose, 2000) and responsive differentiation (Tomlinson, 2003), inclusive teachers deliberately focus on making the curriculum accessible for all learners by removing potential barriers to learning. Such inclusive classroom approaches aim to improve the effect of teaching from the ground up and thus prevent learning delays, learning difficulties and disordered learning. As we will see below, increasing the capacity of students to drive their learning, and building the capacity of families to support their children's learning, is also a focus of preventative approaches that acknowledge the shared power for learning that lies within the team of students, teachers and families.

Provision of appropriate learning opportunities and use of the most suitable teaching strategies are at the heart of effective teaching. Usually this is designed and happens within a whole class context as represented in Figure 1.6, with one teacher and many students. Although this seems to be a very simplistic representation, it is a starting point for considering many aspects of effective learning intervention with both the class and individual learners in mind. Teachers who are successful in including students with disabilities tend to see all of their students as having individual needs (Shaddock et al., 2007). They focus on a class of individual learners. In Figure 1.6 each of these students and the teacher are all represented by an adaptation of the ATRiUM pentagon to emphasise the multidimensionality of humans in classrooms.

In a classroom many interactions are between one teacher and a group of students. Although interactions with individual learners seem to be incidental and

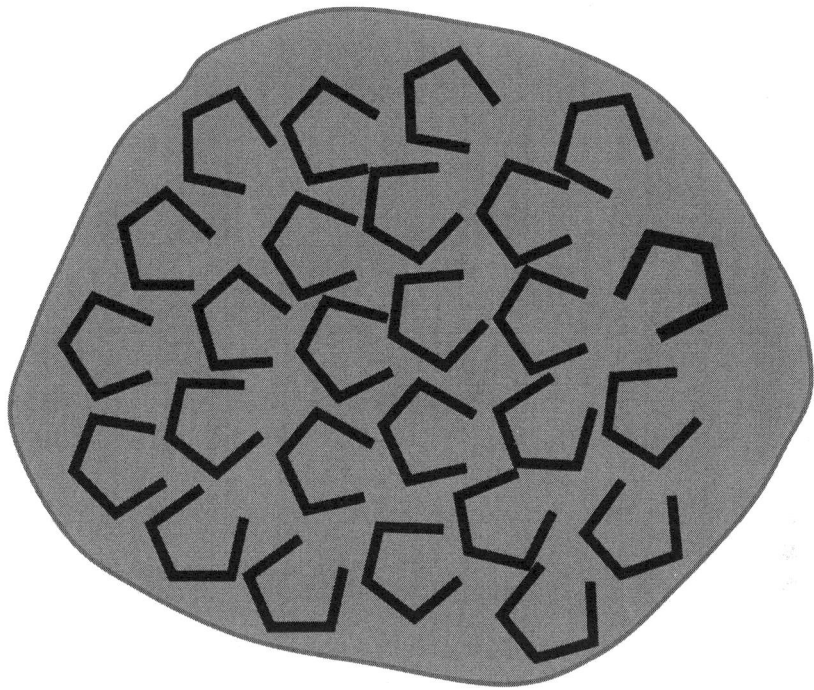

FIGURE 1.6 A responsive teacher's focus on a class of individual learners

happen in the complex busy classroom, they are still central to the learning experience of each student and deserve to be carefully considered. This can be seen by focusing on an individual student (Figure 1.7), which shows how the interactions between that student and the teacher are a mix of the teacher's strategies and the learning strategies put into play by the student.

Both the teacher and the learner draw on their capabilities to support their contribution to the teaching–learning interactions that occur around a learning opportunity. In this representation the interactions are direct and reciprocal and focused closely around the learning opportunity. However, in a complex classroom these will be much more blurred and affected by the many other interactions between the teacher and other students, and between students. While many teaching strategies will be aimed at multiple students, each student experiences these in a particular, individual way. The interactions between teacher and student, which are important in the enacting of specific teaching strategies, are unpacked more comprehensively in Chapter 10.

Prevention and early intervention

Providing the most effective universal instruction and responsive teaching is as much a preventative and early intervention approach as it is about intervention.

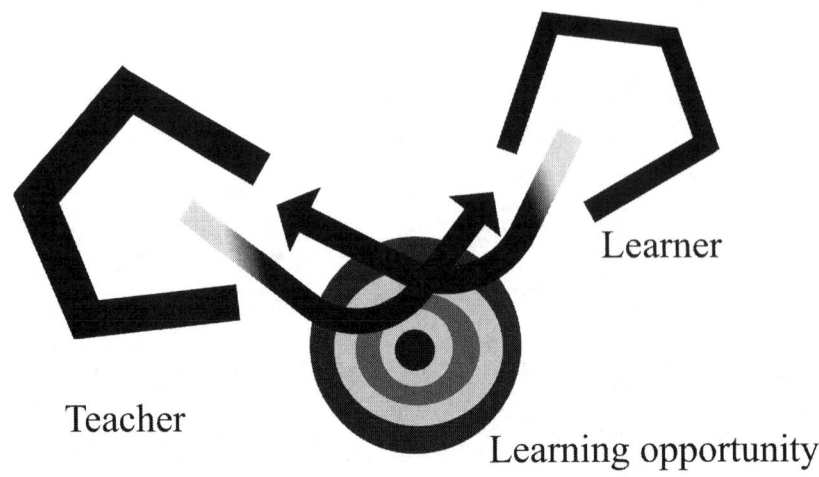

FIGURE 1.7 Teacher–student interactions around a learning opportunity

Prevention and early intervention are explicit in the Response to Intervention (RtI) framework that has grown out of the legislative system in the United States (US). This framework aims to provide intervention in learning through changes in teaching as soon as a need is recognised (Fletcher & Vaughan, 2009; Fuchs & Fuchs, 2006). RtI contrasts with previous US models in special education that required substantial assessment processes and gathered evidence of a Learning Disability (LD) as a deficit within the learner, in order for the student to be eligible for any changes in teaching to be put in place. Often this assessment process informally considered the nature of the learning opportunities the student had experienced. This crucial consideration is now specifically built into RtI, since it aims to understand students' responses to evidence-based instruction. When a student has an unexpected underachievement despite good teaching, or is not responsive to higher intensity intervention, then issues of inherent learning 'disabilities' are explored. However, in this instance the diagnosis of LD is not needed to access intervention, as was necessary in the past.

Instead, promotion, prevention and early intervention (PPEI) now happen irrespective of diagnoses. This is based on the premise that if we are proactive and increase awareness and understanding, we can prevent or intervene early in relation to difficulties in learning, behaviour or mental wellbeing. Promotion and prevention are now included with intervention to capture the notion that if we do PPEI well, there will be less need for the highly structured, expensive intervention that is required when learners experience significant difficulties, disabilities or mental illness (Neil & Christensen, 2009).

Effective universal teaching and early intervention to prevent learning and behavioural difficulties are based on assumptions that the reasons for difficulties are a function of the combination of learner and learning environment, which includes the teaching being offered. This focus on the interaction between learner and learning environment is a distinct move away from the traditional special education and psychological intervention focus on finding and defining deficits in the learner, which assumed that the opportunity to learn has been appropriate. Immediate intervention aims to prevent learning difficulties that may develop because of inadequate teaching. In the context of behaviour, for example, the *Positive Behaviour Supports* (PBS) model (Carr, Dunlap, Horner, Koegel & Turnbull, 2002), is about preventing behaviour problems, by teaching positive behaviours for learning and responding to behavioural difficulties early. This is an example of promotion, prevention and early intervention enacted systematically.

Educational casework

To complement responsive classroom teaching, educational casework is practised in many education systems to support more focused individual assessment and intervention. Educational casework is carried out in schools and outside schools by teachers with specialist qualifications or roles, and by other professionals involved in child development and education.

A close focus on an individual learner, through casework, is usually a reaction to a perceived significant delay or disordered pattern of development, or a diagnosed condition or disability. However, in inclusive schools, there is not, as in traditional special education models, a separation of the educational casework and subsequent intervention from the classroom teaching. Instead, educational casework provides a different lens that aims to complement and strengthen the responsive classroom teaching and thus the learning experiences and outcomes for an individual learner. In the remaining chapters of this book we develop and apply the frameworks introduced above.

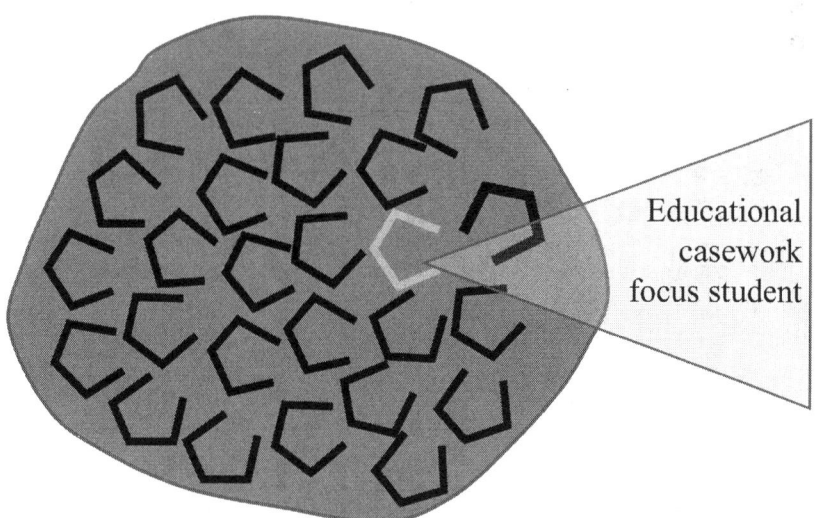

FIGURE 1.8   Educational casework focus on an individual student

The structure of the book

Responsive teaching and educational casework

In Chapter 2 we consider how responsive teaching and educational casework can work together in practice. Essential in our layered model is the need for coherence and alignment between layers. For students who are the focus of educational casework, this means that all intervention strategies and any small group or individual intervention will be linked to the class program in some way and will aim to strengthen learning in the classroom for that student.

Layered learning intervention

In Chapters 3 and 4 we introduce the different layers of intervention and how to scope their prospective use. Learning intervention can be thought of in terms of layers, with every aspect of a student's learning program, whether it is implemented individually or in small groups, in the classroom or outside the school, aimed towards success in the classroom and preparing for lifelong learning. We have already mentioned prevention and early intervention, which are part of the base layer of effective classroom teaching. On top of this foundation are further layers of small group and individual intervention that may be implemented over short- or longer-term periods.

The professional practice that supports layered learning intervention comes from two different perspectives. One is that of the responsive teacher, who has a focus on a class of students, comprising many individual learners. To complement this view is that of educational casework, which has an individual student focus. These two processes work together to influence the design, implementation and evaluation of the layers of learning intervention. How the layers of intervention work together for sustainable learning across the learning environment for any student will be explored in Chapter 3, providing a way to think about educational casework having a broad impact.

Classroom teaching is strengthened through collaboration with colleagues who are more experienced, or have deeper or different expertise. These other people can be learning intervention teachers who take on casework, or other professionals. They may also include teaching assistants or teacher aides who often have a large presence in classrooms and in some students' learning journeys, particularly those with disabilities or who are experiencing behavioural difficulties. The most important collaborative relationship in learning intervention is that between the teacher and students, and, by extension, with families of students. How learning intervention professionals work together with others and make joint decisions is vital to consider. Processes for collaboration in learning intervention are considered in Chapter 3, as part of the glue joining layers of intervention and then again in Chapter 4, as a key aspect of scoping and planning for intervention and deciding who is to be involved and in what capacities.

Research evidence as basis for effective learning intervention

Chapter 5 addresses the evidence base for learning intervention. Learning intervention, from responsive classroom teaching to individually focused intervention within educational casework, is based on careful decision-making. Intervention is not just a matter of selecting a ready-made set of lessons, or activities, but instead involves the expert and careful consideration of the multiple dimensions of any learning–teaching situation and responsiveness to current learning needs. In reality, teachers often simplify this process by choosing a pre-existing program or intervention strategy, so it is important to acknowledge what may have been assumed in making such quick decisions about intervention. Awareness of assumptions and clear processes for monitoring the impact of an intervention can be the difference between an effective way forward for a student's learning or a waste of time. Also important is the consideration of evidence that supports the hypothesis that a particular intervention approach will have a positive impact.

To complement the information about individuals and their responsiveness to teaching, research evidence about learning opportunities and teaching strategies is becoming more accessible for teachers, allowing them to be more informed about how learning activities are best designed and implemented in classrooms. The notion of evidence-based practice is explored in Chapter 5. In that chapter we use a model of multiple types of evidence that need to be combined in order to make the most appropriate decisions about learning intervention. Not only do we see research studies as evidence, we also value the evidence that students and families can provide from their constant involvement in a student's learning journey. As well, we consider that well-designed teaching practice that generates evidence of effect and thus can be evaluated based on data is practice-based evidence. Teachers are becoming more proficient at asking evaluative questions about their practice and setting up assessment processes that will allow the collection and analysis of information that will enable them to respond to those questions validly.

Assessment as foundation for educational casework

Chapters 6, 7 and 8 address the relationship between assessment and intervention. In conjunction with the practices for designing learning opportunities and teaching strategies through PPEI and RtI, individually focused assessment is important in allowing teachers to know more about their students as learners and thus be able to respond to current learning needs across their classes. Within the educational casework process, assessment is integral. In an ideal world, casework would provide not just preliminary assessment information, but also seek to understand how well and in what ways learners respond to teaching and to learning activities. It would then directly inform the provision of those opportunities, and contribute to collaborative planning of assessment throughout any intervention in order to determine the effects and then evaluate the learning intervention. These kinds of assessment decisions are explored in Chapters 6 ,7 and 8. They align with the full cycle of engagement in educational casework, from initial referral to evaluation of any intervention put in place. In reality, however, the casework will often be cut short and this cycle will be incomplete, with teachers left to interpret professional reports and incorporate assessment information into teaching decisions on their own. For many reasons, the valuable information that has been gathered may never really influence the teaching that is provided.

Learning opportunities and teaching strategies

Chapters 9 and 10 show how to develop learning opportunities, and to turn these into learning experiences through explicit teaching. In Chapter 9 we provide structures for designing and selecting appropriate learning activities, and arranging them to best meet learning needs. At the heart of any learning intervention there is the individual student, and the primary relationship between the classroom teacher and the student. This relationship is played out in a very complex context, alongside many other teacher–student relationships, and is complicated still further by the relationship between the teacher and the class as a whole, and as small groups. In Chapter 10, we explore the interactions between a teacher and single student and focus on teaching strategies that can be consciously and deliberately used in those interactions to enhance every learning opportunity.

Professional practice in learning intervention

Humans are naturally reflective, they think about what has happened and try to make sense of it in order to inform their actions in future similar situations. This forensic processing of lived experiences is what supports sustainable learning, and contributes to the constant development of capabilities for life. It is also an inherent part of the professional domains of our lives and has become formalised in those contexts. Professional practice in learning intervention is deliberate, explicit and planned, and supported at every step by aligned assessment. It also relies on an embedded process of reflection. This is in order to practice consciously, so that the best possible educational decisions are made and that all decisions are considered in terms of how they could have been different. The responsive teaching and educational casework frameworks used in this book are deliberately reflective, organised around a set of questions for responsive teachers and educational casework professionals to draw from in their practice. In Chapter 11 we focus on important aspects of reflective practice, and in Chapter 12 we draw together all the frameworks previously discussed in order to support reflective and ethical learning intervention practice.

Summary

Learning intervention is everything that effective teachers do to lead and support the learning of their students in the classroom and the school. Learning intervention starts with what families do to nurture their children's development and learning and extends into what teachers and schools do to expertly design class, small group and individual teaching and learning activities in order to meet students' learning needs identified through expert assessment. Effective teaching is core business across all the layers of learning intervention – in the classroom; with small groups; and with individual learners. Effective teaching, in response to clearly defined learning needs, is central to the achievement of all students. Educational casework complements and builds on the evidence-based and collaborative practices of effective responsive teachers.

References

Bronfenbrenner, U. (1977). Toward an experimental ecology of human development. *American Psychologist, 32*(7), 513–531.

Carr, E., Dunlap, G., Horner, R., Koegel, R., & Turnbull, A. (2002). Positive behavior support: Evolution of an applied science. *Journal of Positive Behavior Interventions, 4*(1), 4–16.

Department for Education (2014). *Schools: Guide to the 0 to 25 SEND code of practice Advice for school governing bodies/proprietors, senior leadership teams, SENCOs and classroom staff.* London: DES.

Dweck, C. (2006). *Mindset: The new psychology of success.* New York, NY: Random House.

Fitzpatrick, M. & Berman, J. (2016). Cultural dissonance in tertiary education: History repeating itself. *MAI Journal: A New Zealand Journal of Indigenous Scholarship, 5*(2), DOI: 10.20507/MAIJournal.2016.5.2.4

Fletcher, Jack M. & Vaughn, Sharon. (2009). Response to Intervention: Preventing and remediating academic difficulties. *Child Development Perspectives, 3*(1), 30–37.

Fuchs, Douglas, & Fuchs, Lynn S. (2006). Introduction to Response to Intervention: What, why, and how valid is it? *Reading Research Quarterly, 41*(1), 93–99.

Graham, L., Berman, J., & Bellert, A. (2015). *Sustainable learning: Inclusive practices for 21st century classrooms.* Melbourne, VIC: Cambridge University Press.

Leggett, N. & Ford, M. (2013). A fine balance: Understanding the roles educators and children play as intentional teachers and intentional learners within the Early Years Learning Framework. *Australasian Journal of Early Childhood, 38*(4), 42–50.

Macfarlane, A., Webber, M., McRae, H., & Cookson-Cox, C. (2014). *Ka Awatea: An iwi case study of Māori students' success: Report for Ngā Pae o te Māramatanga.* Christchurch: Te Rū Rangahau, University of Canterbury. Retrieved from www.maramatanga.co.nz/project/ka-awatea-iwi-case-study-m-ori-students-experiencing-success

Meyer, A., Rose, D., & Gordon, D. (2014). *Universal design for learning: Theory and practice.* Wakefield, MA: CAST Professional Publishing.

Neil, A. & Christensen, H. (2009). Efficacy and effectiveness of school-based prevention and early intervention programs for anxiety. *Clinical Psychology Review, 29*(3), 208–215.

New Zealand Ministry of Education (2000). Special education 2000. Getting it right together. Wellington, NZ: Ministry of Education.

Poananga, S. (2011). *Positive 'Whanau Management': Privileging the centrality of Whanau and culturally specific understandings of child discipline for effective psychological practice with Maori.* Unpublished DClinPsych thesis. Hamilton, NZ: University of Waikato.

Royal Australian and New Zealand College of Psychiatrists (n.d.). Aboriginal and Torres Strait Islander mental health. Retrieved from https://www.ranzcp.org/Publications/Indigenous-mental-health/Aboriginal-Torres-Strait-Islander-mental-health/The-Dance-of-Life.aspx

Rose, D. (2000). Universal design for learning. *Journal of Special Education Technology, 15*(4), 47–51.

Seligman, M. (2011). *Flourish: A visionary new understanding of happiness and wellbeing.* New York, NY: Free Press.

Shaddock, A. J., Hook, J., Hoffman-Raap, L., Spinks, A. T., Woolley, G., & Pearce, M. (2007). How do successful classroom teachers provide a relevant curriculum for students with disabilities in their mainstream class? *A Project to Improve the Learning Outcomes of Students with Disabilities in the Early, Middle and Post Compulsory Years of Schooling.* Barton, ACT: Commonwealth of Australia, 135–175.

Sternberg, R. (1997). *Successful intelligence.* New York, NY: Simon & Schuster.

Sternberg, R. & Grigorenko, E. (2007). *Teaching for successful intelligence: To increase student learning and achievement.* Thousand Oaks, CA: Corwin Press.

Tomlinson, C. (2003). *Fulfilling the promise of the differentiated classroom: Strategies and tools for responsive teaching.* Alexandria, VA: Association for Supervision and Curriculum Development.

Zubrick, S. R., Williams, A. A., Silburn, S. R., & Vimpani, G. (2000). *Indicators of family functioning.* Canberra, ACT: Australian Department of Family and Community Services.

2

EDUCATIONAL CASEWORK AND RESPONSIVE TEACHING

Responsive teaching is what effective teachers do every day in their classrooms. Educational casework, managed by specialist teachers and/or other professionals, works together with responsive teaching to become layered learning intervention. For the purposes of this book, we focus on how educational casework is carried out in collaboration with responsive teachers to ensure that the learning needs of all students are met.

As we have established, the foundation for learning intervention that makes a difference for learners is what happens all day, every day, in every classroom – it is responsive teaching. Responsive teachers have a focus on the learning of a class, and of the individuals within that class, while educational caseworkers see the learning of an individual student. We have represented this in Figure 2.1, with the lens for the classroom teacher being increasingly focused on individual students who are involved in educational casework. In tandem, educational casework starts with the individual learner, and considers learning within the context of the class. Both sets of professionals consider the group and the individual, but from different starting points.

Classroom teachers are always responsible for student outcomes in their classrooms, and this responsibility is not lessened by intervention implemented as part of learning support. A school psychologist or other educational professional may take responsibility for managing a casework process, but the intervention implemented and how it impacts on a student's learning continues to be very relevant for class teachers. Contributing to the casework process and using the evidence from it to respond in class remains part of classroom teachers' responsibilities, albeit in partnership with casework professionals.

In this book, we present a professional practice framework that can be used by educational and allied health professionals in their in-depth casework. The Educational Casework Process has been developed in acknowledgement of the need for "innovative, systematic approach[es] to clarifying professional objectives and evaluating outcomes of professional involvement" (Kelly, 2008, p.16). It has grown out of the Responsive Teaching Framework (Graham, Berman & Bellert, 2015).

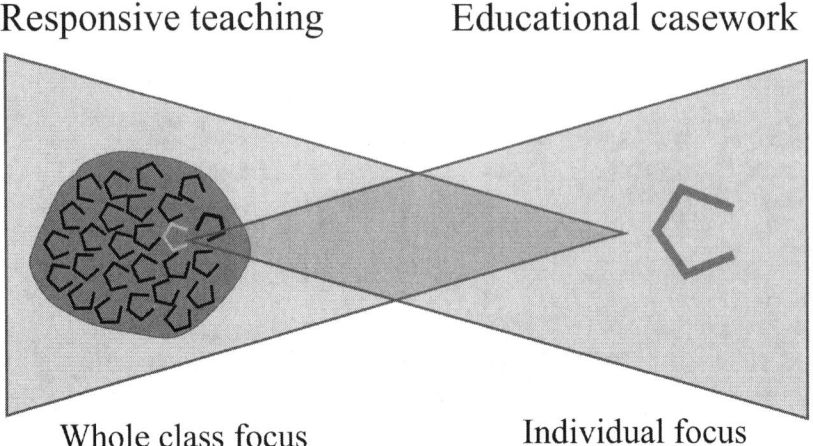

Responsive teaching   Educational casework

Whole class focus   Individual focus

FIGURE 2.1 Responsive teaching and educational casework together in learning intervention

It illustrates how educational casework can complement the processes of teachers and can explicitly support their responsive teaching. We have extended the traditional engagement of many psychologists and special educators, beyond completing assessments and writing and receiving reports, with recommendations for teachers to include developing, implementing and evaluating intervention that targets the specific needs of individual learners in partnership with teachers, students and families. In this model, educational casework professionals will continue to work together throughout interventions and to be part of the implementation team that evaluates and makes decisions about future teaching and intervention.

Responsive Teaching Framework

Teachers bring their expertise, knowledge and skills around child development, learning and teaching to their teaching of a class of students. They work through processes to take into account the complexity of the ecological influences on their work and to make sure they teach within the legal, ethical, professional, systemic and school and community expectations. The Responsive Teaching Framework (RTF; Graham, Berman & Bellert, 2015) is designed around the kind of questions responsive teachers ask themselves as they move through teaching cycles, in order to include consideration of all these dimensions. Eight sets of questions frame responsive teaching by prompting the kind of assessment and information gathering that ensures every teaching decision is well informed and justifiable.

Responsive teaching reflects the increasingly complex role of classroom teaching that is required by contemporary inclusive schools and the considerable variability of learners who are within our schools. The focus on individual learning needs and on generating evidence of impact of teaching is central to inclusive

Clinical Teaching Cycle 	Responsive Teaching Framework
What is the learner ready to learn and what evidence supports this?	1. What frameworks do I need to consider?
What are the possible evidence-based interventions?	2. What do I bring as a teacher?
	3. What do my students bring as learners?
What is the preferred intervention and how will it be resourced and implemented?	4. What do I need to teach now?
	5. How do I teach for all my learners?
What is the expected impact on learning and how will this be evaluated?	6. What did my students learn?
	7. What feedback supports my students' learning?
What happened and how can this be interpreted?	8. How did my teaching support my students' learning?

FIGURE 2.2   The Clinical Teaching Cycle and the Responsive Teaching Framework

Source: McLean Davies at al., 2014; and Graham, Berman & Bellert, 2015.

teaching. It is also reflected in the model of Clinical Teaching (McLean Davies et al., 2015). In the Clinical Teaching Cycle, teachers think through the phases of teaching with a focus on individual learners and consideration of what the learners are ready to learn, what evidence-based teaching will meet their needs, and how to evaluate the impact of that teaching. The decision-making questions in the RTF provide purposeful elaborations of the Clinical Teaching model. Both of these are shown in Figure 2.2.

As is explicitly articulated in the Responsive Teaching Framework, it is imperative for teachers to know about the policies and expectations of the educational setting, and the cultural and social contexts within which teaching is to happen, as well as being conscious of their own skills and limitations. Teachers need to be aware of their competence both as members of a culture and a profession. This knowledge is foundational for understanding students as learners and for teaching responsively.

Educational Casework Process

Traditionally, classroom teaching and educational casework have been distinctive and at times completely separate. Such casework is often at the instigation of teachers, or of families, and is carried out by a range of professionals, including teachers with specific expertise (special educators), speech pathologists, educational and developmental psychologists, medical practitioners and mental health professionals. These professionals carry out assessment and write reports making recommendations for the classroom. The teacher receives the report and takes the recommendations into account in teaching – or that is how this should work.

In reality, what happens is that many teachers look at professional reports and have difficulty translating the information provided into use in the classroom. This may be sometimes because the recommendations cannot be done in a classroom. Alternatively, it could be because more time is needed to develop a shared understanding of the learner and context and that is difficult through a report. Sometimes professionals meet with teachers in the process of report writing, but find allocating shared time is a challenge. Some professionals write individual learning plans and provide these for teachers but never know whether any of their planning has been considered or incorporated into classroom activity.

There are many reasons for this disconnect between other professionals and classroom teachers, not the least of which is time. It takes considerable time to develop deep understanding of the complexity of learners and to engage in professional collaboration, and this time is not always allocated or available in the busy lives of educational professionals.

The process of educational casework aims to increase shared understanding of the nature of learning needs of a student so that intervention can be well founded and will have a positive effect. Usually such casework is focused on problems in development, learning and wellbeing that have been observed, and it happens after teachers and families have tried a number of intervention strategies without success. The complementary processes that classroom teachers and educational caseworkers use in learning intervention are represented in Figure 2.3. The Responsive Teaching Framework is used here as a reference point for the development of an explicit framework for educational casework.

Alignment of responsive teaching and educational casework

Although the two sets of processes are presented in Figure 2.3 as if they are parallel, they are best conceptualised as complementary, and with blurred boundaries, that are combined as appropriate to best meet the learning needs of students. The Responsive Teaching Framework represents the work of inclusive classroom teachers, while the Educational Casework Process is more aligned with the work of learning intervention teachers and other educational professionals.

Both responsive teaching and educational casework go through the same phases of planning, intervening and evaluating, but the relevant phases are framed differently to account for the different perspectives needed. The eight key guiding questions in these frameworks are further elaborated through questions such as those in Table 2.1.

The series of reflective questions within these two processes can act as reference points for responsive teaching and educational casework. Some of these questions may not be relevant at all times and there will, inevitably, be other questions that arise, that can be included to guide the careful consideration of all decisions involved in learning intervention.

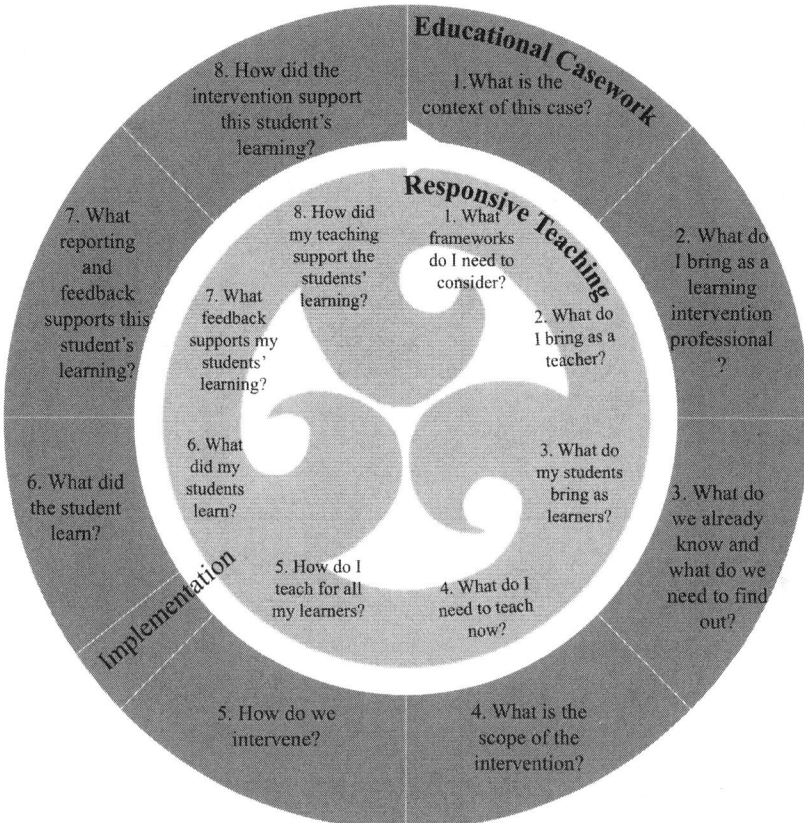

FIGURE 2.3   Responsive teaching and educational casework processes

Source: Graham, Berman & Bellert, 2015.

People in educational casework

As already mentioned, there are a number of professional disciplines that are involved in supporting learners in schools through casework, including learning intervention teachers, educational and developmental psychologists, speech pathologists, physiotherapists, occupational therapists, psychiatrists, paediatricians and mental health professionals. These professionals use a range of approaches to contribute to understanding the learning and developmental needs of individual students, and to put in place interventions that will support learning and development.

Although much of the discussion and structure around casework is applicable to other professionals who work in schools, the focus of this book is more closely aligned to what specialist learning intervention teachers and educational psychologists do in education. It may provoke conversations and consideration about the roles of other professionals who work into educational settings, however, and could be adapted to other professional contexts.

TABLE 2.1 Responsive teaching and educational casework processes elaborated

Responsive Teaching	*Educational Casework*
PLANNING	

1. What frameworks do I need to consider?

What legislative frameworks, curriculum, culture and community contexts, education system policies and procedures, school context, teacher registration requirements and physical environments do I teach within?	What is the context of this case? What legislative frameworks, curriculum, culture and community contexts, education system policies and procedures, school context, professional registration requirements and physical environments do I work within?

2. What do I bring as a teacher or learning intervention professional?

What cultural competence, assumptions about learning, teaching skills and knowledge, assumptions about named disabilities and learning difficulties and levels of responsive and reflective practice do I bring to my teaching?	What cultural competence, professional competence and assumptions about case or context do I bring to this casework?
	Why are we doing this casework? What is the appropriate extent of involvement? What ethical dimensions are to be considered?
	What do I know about this domain of development and learning (this condition, disability, syndrome)? What assumptions are inherent in my knowledge and previous professional experience? What do I understand about what supports and hinders learning for this domain of development and learning? What else do I need to research?

3. What do my students bring as learners?	3. What do we already know and what do we need to find out about this student's learning and development?
What cultural contexts, needs, interests, experiences, capabilities, prior learning and achievements do my students bring to their learning? What is the nature of the learning group they create? What do my students' families bring to each student's learning and our learning group?	What is already known about the student's development and learning? What is known about the other people in the case? What are the priorities of these people (student, family, teacher, others)?
	What dimensions of development and learning are we looking at in this casework? What other assessment information is needed to inform the intervention?

4. What do I need to teach now?	4. What are the priorities and parameters (scope) of the intervention?
What is the next step of curriculum related to intended learning outcomes and ATRiUM capabilities? How is this next step related to what the students bring as individual learners and as a learning group?	What are the priorities for intervention based on the assessment information?
	What is the length of time for the intervention?
	What people are available for the intervention (professionals, teaching assistants, family and other students)? What is the learning environment within which the intervention is to be implemented? What layers of learning intervention are appropriate? How will this be connected to classroom teaching? What factors will support and hinder intervention implementation? What sort of reporting will be required, and to whom?

(Continued)

TABLE 2.1 (Continued)

Responsive Teaching	*Educational Casework*
5. How do I teach for all my learners?	5. How do we intervene?
What common and distinctive learning needs are evident within my class?	What intended learning outcomes (ILOs) are important and realistic? How can these ILOs be targeted in this context? How can sustainability (transfer and maintenance) be built in to the ILOs?
What are the (curriculum-based and ATRiUM capabilities) intended learning outcomes?	What intervention is evidenced in scientific literature, in professional experience (own and colleagues'), and from family and student perspectives?
What learning activities are appropriate? (How will my students view these activities? What range of task difficulty is needed? What modes of delivery are available? What adjustments might be needed for individual students?)	How can these three bodies of evidence be brought together into learning opportunities and teaching strategies?
What is the most appropriate sequence of learning activities?	What learning opportunities (tasks, instructions and materials) are appropriate?
What groupings and effective teaching practices will work best?	How should the learning opportunities be arranged? What intensity of learning opportunities are appropriate?
What organisation and resources are needed?	Who should mediate the learning opportunities?
What on-the-spot adjustments might I need to make?	What should be the size and make-up of the learning group?
What will success look like (clear, appropriately challenging success criteria)?	In what ways can class learning activities and adaptations meet the needs of this learner?
What products and outcomes will demonstrate learning progress? What feedback is most appropriate and when will it be provided?	How are these learning opportunities to be resourced?
	What personnel are needed? How will they work together? What are their responsibilities? What professional development and preparation is needed?
	What factors will support and hinder intervention implementation?
	What on-the-spot adjustments might need to be made?
	What is the assessment plan (outcome measures, processes for monitoring and feedback)?
	Who is involved in compiling and analysing monitoring and outcome assessment information?
ASSESSSING AND TEACHING	IMPLEMENTING INTERVENTION
6. What did my students learn?	6. What did this student learn?
In what ways did each learner and the learning group respond to the instruction in relation to: (i) the intended learning outcomes; (ii) unintended learning outcomes; and (iii) factors that supported and hindered learning?	What does analysis of data from monitoring and outcome measures indicate in relation to: (i) the intended learning outcomes; (ii) any unintended learning outcomes; and (iii) factors that supported and hindered learning?
How was sustainability evidenced (transfer and maintenance)?	How was sustainability evidenced (transfer and maintenance)?

(*Continued*)

TABLE 2.1 (Continued)

Responsive Teaching	Educational Casework
7. What feedback supported my students' learning? What immediate feedback supported learning? What further feedback is needed now about (i) the task; (ii) the processes of learning; and (iii) self-regulation? How can I respond to my students' need to know: *Where am I going? How am I going? Where to next?*	7. What reporting and feedback support this student's learning? How can this feedback best support the intervention? What feedback is most appropriate and when will it be provided? How is the learner to be given feedback? How is the learner's feedback to be gained and shared? How, and to whom, is the effect of the intervention to be reported?

EVALUATING

8. How did my teaching support my students' learning? How effective was my teaching for the group and for individuals with respect to curriculum intended learning outcomes and ATRiUM capabilities? What does this tell me about what my students are ready to do next? How will I build on my students' learning now? What activities can support their consistent and maintained progress? Did feedback lead to increased effort and success?	8. How did the intervention support the student's learning? How effective was the intervention for this student's learning? What is the next step? What implementation factors (competence, organisation and leadership) supported or impeded the effect of the intervention? How did my practice as a learning intervention professional support the intervention?

Learning intervention teachers

The professional expectations of teachers who focus on individual learners in casework are determined in part by the structures in the schools within which they work. In essence, though, learning intervention teachers will seek to develop a deeper understanding of each learner and will have the capacity to design intervention that meets the needs of learners within and outside their classrooms. The model of layered intervention used in this book includes working with classroom teachers to differentiate for individual learners, designing and implementing and evaluating small group and individual short-term intervention, as well as managing longer-term intervention that may be needed for some students who have disabling conditions.

Many learning intervention teachers manage caseloads that include students with identified disabilities, learning difficulties or students who are dealing with the consequences of interruptions to school learning. They also contribute to professional learning for classroom teachers, and provide awareness-raising opportunities for families. Often, learning intervention teachers are the staff members in schools who coordinate the involvement of other professionals in learning intervention. There are many different titles for these learning intervention teachers including support teachers, learning adjustment coordinators, learning enhancement teachers, SEN teachers or coordinators, specialist teachers and resource teachers for learning and behaviour.

Other professionals in educational casework

There are a variety of developmental and educational professionals who become involved in educational casework in conjunction with schools. Their involvement is shaped by many factors, not least of which are the expectations that schools and teachers have of them. Many of these expectations are limited by knowledge about what these professionals can do. For example, the professional expectations of psychologists in education are highly variable. Often psychologists are seen only as assessment professionals, who provide the required assessment information, that is, do the psychological tests necessary to access resources within education systems. In many cases this is seen as the difference between teachers and psychologists; psychologists are allowed to do intelligence tests. However, psychological practice in education has much more to offer in support of classroom teachers and students, and families.

In Aotearoa New Zealand, for example, it is not uncommon for specialist teachers to continue their education to become registered educational psychologists. At the beginning of the internship year, many students cannot see how the work of specialist teachers and psychologists differ, except for their recognition as psychologists. However, at the end of the year, these beginning psychologists do not have any difficulty articulating how they have transformed from teachers to psychologists and now use a different way of seeing their discipline knowledge. This includes an increase in their depth and breadth of understanding, their skills as assessors and analysts of learning and teaching, and their abilities to apply their research capabilities as agents of change through designing, implementing and evaluating interventions for learning.

Although there are pressures within systems for psychologists to leave anything to do with learning up to teachers, in this book we take the stance that psychologists need to know everything teachers know, in more depth and to be able to do complementary assessment (to that done by teachers) when exploring student development and learning. Many psychologists are not teachers, so the skills of teaching are not essential for psychologists, but knowledge about teacher competencies and their efficacy is certainly essential. Psychologists also bring their understanding of all the ATRiUM capabilities, their development and application for learners at different ages and in different contexts. Psychologists should also have the skills to explore, in depth, particular developmental conditions that have implications for learning. Skills for change management and for therapeutic engagement with students and families are also part of their repertoire, as is collaborative expertise that underpins productive work with all others involved in schools.

Professionals specialising in the development of children's speech and language, variously called speech pathologists, speech language therapists and speech therapists, are also often involved in educational casework, both within schools and separately within government, non-government and private practice. Their in-depth knowledge of children's development of speech and language is valuable for complementing the teacher knowledge in many cases, but particularly in cases where there is a significant difficulty, delay or disordered development of the use of the language system (the U in ATRiUM).

Paediatric occupational therapists are also integral to some casework and have much to offer in terms of knowledge and expertise around the motor development of children, from their general mobility to the fine motor skills needed in classroom handwriting and underpinning keyboard capabilities.

Medical practitioners are also often involved in educational casework, either as general practitioners, as paediatricians who specialise in children's development and disordered development, or as psychiatric specialists. These professionals are vital contributors to any casework that needs to explore physiological, genetic and chromosomal, or medical conditions that affect learning. They are also essential team members for any casework that involves mental health, particularly when casework includes individual therapy and the management of medications.

Teaching assistants

There are many other people who work in education, known as teacher aides, teaching assistants, learning support officers and educational support workers who are often seen to be the embodiment of intervention: They *are* the intervention. For example, many students are enrolled at schools after assurance from the education system that a teaching assistant will be provided; inferring that this extra adult will be the support for the learner. There is an assumption that the teaching assistant will provide all that is needed to make the placement successful and to meet the learning needs of the student. There can also often be expectations around the role of the teaching assistant in minding the student, or managing behaviours that may be disruptive in class.

The responsibilities placed on teaching assistants can be enormous and problematic when considered in terms of the needs of students who have significant additional learning needs, high and complex needs, special education needs, disabilities or learning difficulties. Expecting the least qualified educator in the class to teach the student who has the highest needs creates considerable incongruity. We recognise the tensions inherent in this situation: teaching assistants are cheaper to employ, and there is an expectation that their presence will be of great impact, not only in reducing disruptions in classrooms, but also in activating learning. In this book, however, we position teaching assistants as part of a team of educational and developmental professionals. Their involvement constitutes a very valuable human resource, when supported well, to carry out specific roles within an intervention, designed by the educators or other professionals. Teaching assistants need to be provided with appropriate professional learning and supervision to guide their contribution to the implementation of any learning intervention.

Process of educational casework

Educational casework is part of the educational experience of some students all of the time and for other students some of the time. A student who has a particular condition or identified disability that will affect learning and development throughout life may have educational casework as a perpetual and integral part of their school journey. This is the case, for example, for students who have been identified with a general developmental delay as young children, and subsequently with intellectual disability. Long-term educational casework like this operates through the specialist assessment and collaboration processes that accompany classroom teaching and that systematically link class teachers to other relevant professionals and to families throughout a student's school life. In these cases the emphasis is on developing and evaluating individual learning plans at each stage across the school years, and working towards post-school possibilities for these young people.

In contrast, some students have short-term involvement in educational casework that may be necessary to enable the exploration of learning needs through specialist assessment, or to provide some short-term intervention. Often such casework for short-term intervention is instigated because of school access to additional resources such as a grant funding extra personnel. Otherwise the provision of intervention follows a routine process within a school, and within a system that provides short-term intervention for those students identified with the most significant learning and behaviour needs each year.

Educational casework that aims to develop a better understanding of the learning needs of students is typical in education systems. It is triggered by referral for assessment and culminates in a report that will help teachers design more effective learning opportunities. Involvement of an assessment professional, who is often from a health or allied health background, often stops with the report. This situation is problematic in many ways and has contributed to the frustration of both groups of professionals. Instead, in this unpacking of learning intervention we are advocating for an ongoing partnership that continues after the specialist report and contributes to decision-making around classroom teaching and intervention.

Language of learning intervention

Because of the involvement of multiple professionals, students and families in educational casework, the language that is used in learning intervention needs to be clear. In order to establish shared understanding and clarify intentions for learning intervention, well-chosen particular language is used, both to describe the learning needs of students and to discuss the nature of the learning intervention being developed and implemented. As with any professional field there is a specific vocabulary that aims to make our professional conversations more efficient and precise. A shared vocabulary is imperative in facilitating the relationships between classroom teachers and educational caseworkers. Sharing language and understandings is not always straightforward however. For example, while we may assume that we are all using important terms like 'inclusive education', 'special education', 'disabilities', 'learning difficulties', 'learning disabilities', 'learning disorders', 'assessment' and 'intervention' in the same way, there is an enormous variation in how this language is used. There are not only considerable variations in language and understanding within single educational settings but these terms are also used differently around the world in practice and in the research being carried out in this field.

How categories of students are defined for research purposes is also important because the findings from relevant studies contribute to our evidence base. Drawing on relevant research underpins educational professionals' understanding of the learning needs of certain individuals, and informs their instruction where the scientific research provides information about particular ways to teach identified learners. Analysis of international research in learning difficulties, (for example Elliott & Grigorenko, 2014), illustrates the need for us to be constantly questioning the constructs that shape our field and the language we use to describe learners and learning, as well as the activity that is learning intervention.

Labels for learners

In describing learning intervention, many terms are used to refer to 'types' of learners. Although inclusive education attempts to be non-categorical, any education system develops a set of categories or classifications that help manage and organise students and the resourcing of their teaching. Therefore, it is important that all professionals involved in learning intervention are aware of common labels and their meanings, how they are used and the roles they play in the lives of individual learners and their families. It is also important to be conscious of the limits of those labels.

Labels for learners are derived from a number of different sources, and for different purposes. In education we use general terms like 'disabilities', 'learning difficulties', 'special education needs', 'learning disabilities' and 'learning disorders' to refer to the students for whom educational casework is instigated. Under these umbrella terms there are more specific words that come from medical and psychological science that refer to specific patterns of development or to conditions that have been documented. From a positive perspective, such labels aim to, and can, support shared understanding and allow prediction of developmental or learning pathways.

Traditionally, language from the special education paradigm focused on providing descriptors or labels for learners that helped to 'sort' students. These were based on the extent and nature of developmental delays or disorders, or genetic, medical or physiological conditions or syndromes, and patterns of behaviours or responses to the environment. Many terms have been generated in this context that originally supported sorting for placement in different educational settings designed to match the learning needs of particular groups. This practice of special education continues in parts of our education systems (and relates to a further discussion of the uses of assessment for selection in Chapter 6).

In Table 2.2 we have listed some labels that are derived from medical science, psychological science and education systems. Of interest is how these labels may support work in learning intervention. It is also vital, however, to consider the limits of that support, outside which these labels may, in fact, create or contribute to problems themselves.

TABLE 2.2 Sources and examples of labels of variability of human development and functioning

Medical science	Psychological science	Education systems
Spina bifida	Intellectual disability	Intellectual disability
Cerebral Palsy	Mental health disorders	Physical disability or health
Down syndrome	Learning disorders	impairment
Cystic fibrosis	Dyslexia	Multiple disability
Multiple sclerosis	Attention deficit	Vision impairment or blindness
Acquired brain injury	hyperactivity disorder	Deaf or Hearing impairment
Asthma	(ADHD)	Autism/Pervasive
Sensory impairment	Autism Spectrum Disorder	developmental disorder
Quadriplegia	Obsessive compulsive disorder	Psychiatric disability/mental
Chronic illness	Oppositional defiant disorder	health problems
Fragile X	Conduct disorder	Severe behaviour disorder
CHARGE Syndrome	Borderline personality	Severe language disorder
Cornelia de Lange	disorder	Social emotional disorder
Syndrome	Mood disorders	Dyslexia
Angelman Syndrome		Gifted & Talented
Cri du Chat Syndrome		

Source: Adapted from Graham, Berman & Bellert, 2015.

Usually medical and psychological labels are the result of identification, using clinical procedures, of a 'condition' or of a developmental or physiological pattern of significant difference from normal. Such labels that come from medical and psychological bases are often considered to be well-founded scientific categories that have considerable power to explain causes and to provide direction for intervention. As scientific research identifies physiological bases for some differences, they can be examined in systematic ways by testing hypotheses in subsequent cases and documenting evidence. This is the case for some conditions, and within some situations it may be possible to alter physiological or neurological variables and thus have an impact on conditions. Medications, for example, are the cornerstones of many interventions that aim to alter the chemistry of the body in order to change a condition or symptoms associated with a condition.

The process of problem solving and diagnosis that underpins this medical approach is valuable as a basis of assessment and intervention. However, labels used in medical and scientific contexts are often used in other contexts where they may not necessarily have the same validity, nor be able to meaningfully point to appropriate intervention. Specifically, they may not necessarily be applicable to many of the considerations of educational casework so their limitations need to be acknowledged in making decisions about learning intervention.

This issue is exemplified in the case of dyslexia: Elliott and Grigorenko (2014) examined "the extent to which the dyslexia construct operates as a rigorous scientific construct that adds to our capacity to help those who struggle to learn to read" (p.4). Elliott and Grigorenko's work shows that there is no one consistent, evidence-based construct of dyslexia that is acceptable to all interested parties. They found that when the definitions that were used for dyslexia in research across scientific disciplines were gathered, and the purposes for which the definition was used were explored, the variation between definitions made consideration of dyslexia as a scientific construct quite problematic and, in turn, challenged the usefulness of all associated research findings.

It is unarguable that a consistent definition or set of criteria for any category or group of subjects is needed for *scientific research* purposes, that is, when researching as well as when using research findings. Without this consistency, it is impossible to build on or to compare research findings, or to combine them into meta-analyses. This issue is crucial for the utility of the evidence base that we draw on to inform professional actions. Because scientific research is carried out in many disciplinary contexts, and published in many different forms, however, there are different expectations about the definition of constructs and the selection of participants in studies. It seems impossible to agree on a definition for a condition that is not easily determined, and so research needs to specify how the term is used in each situation.

An important consideration arising from Elliott and Grigorenko's (2014) work relates to the other uses of labels that are relevant to learning intervention, not only as a construct in scientific research, but also as a category for the allocation of educational and social resources; as a focus of advocacy to gain formal legislative recognition; and to support a shared understanding of learning needs, intervention and teaching.

There is always a need to determine who will access the limited *educational and social resources* available in schools or to have supports in the community for everyday living. Educational and social systems usually set up categories that have specific criteria and use agreed-upon processes to establish who meets these criteria. Such definitions of conditions may vary, and be broadened or narrowed over time or to suit particular situations. Access to diagnostic services then reciprocally influences who may be deemed eligible for additional services based on diagnostic criteria. Issues of social equity are important in these situations because a divide exists between students whose families have the resources to engage the expertise of medical or psychological professionals to pursue diagnoses compared to those families who do not.

Similarly, there are many advocacy groups that set out to highlight the consequences of specific learning problems and to gain formal *legislative recognition* that will translate into education and social system processes and services. This situation is evident in the international, national and state legislation and policies around disability that guides access to provisions for students with disabilities in education systems.

The fourth purpose of labels identified through Elliott and Grigorenko's (2014) work is to serve as a foundation for a *shared understanding of learning needs and intervention*. In inclusive education, responsive teaching and educational casework, this is the main purpose of labels. However, it must be understood that labels are not helpful in isolation and are only the beginning in terms of educational casework. Although diagnostic categories can help explain common characteristics of students with particular syndromes or disabilities, much variation is evident between the skill sets of individuals who are considered to be in the same category.

Tensions in the use of labels

From a teaching point of view, it is most useful to consider students' learning abilities as resulting from their individual combinations of physiological, psychological, social and cultural factors – factors that either support or hinder learning in the classroom. Teachers need to know, through assessment and observation, what their students' learning needs are irrespective of a particular label or diagnosis. Then teachers can investigate and make sense of influences on learning for individuals in their classrooms in order to provide responsive teaching. This move towards responsiveness of learning is in line with contemporary developments in medicine and exercise, which are both becoming more individually specific through the use of fine-grained assessment and technology, including genetic testing and analysis (see, for example, Timmons et al., 2010).

Many families express relief when a label is attached to what they are experiencing with the development and learning of a child. Similarly, there are many stories about the relief adults feel when they can put a label on their learning difficulties to help explain what they could not understand as they were living through difficult school years. In both of these situations, the shared understanding that comes with the label assists the family or adult to find ways for managing learning and living more successfully. While we try to make sense of uniquely different learning needs, we also seek to find similarities and capture those through labels. This allows people with similar labels to connect with each other and to learn from others' experiences. In the context of young learners, the frustrations associated with experiencing little success from classroom teaching and other small group or individual intervention in schools without a full exploration of possible explanations is considerable for learners and their families.

There are also problems with the use of labels including overdiagnosis and misdiagnosis, as well as the potential for the allocation of a label to be seen as the end of the educational casework when, in fact, it is just the beginning. If diagnostic work opens doors to better teaching and learning, it is valuable. If it is seen as the answer itself, however, that is problematic and can restrict learners' opportunities. For example, if an assessment process results in the determination of intellectual disability, this can act as an explanation for the delayed development and learning that has been evident. From a responsive teaching perspective, however, it is then necessary to ask about how this helps design learning opportunities and teaching strategies for this learner in his/her class context. This step is much more important to instructional decision-making than the diagnosis itself.

In learning intervention we are working towards defining and then address-ing individual learning needs. The term *learning needs* has different interpretations. Many people in special education still see 'learning needs' as only being relevant to learners with difficulties or disabilities. Often it is only used when a student is iden-tified with learning difficulties or disabilities that generate 'special' needs. Funding for students with disabilities or learning difficulties, for example, depends on clear articulation of the 'additional' or 'special' needs that justify additional resources. This tension between seeing all learners as individuals with their own unique package of learning needs, and seeing some students only as having learning needs, or as having additional or special needs, is a reality that calls out for resolution.

In this book, the term *learning needs* is used in relation to all learners. All learners have learning needs that are relevant to them at any particular time. We all have, and continue to have, learning needs throughout our lives. It is what we need to learn next. We will not be using *additional* or *special*, since these are subsumed into the more general and universally applicable notion of individual learning needs. A key part of responsive teaching and educational casework is making sense of the individual learning needs of each of our students so that we can respond to them through our decisions.

Language of learning intervention practice

The other usage of terminology that is relevant in educational casework and respon-sive teaching is around professional activity, and relates to terms such as *intervention* and *interventions*. The term *intervention* is used in this book to include all activity or processes that professionals use to support the learning of students. We have framed learning intervention as the combination of educational casework and responsive teaching in order to meet individual and class learning needs.

There is also recognition, though, that learning intervention will include what can also be referred to as *interventions*. These are components of learning inter-vention that are bounded by defined changes to the environment for a particular learner or a class of learners; or a set of learning opportunities or teaching strate-gies implemented in response to individual or small group learning needs. These interventions have a beginning and an end, and incorporate assessment to see what impact they have had over that time. This term is also relevant in the context of packaged, sometimes commercial, programs that are often referred to as interven-tions. Interventions are used as needed within both responsive teaching and edu-cational casework. It is vital that educational professionals constantly check that they are using such terms with mutual understanding, as this underpins successful collaboration with colleagues and families.

Summary

Playgroups and early childhood settings, primary and high schools, and tertiary and workplace settings are all formally organised learning environments that depend on professionally qualified teachers to carry out responsive teaching that leads to sustainable learning. To complement this expertise, educational casework is practised across the range of educational settings by a range of professionals who take on many roles. Learning intervention teachers teach classes, small groups and individuals, work as consultants for classroom teachers, collaborate with other educational professionals and manage individual educational casework. Other professionals, including psychologists, speech pathologists and other allied health workers, draw on their particular domain of expertise to work together with classroom teachers, learning intervention teachers, families and students to design and implement intervention at many levels.

The responsive teaching and educational casework practice frameworks outlined in this chapter aim to guide practice. We will refer to both of these in the rest of the book, but with emphasis on unpacking the Educational Casework Process: Steps 1 and 2 will be explored further in Chapter 4 as part of scoping for learning intervention; Steps 3 to 8 all involve assessment and will be unpacked in Chapters 6, 7 and 8; Step 5 shines the spotlight on the evidence base (Chapter 5) used by teachers in providing learning opportunities (Chapter 9) and choosing teaching strategies (Chapter 10). Following on from these chapters, Chapter 11 focuses on evaluating learning intervention and Chapter 12 brings together the frameworks and processes for planning and documenting educational casework.

References

Elliott, J. & Grigorenko, E. (2014). *The dyslexia debate.* New York, NY: Cambridge University Press.

Graham, L., Berman, J., & Bellert, A. (2015). *Sustainable learning: Inclusive practices for 21st century classrooms,* Melbourne, VIC: Cambridge University Press.

Kelly, B. (2008). Frameworks for practice in educational psychology: Coherent perspectives for a developing profession. In Kelly, B., Woolfson, L., & Boyle, J. (Eds.), *Frameworks for practice in educational psychology: A textbook for trainees and practitioners.* London: Jessica Kingsley, 15–30.

McLean Davies, L., Dickson, B., Rickards, F., Dinham, S., Conroy, J., & Davis, R. (2015). Teaching as a clinical profession: Translational practices in initial teacher education – an international perspective. *Journal of Education for Teaching, 41*(5), 514–528.

Timmons, J., Knudsen, S., Rankinen, T., Koch, L., Sarzynski, M., Jensen, T., & Bouchard, C. (2010). Using molecular classification to predict gains in maximal aerobic capacity following endurance exercise training in humans. *Journal of Applied Physiology, 108*(6), 1487–1496.

3

LAYERS OF LEARNING INTERVENTION

Learning intervention in homes and communities occurs in a range of settings as well as in different sized groups – large group, small group and pairs – as appropriate. There are also opportunities for members of small groups to learn from and with each other, such as when families go on holidays, or participate in activities with a social, cultural, sporting and environmental focus. For example, families teach music to their children through individual tuition, small group and family music-making sessions, formal orchestral, choral or chamber music groups, as well as using individual practice sessions. Similarly, a key aspect of learning intervention practice is the strategic and careful use of different groupings and contexts for learning, and we see these as layers of intervention. The conceptualisation of layers of learning intervention presented in this chapter derives from the Response to Intervention model that is used in many schools, but we emphasise the dynamic contribution of different types of learning opportunities to the main game of classroom learning.

The Response to Intervention model

Response to Intervention (RtI) is a model of tiered intervention that was designed to replace the conventional process for diagnosing Learning Disabilities within the US legislative context, which was based on a measurement of the discrepancy between ability and achievement. The model was developed to move the emphasis of the intervention process onto early intervention, and to use the assessment information gathered while such intervention is in progress to more solidly support determinations of Learning Disabilities. Two key ideas drove this framework:

1   Education should not wait for a diagnosis of Learning Disability (LD) before providing what we know is appropriate intervention. Instead we should provide evidence-based intervention as early as possible in a child's learning

journey; as soon as it is noted that the current instruction is not producing the learning outcomes that were intended. In providing this intervention we would gather assessment information to indicate how well the student was responding to the intervention. This would help guide the intervention as well as becoming evidence for subsequent assessment of LD if appropriate.

2 Assessment for the purposes of determining LD would be able to draw on information gathered during the provision of early intervention, to help make determinations about what was hindering learning and to determine whether the learner had appropriate opportunities to learn. Many determinations of LD have been made over the years without knowing this crucial piece of information, and therefore some psychoeducational decisions have not been fully informed. The practical outcome of such an incomplete process of assessment is that many learners have been defined as inherently deficient, when in fact their lack of opportunity to learn was the key factor.

Three tiers of intervention

The representation of this RtI model is a triangle divided into three tiers (Figure 3.1). The separate tiers of the triangle indicate the proportion of people who will learn effectively with increasingly targeted and intensive intervention. Tier 1 is seen as generic or 'universal', teaching that will provide for most (75–90 per cent) learners. Tier 2 is when some changes are made to cater for those who did not learn

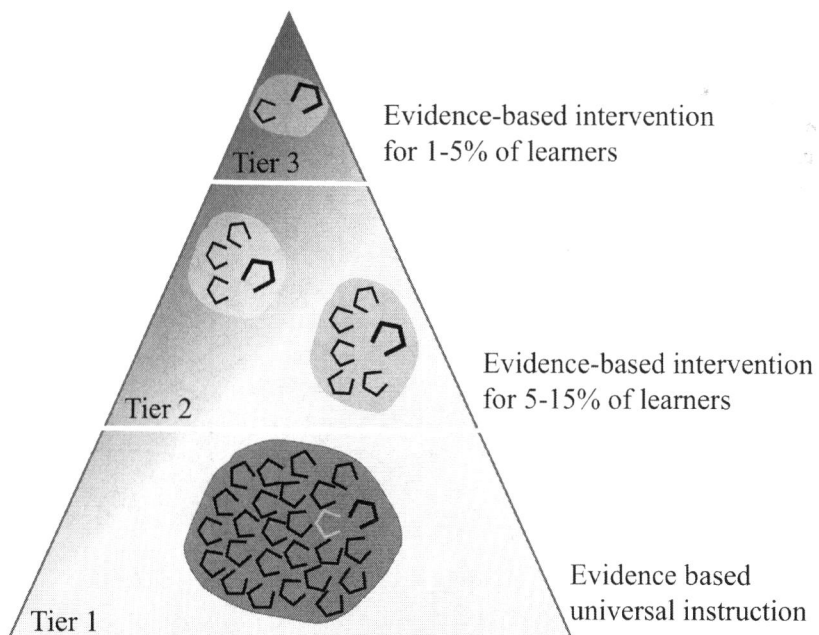

Tier 3 — Evidence-based intervention for 1-5% of learners

Tier 2 — Evidence-based intervention for 5-15% of learners

Tier 1 — Evidence based universal instruction

FIGURE 3.1 Tiers of evidence-based intervention

as expected from the generic version of teaching (5–15 per cent). Tier 3 is a more focused, individual intervention for those learners who were not successful in Tiers 1 or 2 (1–5 per cent).

Many schools use the simple framework of tiers in their organisation of learning support, with Tier 1 being core classroom instruction, Tier 2 supplemental instruction and Tier 3 instruction for intensive intervention (Mitchell, 2014, p.245). When a learner is not responding as anticipated to instruction in the classroom, it is appropriate to increase the intensity of instruction and to more specifically target learning needs with the next tier of instruction. In order to do that, more fine-grained assessment is needed, as well as information about the student's responses to the previous instruction. All this is taken into account in designing the next level of instruction or intervention. What also happens is a reduction in the number of learners being involved in the next level of instruction or intervention, as many higher-level interventions are designed for small groups or for individuals.

This multi-tiered model of learning intervention can be seen as a model of prevention and early intervention, and of increasingly focused, intensive intervention. An *if–then* process is central to this notion: *if* this doesn't work, *then* let's do something more focused or more intensive. However, since responsive teachers design and implement interventions at all three tiers, and educational caseworkers design and support implementation of intervention at all three levels, strict *if–then* thinking is not necessarily helpful. Instead, in this book we are using the notion of multi-levels of intervention more fluidly and flexibly. All tiers are to be considered as part of the wider design of appropriate intervention, from universal classroom instruction and responsive differentiation, to small group and individual evidence-based intervention that may be short or longer term.

Three layers of intervention

In a context where diagnoses of Learning Disabilities are not a part of the education system, RtI is instead used as a problem-solving decision-making process using evidence-based, increasingly intensive intervention and close monitoring (Riccomini & Smith, 2013; Symes, 2014). We therefore present a model derived from RtI that has layers of learning intervention, all of which need to be considered in educational casework decision-making. This conceptualisation is a more fluid representation of learning intervention and includes consideration of the best way of providing targeted intervention, within class teaching, in small groups or individually. Referral for assessment and educational casework will not necessarily result in an individual or small group intervention, remediating or compensating for an individual learner's so-called deficits. Instead, it may be most appropriate to support the teacher in more efficacious universal teaching, by strengthening universal design and responsive differentiation. As well, small group and individualised instruction within classes, and separate from classes, can be used as appropriate to best support learners at different times in their learning journeys. Decisions around these aspects of intervention are to be supported by the evidence that is available in relevant research, as well as in light of consideration of all the factors that will affect implementation in any particular context.

This approach, represented in Figure 3.2 has a focus on different sized groups of learners, from large classes, to small groups and individuals. In fact, the whole class and individual are the two fixed perspectives, with the other groupings created and adapted as and when needed. Teachers manage class programs and are responsible for each individual learner in the class. They get to know the class as a group of learners, and they get to know individual learners as well as possible. Based on those relationships, responsive teachers then draw flexibly on different groupings to meet the ever-changing learning needs of their students. There are many ways to group learners to optimise learning. Learners need to see that they are placed in groups using multiple criteria so that notions of all-round best or slowest group are not entrenched.

The notion of 'layers of intervention' is useful when thinking about options for designing and implementing instructional responses to student learning needs. Layers do not operate separately, instead they combine to provide learners with instructional opportunities that are tailored to individual and group learning needs. All layers contribute to the learning journey of individual students. This model depends on collaboration between classroom teachers and educational casework professionals to support the flexible use of layers of intervention. Sustainability of learning in this model is reflected in a combination of transfer of learning through the layers, as well as the maintenance of learning over time.

- In Layer 1, teachers provide evidence-based inclusive teaching, incorporating multiple modes of access to the curriculum (the Universal Design for Learning (UDL) model, outlined below), and noticing how students are responding

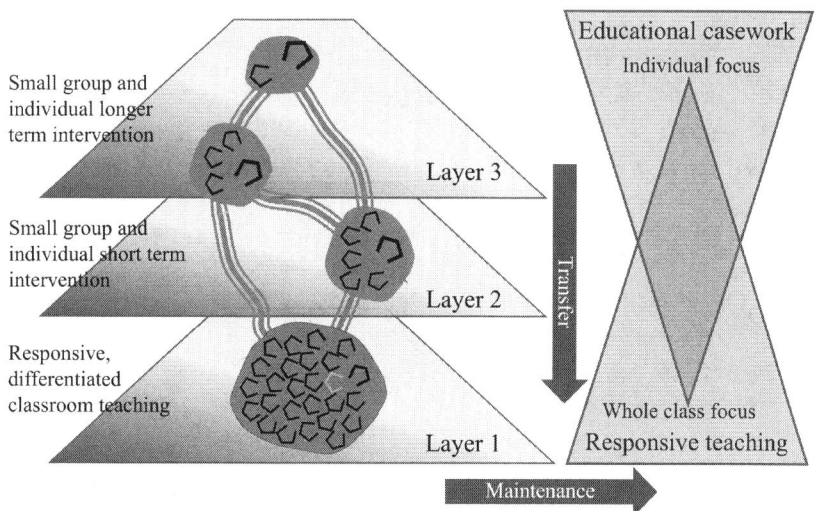

FIGURE 3.2   Layers of learning intervention

through careful monitoring and evaluative assessment. They then use increasingly responsive differentiation, designing learning opportunities and teaching strategies to match the actual variability of learning needs in the class, targeting group and individual learning needs.

- In Layer 2, teachers use short-term, flexible, small group and individual teaching within their class program, or elsewhere, that complements the class teaching.
- In Layer 3, individual or small group longer term intervention complements classroom teaching. In this layer, teachers collaborate with other professionals to make individualised adaptations for students in light of educational casework that involves specialised assessment and expertise.

Responsive classroom teaching extends into all three layers of learning intervention. Teachers often manage flexible grouping of the learners in a class, which is derived from the class program, along with short-term interventions that are happening as part of whole school support for learning. As well, some students in the class may have long-term intervention that is carried out within the class, or separate from it, that will influence consideration of the most appropriate learning opportunities and teaching strategies for that individual student.

Educational casework touches all layers as well. Although a learning intervention teacher or other professional is working within an individual case, the assessment information and any outcomes of intervention in small groups or individually within that casework have considerable implications for the base layer, the responsive teaching in the classroom. Ideally, collaboration between the class teacher and the caseworker will support well-founded decisions about the classroom learning opportunities and teaching strategies. Such casework will also support consideration of the possibilities of small group or individual short-term or longer-term intervention for any particular student.

Layer 1: Responsive classroom teaching

The foundational layer of learning intervention is inclusive class teaching. Its ultimate aim is that every learner's needs are met in the classroom. This is a worthy aim, and, as we have already established, a step towards this is to employ a responsive model of teaching that involves the flexible use of small group and individual learning experiences and is complemented by the kind of systematic educational casework that can strengthen classroom instruction.

Traditionally, learning opportunities in formal education have expected students to listen to or read information and then respond to that information in spoken or written form. Teachers have provided access to books, lectures or topic notes and then sought some structured response from their students, often in a written task. Many sets of textbooks are available to support this approach to teaching, and many schools rely on these commercially available books or programs to provide the curriculum content, structure the delivery and shape student responses for assessment.

Teaching of groups of students still relies on such conventional learning opportunities, although topic information is increasingly provided through multimedia.

The main framework for class lessons is often through the availability of multiple means for students to access information, to engage with it and to respond to it. Such provision of multiple means of access using frameworks like Universal Design for Learning aims to reduce barriers that may be present for some learners.

Universal Design for Learning

The Universal Design for Learning model (UDL: Meyer, Rose & Gordon, 2014; CAST, 2017) grew out of the discipline of architecture in which the principle of 'universal design' provides for anyone who needs access to the built environment. It relies on the idea that if a building is fully accessible by certain people, for example those who are in wheelchairs, then it will be accessible to everybody else. The same notion of making the curriculum and classroom learning activities accessible for all learners underpins UDL. This idea is often reflected in statements such as "if you make it right for children with disabilities, it will work for everyone". This approach acknowledges the fact that many disabilities are defined by aspects of the environment, and by the interactions of learners with their environments, rather than by inherent characteristics of the learners. It is, therefore, important to reduce any barriers that may be inherent in educational settings, before considering other compensatory or alternative strategies to meet learner needs.

One of the drivers for UDL is the anticipation of possibilities, since the learning needs of all students who come to the door of the classroom are not always known. Initially, class teaching is based on limited knowledge of a group of learners. This has always been the case, where teaching has been targeted towards what is expected of students in a particular grade and at a particular age and time of year based on the curriculum, but not based on knowing the individual learners. This teaching to the 'middle' of the class and expecting that some students will need more time to understand specific content, and that some students will need extension activities or deeper explanations was a standard approach. While this is a useful starting point it needs to be enhanced, and can be by using the UDL approach that focuses on how students access the curriculum, based on three principles:

- providing multiple means of representing the curriculum material to allow access for all (perception, language, mathematical expressions and symbols, and comprehension);
- providing multiple means of engagement (physical action, expression and communication, and executive functioning); and
- providing multiple ways for learners to manage and express their learning (recruiting interest, sustaining effort and persistence, and self-regulation) (CAST, 2011, p.5).

It can be useful to consider the nine aspects of these three principles in terms of ATRiUM capabilities, as shown in Figure 3.3. These principles map broadly across the ATRiUM capabilities, showing that they take into account all aspects of active learning. Similarly, that UDL principles can also be mapped against information

A **T** R **iU** M	1. Options for perception
A T R **iU** M	2. Options for language, mathematical expressions and symbols
A **T** R **iU** M	3. Options for comprehension
A T R iU M	4. Options for physical action
A **T** **R** **iU** M	5. Options for expression and communication
A **T** R iU **M**	6. Options for executive functioning
A **T** R iU M	7. Options for recruiting interest
A T R iU **M**	8. Options for sustaining effort and persistence
A T R iU **M**	9. Options for self-regulation

FIGURE 3.3   UDL and ATRiUM capabilities

processing theory (La Berge & Samuels, 1974) is a useful way of making sense of how these work to reduce barriers to learning. In simple terms, information processing is the taking in of information from the environment, thinking about it, and then producing information using action or language (Figure 3.4).

As Table 3.1 indicates, UDL guidelines relate to these main organising features of the information processing model of learning: how information is received; thought about; and responded to. More specifically, the emphasis in UDL is not only on multiple modes of presenting information for students to access (input) and demonstrate learning (output), but also on aspects of engagement (interest, autonomy, effort, persistence, collaboration and self-regulation) and action (goal setting, planning and strategy use, monitoring). In this way the UDL framework can be shown to acknowledge much more than the notion of access to curriculum content. It can map onto the full breadth of the ATRiUM capabilities for supporting learners and include the complexity of learners as emotional and social beings.

The UDL approach means that learning opportunities in classrooms can be much more diverse than they may have been previously. Although universal design was developed specifically to reduce barriers to building access for people with sensory or physical disabilities, it now underpins an educational approach that opens access to learning opportunities for everyone, including those learners who do not necessarily appear to need adjusted instruction, yet thrive when provided with a range of opportunities for learning. The bottom line is that teachers need to be prepared to teach a range of learners in any group, and can be proactive in providing multiple ways for students to become engaged, to access what they need and to demonstrate their learning.

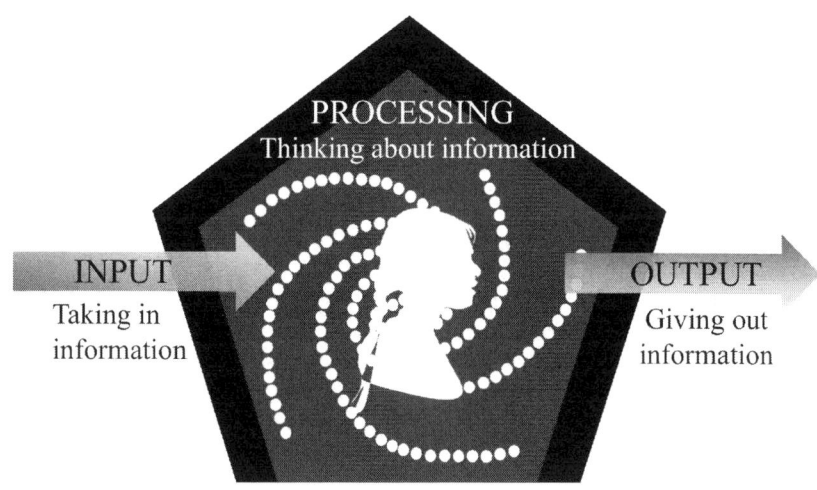

FIGURE 3.4   Information processing

TABLE 3.1 UDL and information processing

UDL guidelines (CAST, 2011)	*Information processing*		
	INPUT Taking in information	*PROCESSING* Thinking about information	*OUTPUT* Giving out information
1. Options for perception			
2. Options for language, mathematical expressions and symbols			
3. Options for comprehension			
4. Options for physical action			
5. Options for expression and communication			
6. Options for executive functioning			
7. Options for recruiting interest			
8. Options for sustaining effort and persistence			
9. Options for self-regulation			

Frameworks for universal design

Developing lessons, weekly plans and term programs involves making many decisions about learning opportunities and teaching strategies and their arrangement and intensity. There are many frameworks that can support teachers' creative planning of multiple learning opportunities, of universal design, for their classes, including Gardner's multiple intelligences and Bloom's taxonomy.

Gardner's model of multiple intelligences (1983, 1999) has been used by many teachers to provide a matrix of human activity against which teachers can be creative in the provision of learning opportunities. While we do not have room to critically explore the theoretical issues around defining multiple intelligences in this book, the domains of human activity and interests articulated in this model can be used to generate interesting ways of engaging students with school curriculum. By including learning opportunities that require logical–mathematical, linguistic, musical, spatial, bodily–kinaesthetic, interpersonal, intrapersonal, natural and existential (Gardner, 1999) activity, teachers optimise the possibilities for engagement across a class of students. The logical extension or real life application of this approach is through cross-curriculum learning activities, that draw on content and processes from multiple disciplines at the same time.

Similarly, Bloom's taxonomy (Anderson et al., 2001; Bloom, 1984; Bloom et al., 1956) can be used to generate multiple classroom activities that involve a range of thinking skills: knowledge and comprehension; application; analysis; synthesis; and evaluation. Creative teachers have taken such frameworks and elaborated on them to provide prompts for generating multiple learning opportunities. Wheel Work (Mackay & Hoy, 2002) is an example of such an approach using Bloom's taxonomy to structure options for learning activities. In this model, which is used collaboratively with students, the five types of thinking are explicitly presented, along with activities and the products of those activities that can be used as learning opportunities. Multiple activities and various options for products of learning extend the richness of instructional opportunities and are used by teachers, strategically, for extending or consolidating particular learning outcomes for their students. For example, analytical thinking can be engaged in through activities that include surveying, contrasting, classifying, comparing, separating or dissecting, and this activity can be evidenced in products such as diagrams, graphs, charts, questionnaires and reports.

From universal design to responsive teaching

Knowing about universal design and the proactive provision of multiple learning opportunities is just the beginning, since it is very rare not to know anything about the learners in a class we are teaching. We usually have some preliminary knowledge and with every lesson we get to know more about the learners that we can take into account when planning subsequent teaching. It is vital for teaching to connect with what the learning needs are across the class and for teachers to be responsive to what is known about their learners.

Teaching decisions are shaped and refined in response to increasing understandings of the learning needs of the group. Individuals in such groups become better known as teaching–learning relationships develop and the teacher gathers more information about the group and about individual learners.

Finding out about learners as students depends on effective assessment. It is not just assessment events like tests or assignments that can provide evidence of what each student knows and can do, it is every interaction in a classroom. Noticing student interactions and engaging in interactions will provide valuable evidence about how students engage with their learning environment, relate to others, think, manage themselves and actively learn.

Step 3 of the Responsive Teaching Framework (see Chapter 2) asks, 'What do my students bring as learners?' It means that teachers need to consider their students in every decision that they make. Teachers must ask this question perpetually, expecting different answers at different times because each learner is a dynamic human who is developing in a complex world. Sensitivity to how life experiences affect each learner is fundamental to being an effective, responsive teacher, and to having strong relationships with students. Some guiding questions are:

1   What community and family contexts do my students bring with them?
2   What interests do the students have and how do these change or stay the same?
3   What prior experiences have they had as individuals and as a group of students?
4   What achievements and patterns of learning have they demonstrated?
5   What individual personalities are evident? What attitudes to each other are visible?
6   What is the nature of the learning group (range of achievement, receptiveness to teaching, behaviours for active learning)? How do the students relate to each other?
7   What expectations do the students have about learning, teaching and assessment?

Teachers notice constantly, both consciously and unconsciously, the actions of students as learners and their complexity in a learning group. Interactions with students influence teachers' planning for learning. It is what makes a teacher truly responsive to group and individual learning needs. It is reflected in teachers' 'with-it-ness' in the classroom (Kounin, 1970).

What we are really assessing once our teaching is underway is the students' responsiveness to the learning opportunities and teaching strategies. Teachers take this information into account in planning the next learning opportunities and selecting the most appropriate teaching strategies.

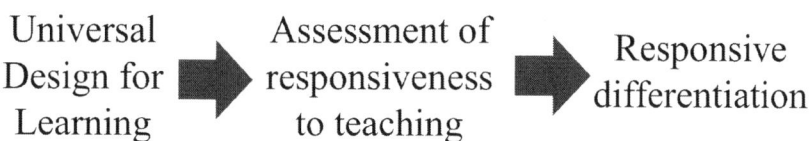

FIGURE 3.5   From UDL to responsive differentiation

Responsive differentiation

Differentiated instruction is "an approach by which teaching is varied and adapted to match students' abilities using systematic procedures for academic progress monitoring and data-based decision-making" (Roy, Guay & Valois, 2013, p.1187). Differentiation in education is anchored in international conventions, such as the United Nations Convention on the Rights of Persons with Disabilities (UNCRPD) (United Nations General Assembly, 2007), in national legislation and regulations such as the Australian Disability Discrimination Act, (1992) and National Standards for Disability (Commonwealth of Australia, 2006), and is translated into education system policies and practices. For example, the Australian Professional Standards for Teachers (AITSL, 2011) specifically include differentiation in one of the Standards (1.5 Differentiate teaching to meet the specific learning needs of students across the full range of abilities), which clearly makes differentiation core business for all teachers. It is part of a teacher's job to respond differently to students' diverse learning needs.

Differentiation aims to reduce the barriers to learning that are often associated with particular impairments or conditions. It is easy to consider this notion of differentiation of instruction in the context of, for example, learners who have physical or sensory impairments because there is considerable expertise in assistive and augmentative communication. For example, by using visual and auditory information together to ensure anyone with vision or hearing difficulties will be still able to access information; and in using cleverly designed furniture and equipment that allows learners with physical disabilities to be able to move independently around learning spaces and to access materials. However, when less visible impairments or differences are considered, differentiation becomes less clear. The process of considering what helps and hinders learning, though, is still as important. It is essential in designing learning activities in classrooms that are not in themselves barriers to learning.

The practice of universal design grew out of a need to provide alternatives for learners who could not engage, act or demonstrate learning using the conventional strategies in classrooms, and this is still one of the situations in which it is essential. However, it is also the job of teachers to engineer instruction in such a way so that each learner is stretched and becomes increasingly independent. As an example, by always providing spoken instructions teachers may build a reliance on them as instructors. Alternatively, by always providing visual and written instructions an expectation may be set that these will always be available. Such reliance on particular strategies can be as limiting as not providing them.

As teachers get to know the learners in their classes it may be that some of the options for student engagement are not used much, while others are used frequently. Teachers need to consider all options and make decisions about whether some or all learners, in fact, need to experience other ways of engaging, or being active or of demonstrating learning. Careful and considered decisions about how far to lead learners out of their comfort zones is integral to extending them and is central to decision-making about differentiation. Teachers can, for example, use carefully engineered option or choice boards, and keep records of student choices, so that the pitfalls of providing multiple opportunities are noticed and managed. All students, for example, need to practise academic written responses that provide opportunities for receiving targeted feedback and refining skills.

Considering how to differentiate instruction raises a key issue for educators that relates to how we know what is needed to support our students' learning. As teachers support the increased self-management of learning for students, they move towards accessing student voice and negotiating appropriate learning opportunities. That means teachers facilitate the expression of student opinions, and take their perspectives into account in teaching decisions about differentiating for depth and quality of learning, and when making planned or on-the-spot adaptations.

Differentiating for depth and quality of learning

The SOLO taxonomy is a framework used widely for developing learning opportunities that cover a range of quality of cognitive learning or levels of thinking within a class. This theoretical basis for distinguishing between increasing levels of the quality of written work from school students was developed by Australian researchers John Biggs and Kevin Collis in the 1980s. Biggs and Collis (1982) systematically explored what it is that makes some students' work judged to be of a better quality, and thus evidence of deeper learning. By examining many student responses to typical school questions, the patterns of development of thinking were revealed as Structure of Observed Learning Outcome (SOLO) levels. This theory has been expanded to focus on the development of thinking skills and can be used to plan teaching for higher quality thinking (See Chapter 9).

Other models assist with teaching for greater expertise. The Dreyfus model of adult skill acquisition (Dreyfus, 2004) outlines five stages that have been extracted from analyses of tasks (See Chapter 9). This model has been applied to teaching in many professional learning contexts, including medicine, and has resonance with teaching skills to younger students, as it maps the journey of learning from novice, to advanced beginner, to competence, to proficiency and finally to expertise. The first stage is to remove a task from its context and pull it apart – deconstruct it into "context-free features that the beginner can recognize without the desired skill" (Dreyfus, 2004, p.177). This aligns with a typical task analysis approach in special education (Allinder, 1994).

Making planned adaptations

Differentiation is not just something you do by making adjustments to teaching plans, although that is how this whole process began, and is still appropriate in some contexts. The focus on adjustments to a teaching plan is derived from the idea that there is some form of generic teaching that is appropriate for most learners and that we can tweak for those learners who are not 'typical'. Many teachers teach to the middle of their classes and plan to stretch forward or extend some students and re-teach others. In this book, we want to move away from such a normative approach to one that begins with the intended curriculum learning outcomes and then immediately prompts teachers to generate a range of learning opportunities that provide for all their students. The aim is achieving those learning outcomes for all learners in our charge. Although teachers might start with a large range of learning opportunities, as they get to know their students they will be able to refine the range of learning opportunities so that their responsive teaching becomes more targeted to their students' particular needs.

Teachers need to make decisions about what is the right level of challenge for each learner or group of learners. They need to match learning opportunities to particular learners, based on hypotheses about what will provide the best learning for them. Allowing students to always select activities or modalities that are comfortable for them may restrict their learning just as much as providing the wrong opportunities. Good teachers determine which learning opportunities are just right at any particular time and support their students in taking risks and making the most of them. Teachers can also take prepared learning opportunities and adjust or adapt them to work better, based on what they know about their students as learners.

Planned adaptations are made based on information provided by previous teachers, other professionals, parents and the students themselves. Teachers may have access to comprehensive reports and files of information about particular learners that provide insights to inform planned adaptations. They can also use their insights that have been formed by experience with individual learners, particularly by reflecting on the on-the-spot adaptations made during previous teaching and learning interactions.

This planning can also incorporate the focus of individual teaching plans (e.g., Individual Education Plans (IEPs), Individual Learning Plans (ILPs), Personalised Learning Plans (PLPs), etc.) that have been developed for some students. Education systems have requirements that specify the development of individually focused intervention plans for some students. These requirements depend on different criteria and circumstances. A challenge for teachers is including the information that is a part of Individual Learning Plans into the whole class program.

Any teacher can generate a creative range of learning activities and present them to a class of students. But it takes a responsive mindset to take this universal approach to the next step, to make sure that the learning opportunities match the sets of learning needs that exist in the class. Considerable planning and documenting of evidence is required to make that responsiveness visible. Development of inclusive classroom programs (Graham, Berman & Bellert, 2002) as flexible, living documents supports not only the immediate functioning of the classroom but also the sustainability of planning across teachers. Essential aspects of inclusive classroom programs include intended curriculum learning outcomes, focus content, teaching/learning activities, indicators of learning, evaluation and individual focus. The individual focus comes from the educational casework that works in partnership with the classroom teaching, which has a focus on individual learning needs of students.

Making on-the-spot adaptations

Teachers also make on-the-spot adaptations to differentiate instruction throughout all their teaching. There can be mismatches between what we anticipate will be engaging and appropriate for our students and what works on the day. In such cases, teachers have to be expert at making adjustments and adaptations to ensure success for students. Effective teachers also make on-the-spot adaptations all the time to tailor interactions with learners in their classes.

Decisions about how to organise responsive differentiation are based on knowledge of what students bring as individual learners, as well as how they fit together as a group of learners. This is Step 3 of the Responsive Teaching Framework. This complex activity can be organised through the ATRiUM model. Knowledge of learners is not just knowing levels of achievement in learning, it is also about how each learner actively engages, thinks, relates to others, uses language and other symbol systems and manages him or herself – how the ATRiUM capabilities are enacted. We do not know all this information when we first plan for teaching, but we do get to know more about each learner and about group functions as we engage in teaching and learning interactions. We also use a range of conceptual models or theories based in our own knowledge to make sense of, and to share understanding of, these capabilities.

In essence, what we are describing here is how we teach in response to what we know about our group of learners and each learner in that group and how we match learning opportunities to the learning needs of each of our students. This is an approach that needs to be inherent in everything we do as teachers, in response to what we know about the learners for whom we are providing learning opportunities. This responsive teaching is supported by assessment knowledge as well as by use of evidence-based instruction and differentiation processes. It is also influenced by reflective practice and evaluation of teaching, when we continually return to consider what effect our teaching has had on learners.

Layer 2: Small group and individual short-term intervention

The second layer of learning intervention involves small group or individual teaching for short periods of time. There are many reasons for this focus, including priorities and resources of governments, education systems, communities, families and schools, and perceived needs of particular students. Learning opportunities in small group work will mirror those available in classrooms. They relate to those outlined in the previous section. As well, the focus here can be on learning opportunities that can be provided in individual teaching; one teacher and one learner in the short term. The first step is to put small group and individual learning opportunities into contexts.

Many schools organise intensive and targeted small group or individual teaching for short periods of time to meet particular learning needs. Some casework is also short term and follows the process of developing a responsive intervention aimed at compensating for a short-term need. This type of intervention is central to a learning intervention approach which seeks to find an intensive, explicit systematic intervention that can compensate for delays or disorders in learning. This emphasises the underpinnings of this approach related to intervention – the belief that we can compensate for many learning difficulties and provide learners with the skills and confidence to engage with classroom instruction.

Flexible grouping, as a way to organise differentiation, is a part of inclusive classroom planning. Such flexible responsive teaching is deliberate and based on what is known about the learners as a group and as individuals, and is determined in relation to pragmatic factors that are in play in every teaching situation. Teachers need to plan the best groupings and make decisions about whether students work with teachers or tutors for every learning activity in order to get the best results for their students. Assessment that supports this finer grained instructional differentiation may include more targeted and individualised assessment, particularly for learners with identified disabilities or learning difficulties, who may also bring with them assessment reports from medical and allied health professionals that can assist in developing a deeper understanding of their educational needs.

Sometimes short-term interventions are developed, not by a systematic casework process that determines the need for intervention, but through access to resources and the opportunity to provide more intensive resourcing to learning support for a period of time due to the availability of government grants and changes in funding priorities. When school staff have to find the appropriate students to match the intervention that is being funded and offered, it is 'the wrong way around' but certainly a real circumstance that affects schools. This raises questions about what happens in response to additional resources for intervention, and how sustainable the outcomes may be, not only for learners but also for school-based professionals. In such situations it is important to consider the best ways to provide useful, relevant short-term intervention for groups or individual students so their needs are met as well as the needs of the system.

This situation is also the case when higher degree professional students are required to complete short periods of practicum in learning intervention that include a casework focus on individual students. Ethically, it is important for such short-term, discrete casework interventions not only to meet the needs of the practicum student but also to contribute meaningfully to the learning of the school student.

Layer 3: Small group or individual longer-term intervention

This third layer of learning intervention refers to small group or individualised intervention for longer time periods that is experienced by some students. The students for whom this kind of support is a reality are usually those with significant disabilities or developmental delays that have been recognised as needing intervention throughout the school years. They can also be learners who experience significant ongoing learning or behavioural difficulties. In these instances, these students are the focus of ongoing casework, which every year reconsiders what type of intervention is most appropriate at this time for these learners.

Allied health and education professionals such as Teachers of the Deaf, speech pathologists, occupational therapists and physiotherapists often work individually or with small groups for long periods of time to support development of particular speech and language or physical skills. These skills need to be practised in the classroom context to have a continuing effect on student performance.

Some children will be engaged in individual intervention from birth because of identified developmental needs related to hearing or vision impairment, developmental disorders or syndromes. Other students will be identified in early childhood settings as having differences in development and responsiveness to teaching that indicate the need for more intensive or systematic early teaching. This issue cannot be separated from the evidence that shows clearly that from early in their lives learners are on learning trajectories, influenced by their family and community resources, their indigeneity and other factors well before formal schooling starts. Many students remain on those trajectories despite the heavy investment that schooling puts into enhancing their development.

For some children small group and individual intervention with early childhood teachers and paediatric allied health workers (e.g., psychologists, speech pathologists, occupational therapists and physiotherapists) is usual and continues to be a part of the layers of learning intervention experienced by them throughout school. These students will experience learning intervention in all layers; responsive teaching and differentiation in the classroom as well as small group and individual intervention. Sometimes small group or individual intervention is with a consistent professional such as a speech pathologist. Sometimes it is inconsistent and draws on whoever is employed and rostered at the time, often with a teaching assistant.

Teaching assistants working with students with disabilities

Although teaching assistants (teacher aides, education support workers) can be involved in students' learning across all layers of intervention, they are often significant in Layer 3. This happens when teaching assistants are employed to support individual students whose profile of learning strengths and weaknesses meet the criteria for a disability, or high support needs, within an education system. In this particular situation, the individual intervention is carried out over the long term, throughout their early childhood and school years.

Another facet of learning intervention that can create considerable inconsistency in individual intervention is the deployment of teaching assistants in schools, many of whom are expected to manage individual teaching sessions, sometimes for years with one student, sometimes with whomever is eligible each year. This situation raises questions around the skills of teaching assistants in carrying out teaching, something that is otherwise considered a skill set of registered graduates of higher education. Ethical and professional issues around this practice need to be considered by learning intervention professionals.

Responsive teaching requires teachers to make careful decisions about how best to use teaching assistant time to support student learning. There needs to be planning time together and the active supervision by teachers (Butt, 2016). From a teacher's point of view, it is important that everyone working with students provides just enough support to scaffold learning and knows when to withdraw support and encourage independence. Based on Vygotsky's (1978) ideas of scaffolding, providing just enough support and then consciously withdrawing it assists learners to become more self-managing. In this way, teachers and parents find opportunities to assist students to become independent learners. It is important, also, to consider the role of teaching assistants through this lens and how they provide scaffolding, and yet not hinder the development of self-regulation for the students they support.

Homework

In many education systems children go home with activities to do. Sometimes this work is exploratory or research focused and can be collaboratively done with parents and siblings. At other times it is work to be done independently, often with the aim of consolidating or practising skills or applying what was learnt in class in an extended problem. Handing in this homework to the teacher is a usual part of many classes. This practice of extending school work into out of school hours is in fact Layer 2 or 3 learning intervention in an informal way. Although homework is designed as an extension of the class teaching program, for many students, and particularly those with learning difficulties of any sort, it can become individual intervention with family members as tutors. For example, requests by teachers for parents to help their child practise multiplication tables or number facts falls into this layer of individual intervention that complements classroom teaching.

The effect size of homework on academic achievement is very low, at 0.29 (Hattie, 2009, 2011, 2015) and it has been found to be most effective in grades 7 to 12. Many factors contribute to these effects. A summary of evidence suggests that teachers need to design homework with quality and interest in mind rather than quantity. Its purpose should be to link the tasks to the classroom and provide explicit support for managing homework activities and to have conversations with students about their homework, providing timely, individual feedback (Xu, 2013).

Many schools provide support for families around homework, with pamphlets and information sessions at school, about how to support young children learning to read or do mathematics. This approach to partnering with parents is a way to increase the impact of classroom learning, by having families use the same strategies and language that are used in the classroom (and that are probably different to that used when those parents were at school themselves). Explicit strategies are sometimes encouraged, for example, the process of *pause, prompt, praise* (McNaughton,

Pause to give your child time to work out the word

- *What do you think the word could be? (D, V) Does this make sense? (C)*
- *What sounds could these letters (groups of letters) make? (D)*
- *Listen, the sounds in that word are (e.g.) r-e-st what word does that make? (P)*

Prompt	- *Does it look like another word you know? (D & V)*

- *Read on and see if we can work out what word might make sense. (C) Does it look like it could be that word? (D)*
- *Go back to the beginning of the sentence. (C & F)*
- *What does the picture tell you? (C & V)*
- *Tell your child the word (V)*

Praise your child for effort and for using different strategies

FIGURE 3.6   Pause, prompt, praise and key literacy competencies

Glyn & Robinson, 1981; Wheldall & Mettem, 1985) when listening to a child read is often found in resources for parents. The example in Figure 3.6 shows how these prompts can explicitly reflect the five key competences in literacy – phonemic awareness (P), decoding (D), vocabulary (V), comprehension (C) and/or fluency (F) (National Reading Panel, 2000).

Home programs, commercially available workbooks, Internet and apps

In some situations, families are the intervention tutors for programs provided by allied health or educational professionals that work better if there is daily practice. For example, speech pathologists may have taught a parent how to model and shape articulation in speech and asked that the parent provides opportunities for practice and feedback daily in the home. This is often also the case in situations of physical therapies.

Intervention for learning is also a commercial business and many families choose to purchase access to programs for their children that are separate from school. Many families organise out of school tutoring that continues for longer time periods aimed at preparing children for opportunities such as selective school examinations.

Other families have taken on the role of complementing school learning by accessing resources to use in teaching at home. Commercially available workbooks have been available forever, and the range of them continues to grow. They focus on curriculum topics and include activities that can be done at home, often in the form of worksheets to be completed. There is also a large range of books that provide preparation for the large-scale testing that is a part of some education systems.

Children are accessing computers and tablets and are being introduced to apps (applications) earlier than ever. While many adults learnt their computer skills as children or adults, the current and future generations are beginning to learn these before they can talk. There are thousands of apps available that claim to teach particular domains of knowledge or skills and these are being used intensively in homes and cars. In these cases the role of tutor or teacher is taken up by a computer program and the effort put in by the young child depends on the feedback from the program in response to the inputs of the child. Though beyond the scope of this book, this is an increasingly significant part of the context of learning for many students and needs to be taken into account.

Flexible use of layers of learning intervention

Educational casework is focused on an individual learner. However, such casework can result in changes to teaching at any level: from universal classroom teaching to intensive individual instruction. In this book we provide a way of thinking about how educational casework can support learning intervention at all three layers, in conjunction with responsive classroom teaching. This works best when other professionals team with the teacher throughout the casework to negotiate the focus of

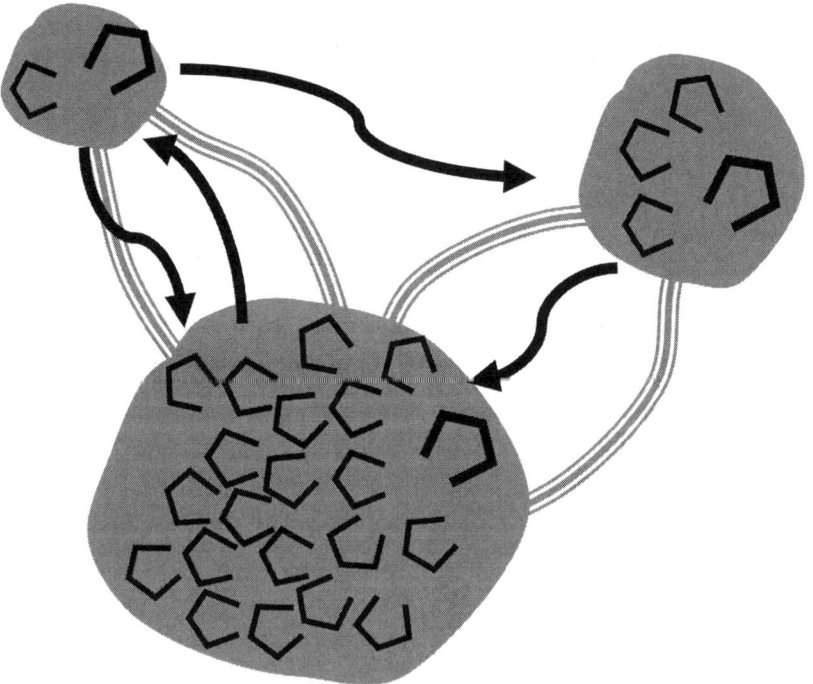

FIGURE 3.7   Flexible use of individual and small group teaching connected to the classroom program

the casework and the realities of the classroom and school within which intervention is to be implemented.

The mixture of individual, small group and large group learning at the heart of the 'layers of intervention' model emphasises that it is essential to have strong links between what is being taught in individual or small group sessions and what is being taught in the classroom. For example, strategies such as pre-teaching during intervention sessions can be used strategically to prepare learners for the content that is to be introduced later in the class. Similarly, small group or individual teaching can assist with the consolidation of classroom introduced learning.

All learning intervention has to be aimed at making responsive classroom teaching as effective as possible. Educational casework needs to consider how to support targeted differentiation in response to what is known about a learner, through sharing information from assessment with the classroom teacher in order to shape appropriate differentiation. The use of small group and individual intervention can be within classroom differentiated instruction or separate, and may be appropriate for a short term or a longer term.

Each school sets up processes for offering and managing different layers of intervention that is influenced by a number of key factors. One factor is how school systems organise their response to the variability of learning needs amongst students and the allocation of funds or resources distributed in response to how schools demonstrate their level of resourcing need.

Individual schools also set up systems and procedures, and spaces and places, that frame how they provide support to learners with learning difficulties and disabilities. For example, some schools have well-resourced learning intervention departments, variously called 'learning support', 'learning enhancement', 'the learning centre' or 'special education' that provide intervention for a number of students. Each school develops a system for identifying and selecting those students who will access the intervention services.

Schools also have a range of systems and processes that determine the alignment that exists between classroom teaching and specialist intervention. In many government school systems there is a move toward deploying learning intervention teachers as consultants rather than as teachers. In these schools, specialist teachers may team teach to provide support in classrooms. This is the typical approach used in many education systems that are working towards inclusion and the equitable allocation of limited resources available for supporting learners with learning difficulties or disabilities. Such an approach increasingly places the expertise of the learning intervention teacher in classrooms for as much time as possible, and expects considerable collaboration between teachers and other professionals such as psychologists or speech pathologists. The aim is to increase the capacity of all those involved to better support the classroom learning of all students.

In contrast, some schools employ learning intervention teachers to exclusively provide individual and small group intervention for selected students. The nature of the intervention may be predetermined, it may be through a commercially available literacy program, or it may be developed in response to the psychoeducational assessment of individual learning needs and part of subsequently developed evidence-based individual learning plans. Compartmentalising learning can occur in such situations and bring with it all the problems of generalisation. Other challenges include the nature of collective responsibility for the efficient and effective use of expertise to make positive differences. Such differences in frameworks in practice raise issues around equity, efficiency, responsibility, collaboration and efficacy.

There can also be confusion about the meaning of *inclusion*. In some schools there is a belief that all teaching and intervention has to occur in the classroom – that this location 'means' inclusion. Certainly, inclusion aims to build teacher capacity so that all learning needs can be met in usual daily practice, but translating this goal into the belief that everything has to happen in the same room is simplistic. It may not be effective to organise all small group and individual teaching in classrooms for pragmatic reasons, such as space and noise. Determining an appropriate space for each learning activity is part of effective decision-making in learning intervention. Just as it is not appropriate for a student of the violin to have individual lessons or to practice in the same room as everyone else, it is also not appropriate for all learning to happen in the classroom. Instead, careful consideration of the best place or space for teaching and learning is essential.

Educational casework and layers of learning intervention

Educational casework can contribute to responsive teaching at all three layers, but this is not always what happens. Although considerable work can be done in casework, it may or may not contribute to making teaching more responsive and effective in the classroom. Even in the same education setting it is not uncommon for learning intervention staff to work completely separately from classroom teachers. They may provide small group and individual intervention within a timetable, but not necessarily consult with others, or negotiate what is to be targeted, and how best to teach it. Instead, many schools have program-based intervention, implemented by specialist teachers and teaching assistants, which is assumed to be sustainable and transferable to the classroom. Such logic is based on assumptions that evidence-based (or sometimes not) programs can be effective without being connected to the main game of classroom learning. While this may be possible, the large investment that goes into such multilayered intervention would be much more effective if there was collaboration, and negotiated programs that linked learning opportunities in the classroom with those provided through small group or individual intervention. Similarly, in cases where students are engaged in out of school small group or individual intervention, alignment and connection increases effect, and supports the student in making links between what is learnt in both settings and how to combine these to realise more effective learning.

Responsive teaching and educational casework are not solo tasks, they are aligned to support the best possible teaching across all layers. Drawing on multiple professional disciplines is an inherent part of intervention for learners experiencing learning difficulties or disabilities. These professionals assist teachers and families to make decisions about the most appropriate focus and level of intervention, to establish ways to assess the subsequent learning and to evaluate the intervention as the basis for subsequent decisions about intervention. One of the highest ranked factors identified as important to student achievement by Hattie (2016) relates to *collective efficacy*, the notion that the collaboration of people and their sense of being able to succeed through working together enhances educational endeavour.

The core people at the centre of any learning intervention are the learner and the teacher. This happens at multiple levels. It begins as a general relationship with the class group of learners and is refined into many individual relationships as the teacher gets to know individual students. The fluidity of relationships is the essence of being a responsive teacher who can draw on whichever level of intensity and/ or group size is considered to best meet learning needs at any time. There is a real skill in being able to establish and nurture a sound relationship that is perpetuated through intermittent connections such as those that occur in high schools.

But there are many other people who are variously involved in the processes of intervention through responsive teaching and educational casework. Taking advantage of the expertise of the many people interested in learning and development of students is important. It enriches the decision-making and creates a shared responsibility for implementing intervention. As already noted in this chapter, there can be many people involved with students who are the focus of casework in education. These include educational psychologists, speech pathologists, mental health professionals, counsellors, social workers, paediatricians, medical professionals, teachers (from graduate, to competent, highly proficient and lead), executive teachers, special educators, early intervention specialists, disability support staff, welfare personnel, social support workers, parents, caregivers, extended family, siblings and other students.

Collaboration in educational casework can be complicated, because it draws on the expertise of many people from multiple disciplines. Including professional voices in assessment supports a much more rounded picture of the factors affecting the learning and development of a student. The mere act of asking questions of people serves as intervention, raising consciousness of issues and seeking input. Such multi-professional input into casework provides multiple lenses that enrich the analysis of developmental and learning needs and the generation of ways forward for intervention for students experiencing learning difficulties, disabilities and behavioural and mental health issues.

In line with the dynamic systems view of human functioning, disciplines, researchers and professionals are realising that it is more efficacious to draw on whatever is known about development, health and learning in order to provide more grounded and broad interventions. That means linking medical and health knowledge with educational and therapeutic knowledge from psychology to help design multidimensional interventions.

When teachers and other professionals work together, with shared understanding of learning needs and aligned goals, there will be a better outcome. Schools vary in terms of expectations for the degree of communication and collaboration that occurs between teachers and between any specialist department and classroom teachers. However, some schools see these two groups of educational professionals as separate, each having discrete responsibility for classroom teaching or intervention, and, therefore, no attempt at professional collaboration is encouraged. Including multiple people in implementation of intervention is challenging but supports more efficacious intervention.

Summary

In this chapter we have explored the three layers of learning intervention that work together to support classroom teaching and learning. The foundation layer is the provision of universal instruction that is designed to maximise access to learning for all those who are in the class. Extending that access as more is known about individual learners in a class requires careful, responsive differentiation of learning opportunities and teaching strategies that is managed by a responsive teacher in order to provide appropriate challenges for all learners. Complementing differentiated classroom instruction are two layers of small group and individual intervention. Short-term intervention is instigated by classroom teachers, or within educational casework, and aims to support learning in the classroom. Longer-term individual or small group intervention is common for students who have identified disabilities and who may be supported by allied health professionals or by teaching assistants within classrooms. All of these layers can be used flexibly to better support learning within classrooms for all learners.

References

Allinder, R. M. (1994). The relationship between efficacy and the instructional practices of special education teachers and consultants. *Teacher Education and Special Education, 17*(2), 86–95.

Anderson, L., Krathwohl, D., Airasian, P., Cruikshank, K., Mayer, R., Pintrich, P., et al. (2001). *A taxonomy for learning, teaching, and assessing: A revision of Bloom's taxonomy of educational objectives (Complete edition)*. New York, NY: Longman.

Australian Institute for Teaching and School Leadership (AITSL) (2011). *Australian Professional Standards for Teachers*. Melbourne, VIC: AITSL. https://www.aitsl.edu.au/docs/default-source/apst-resources/australian_professional_standard_for_teachers_final.pdf

Biggs, J. & Collis, K. (1982). *Evaluating the quality of learning: The SOLO taxonomy (structure of the observed learning outcome)*. New York, NY: Academic Press.

Bloom, B. (1984). *Taxonomy of educational objectives: Handbook of cognitive domain*. New York, NY: Longman.

Bloom, B., Englehart, M., Furst, E., Hill, W., & Krathwohl, D. (1956). *Taxonomy of educational objectives: The classification of educational goals. Handbook I: Cognitive domain*. New York, NY: Longmans Green.

Butt, R. (2016). Teacher assistant support and deployment in mainstream schools. *International Journal of Inclusive Education*, 1–13. Retrieved from http://dx.doi.org/10.1080/1360311 6.2016.1145260

Centre for Applied Special Technology (CAST) (2011) *Universal Design for Learning guidelines version 2.0*. Wakefield, MA: CAST.

Centre for Applied Special Technology (CAST) (2017). *About universal design for learning*, www.cast.org/our-work/about-udl.html#.WZN6OHcjGV4

Commonwealth of Australia (2006). Disability standards for education 2005 plus guidance notes. Barton, ACT: Australian Government.

Dreyfus, S. (2004). The five-stage model of adult skill acquisition. *Bulletin of Science, Technology and Society, 24*, 177–181.

Gardner, H. (1983). *Frames of mind: The theory of multiple intelligences.* New York, NY: Basic Books.

Gardner, H. (1999). *Intelligence reframed: Multiple intelligences for the 21st century.* New York, NY: Basic Books.

Graham, L., Berman, J., & Bellert, A. (2002). Practical literacy programming for students with disabilities: Making IEPs work in the classroom. In Gordon, B. (Ed.), *Practical literacy programming.* Sydney, NSW: Primary English Teachers Association (PETA), 121–135.

Hattie, J. (2009). *Visible learning: A synthesis of over 800 meta-analyses relating to achievement.* Abingdon: Routledge.

Hattie, J. (2011). *Visible learning for teachers: Maximising impact on learning.* London: Routledge.

Hattie, J. (2015). The applicability of Visible Learning to higher education. *Scholarship of Teaching and Learning in Psychology, 1*(1), 79–91.

Hattie, J. (2016). *Shifting away from distractions to improve Australia's schools.* Jack Keating Memorial Lecture, University of Melbourne, June.

Kounin, J. S. (1970). *Discipline and group management in classrooms.* New York, NY: Holt, Rinehart & Winston.

La Berge, D. & Samuels, S. J. (1974). Toward a theory of automatic information processing in reading. *Cognitive Psychology, 6*(2), 293–323.

Mackay, B. & Hoy, L. (2002). *Wheel Work: An educational approach to life long learning.* West Tamworth, NSW: Coolabah Publishing.

McNaughton, S., Glyn, T., & Robinson, V. (1981) *Parents as remedial reading tutors: Issues for home and school.* Wellington: New Zealand Council for Educational Research.

Meyer, A., Rose, D., & Gordon, D. (2014). *Universal design for learning: Theory and practice.* Wakefield, MA: CAST Professional Publishing.

Mitchell, D. (2014). *What really works in special and inclusive education: Using evidence-based teaching strategies* (2nd ed.). London: Routledge.

National Reading Panel (US), National Institute of Child Health and Human Development (US) (2000). *Report of the National Reading Panel: Teaching children to read: An evidence-based assessment of the scientific research literature on reading and its implications for reading instruction: Reports of the subgroups.* Washington, DC: National Institute of Child Health and Human Development, National Institutes of Health.

Riccomini, P. & Smith, G. (2013) Response to intervention: The sum is greater than the parts. In Hattie, J. & Anderman, E. (Eds.), *International guide to student achievement.* New York, NY: Routledge, 345–346.

Roy, A., Guay, F., & Valois, P. (2013) Teaching to address diverse learning needs: Development and validation of a Differentiated Instruction Scale. *International Journal of Inclusive Education, 17*(11), 1186–1204.

Symes, R. (2014). *An exploration of ways in which Waikato primary school principals address the multiple learning requirements of children with special educational needs.* Master of Educational Leadership Thesis. Hamilton, NZ: University of Waikato. http://researchcommons. waikato.ac.nz/bitstream/handle/10289/8724/thesis.pdf?sequence=3

United Nations General Assembly (2007). *Convention on the rights of persons with disabilities.* Geneva: UNGA.

Vygotsky, L. S. (1978). *Mind in society: The development of higher psychological processes.* Cambridge, MA: Harvard University Press.

Wheldall, K. & Mettem, P. (1985). Behavioural peer tutoring: Training 16-year-old tutors to employ the 'pause, prompt and praise' method with 12-year-old remedial readers. *Educational Psychology, 5*(1), 27–44.

Xu, J. (2013). Homework and academic achievement. In Hattie, J. & Anderman, E. (Eds.), *International guide to student achievement.* New York, NY: Routledge, 199–201.

4

SCOPING LEARNING INTERVENTION

Learning intervention is highly complicated. It is not a matter of using an algorithm into which we place what is known about the learner and out pops a teaching plan. Learning intervention is multidimensional and needs to be directed at the changes or learning that we intend to activate. It also needs to take into account the factors that influence specific instances of learning because individuals' learning needs keep changing. Learning intervention is about providing opportunities to learn and involves the consideration of a number of key dimensions of decision-making relevant to responsive teachers and their collaborators. Throughout this book we delineate many of the dimensions of learning intervention, along with the kinds of questions that educational professionals ask as they design these kinds of learning opportunities. In this chapter, we discuss what is involved in defining the scope of an intervention so that it is manageable and has clear boundaries around it.

The scope of the intervention, its priorities and parameters, need to be clarified as they underpin decisions about the use of evidence bases, assessment planning, learning opportunities and teaching. The following guiding questions help determine the priorities and parameters of learning intervention.

1 How was this learning intervention instigated? What sort of reporting will be required?
2 What is the focus of the learning intervention in reference to curriculum and the ATRiUM capabilities?
3 What is the context within which the learning will be applied?
4 What is the time frame for the intervention?
5 What people are involved in the intervention (professionals, teaching assistants, family and other students, professional education student)? What is the current learning group?

6   What is the learning environment within which the intervention is to be implemented?
7   What layers of learning intervention are appropriate? How will these be connected to classroom teaching?
8   What factors will support and hinder intervention implementation?

Instigation of the intervention

This is an important preliminary issue that frames educational casework and intervention. It is necessary to be clear about how the learning intervention was instigated as this reveals the initial 'problem', or set of learning needs, to be addressed. It is also a way to clearly define for whom this intervention is most important and how this relates to the focus student.

In an ideal world the education system would be responsive to the learning needs of all students and able to provide resources for flexible, layered learning intervention as needed. However, there is not always alignment between the resources available to implement learning intervention with small groups or individual students and the need for such intervention. Politics and economics often play a large role in this process, taking the focus from the learning needs and putting it on other factors such as extra funding or more personnel to be able to provide short-term small group or individual intervention to complement classroom learning. As we have already noted, responsiveness depends on the flexibility of layered learning intervention that can be used to address current learning needs.

There are times in the political cycle, for example, when schools can access additional resources to provide more layered learning intervention. When this does happen, schools sometimes scramble to make the most of these additional resources. Sometimes the resourcing is allocated based on needs at a state or national level, or in response to lobbying from particular community and advocacy groups. Extra funding usually comes with criteria for selection of students to participate, which may not be resonant with a school's current way of working. This can make it difficult to accept support for some students, while others, who may be seen to be more in need, miss out. This situation may cause the school to shift resources to balance what is being provided, so that access to learning intervention is seen to be more equitable than it may otherwise have been.

If a school has a model of flexible layered intervention, however, it may be better equipped to be responsive to policy changes. In all such situations, the purpose is to provide the best layered learning intervention that resources allow, and at the same time strengthen the capacity of school staff members so that impact on student learning is sustained. With this in mind, it is particularly important to take opportunities to build the capacity of classroom teachers, who will still be responding to the students' learning needs when any extra resourcing has finished.

Notice that we have not yet mentioned the learners in this unpacking of learning intervention! Staff of responsive schools will know their students and their learning needs and will be able to quickly identify those students for whom intensive, small group or individual short-term intervention will be most valuable. Ideally, they will also be able to adapt in order to make the most of any opportunity to provide layered learning intervention.

Individually focused educational casework happens in response to a referral of some sort. Schools have processes for referring individual students for more intensive educational and developmental assessment in order to base their educational decisions on more substantial evidence than may be available through usual assessment practices. Teachers and families often wonder about a child's learning and development, and then seek to find out more in order to understand how best to support learning.

Referral for further assessment is often associated with RtI Tier 3 in schools (see Chapter 3), when in-school small group intervention has been used to some extent and there are still questions about the nature of learning and how best to teach an individual student. Reporting on assessment results will be shaped by the nature of the referral and the people involved in the responsive teaching or the educational casework. It will also respond to the requirements of the school and education system. Discussing the response to a referral will again require more collaboration between the class teacher, the student's family and educational professionals.

The focus of the intervention

Referrals for learning intervention come in many shapes and sizes and are influenced by the referrers' perceptions of the problem, their previous experiences and what they understand to be available as learning intervention. What is needed is for those involved in the intervention to establish a shared understanding of the focus as a starting point. Generally, the focus begins with learning or behavioural needs that become more defined as they are clarified within the framework of the curriculum and the ATRiUM capabilities.

Sometimes the focus of the referral is exactly appropriate and can be the basis of responsive teaching or casework. As an example, a student may be referred for literacy intervention because the teacher, the student and the family have identified this specific area of need that is hindering a learner's access to the curriculum in the classroom. For example, the student may have withdrawn from class activities and has expressed frustration to family members, and teacher assessment has established the extent of the gap between current reading skills and expected classroom performance, and, further, has articulated that this is a significant difficulty. In this case, the intervention is well framed and set up.

Many referrals for learning intervention, however, are not as clear and appropriate. Sometimes the description of the 'problem' may be well off-target and after careful use of expertise in preliminary assessment, a reframing may be necessary before an intervention is considered. For example, a referral for behavioural difficulties in class could turn out to be stemming from exactly the same need as in the previous example – a literacy difficulty. In this case, the learner is externalising frustration and emotional distress related to reading in a way that is disruptive and has, therefore, been referred as a behaviour problem. Both students may need exactly the same literacy intervention, but the need has been identified in very different ways.

The clarification of the reasons for referral through preliminary assessment is vital to implementing worthwhile intervention. The following questions based on ATRiUM capabilities act as a guide:

- What supports and hinders the active learning of this student?
- What supports and hinders the thinking of this student?
- What supports and hinders this student in relating to others?
- What supports and hinders the development and use of language, symbol systems and ICT?
- What supports and hinders the self-management of this student as a learner?

Context within which learning will be applied

No knowledge or skill is separate from the context within which it is to be used. When designing intervention it is important to understand not only the knowledge and skills of interest, but when and where these are to be drawn on by the learner and the context within which skills will be applied. The following aspects of intervention are important to consider:

1 The classroom use of the learned skills or knowledge.
2 The place of these learned skills and knowledge in the functioning of the whole student.
3 Possible changes in the learning environment that can support sustained learning.

In the first instance, the context of a particular skill set or knowledge is pertinent. For example, an intervention focusing on functional numeracy will be best developed if the particular situation in which numbers are to be used is known and used to shape the learning opportunities as well as the assessment tasks. It is not uncommon for a student to participate in an intensive intervention focusing on a skill and then not be able to apply that skill within usual classroom learning activities. It is important to address the transfer of skills from the start.

The second consideration is the learning profile of the individual learner who is engaging in the intervention. How does the target skill or knowledge fit into the set of capabilities that the individual student has? This consideration of the whole learner is vital. While dimensions of learning and learners are often considered incidentally when designing intervention and assessing effect, these need to be made explicit. For example, any experience of learning difficulties and the associated shame and embarrassment that often happens will influence how learners are able to take what is taught in a learning intervention and use this learning successfully in other aspects of their lives, both in the classroom and in out of school contexts.

Many of the learners who are referred for learning intervention have experienced years of failure and have built up coping mechanisms to protect them from the feelings of failure and constant feedback that marks them as less successful than their peers. Often these coping behaviours block engagement in learning, and in extreme cases create significant behavioural and mental health issues.

The third consideration is the relationship between learners and their classroom learning environments. If we provide specific intervention that builds skills and knowledge but do not support the learners' use of these skills back in their classrooms, we could be wasting time and energy. Also, if we provide intensive intervention for a domain of learning that is not being successfully learnt in a classroom but do not do anything to alter this main learning environment to optimise future learning we are also wasting time. We need to do whatever is possible to change the learning environment so that learning is sustained in students' usual settings. We have a responsibility to consider what changes to the classroom learning environment might better support the learning of the casework students and to collaborate with classroom teachers to consider possible changes. Activating changes in both learners and their environments takes time and collaboration, but is the way to work towards lasting change.

Once a clear definition of the intended change is available, it guides the rest of the process of designing and implementing the intervention. Everything depends on the clarified focus and the context within which the desired learning outcome is relevant. These are the foundations for clearly defining what it is that is to be learnt.

Time frame for the intervention

The length of time available for any learning intervention is an important aspect to be taken into account. This is a pragmatic component that needs to be made explicit as a parameter of learning intervention. Many interventions in education are implemented within limited time frames that influence how they are designed and implemented. Factors that influence the length of time available for intervention include the time frame for the funding that is being used, the availability of staff and other resourcing factors. Usually school calendars help determine sensible time frames for intervention, although the regular timing of sessions are often affected by school community events that need to be taken into account.

Time frames can also be determined according to when a student will need to apply the outcomes of the intervention in another context. For example, pre-teaching of specific content vocabulary for individual students should be completed prior to specific topics being introduced in class lessons, since equipping students with this knowledge is the purpose of the intervention. It may also be useful to have some overlap in timing to assist with the consolidation of knowledge as the topic is dealt with in class.

Many packaged intervention programs bring with them specific time frames. For example, Reading Recovery (Clay, 1979) specifies 20 weeks of intervention, with the expectation that students will have achieved significant progress in that time and will be able to move from the intervention back into their classes to better engage with literacy learning opportunities.

In some situations only a few weeks may be available to complete the full cycle of educational casework intervention and, therefore, some shortcuts will be needed to meet the requirements and to make the intervention useful for the target student. In this instance, the learning intervention professional may have to design intervention without fully knowing what resources are available, and what learning environment is important for their student. Again, assessment information is key in identifying a clear focus on an important area of basic academic skills (e.g., word recognition, decoding, basic number facts, vocabulary instruction). Some discussions of learning strategy interventions by Daniel Willingham, for example, point to comprehension strategies as areas that are responsive to intervention over a limited period of time (Willingham, 2010).

People involved in the intervention

The student is the central person in the learning intervention process. As the initial assessment aims to understand and define the focus for intervention, it includes a consideration of the student's learning needs and processes for seeking input from the student. In scoping learning intervention it is important to acknowledge all the people who may be involved and the nature of their responsibilities. Professionals involved will include the responsible classroom teacher, as well as other teachers who teach or have taught the student, specialist teachers, executives in the education setting and other professionals such as school psychologists, speech pathologists and occupational therapists. There may be teaching assistants who work with the student and who will be very close to everything that is happening on the ground. There may also be professionals outside the school setting who are integrally involved, including other health and allied health professionals.

Although the design of the intervention and its oversight needs to be done by the professionals involved, the teaching activity of learning intervention can be carried out not only by teachers and other professionals but also by teaching assistants, parents and other students. Consideration of who should do which aspects of the learning intervention is important, as is ensuring that the skills of the person providing the intervention match those that are needed.

A criticism that is aimed at the role of teaching assistants in schools is that many learners with the highest needs are provided with the least qualified professionals to teach them. In packaged intervention programs there can be significant training and supervision required so that it is possible for these programs to be implemented by teaching assistants. However, it is always essential to have regular processes of support and supervision by professional educators. There are situations that occur where a teaching assistant continues with the implementation of a program despite a lack of impact. In such situations it is vital to have professional educators involved in making decisions about whether a particular program is suitable for a learner and, when necessary, how to alter the intervention so that it does have an effect, or discontinue it and try something else. Such decisions need to be made by those with appropriate expertise, and taking into account the information collected before and during the intervention.

Families are integral members of the learning intervention team. Indeed, they are the most consistent members of that team for their children. They may take on considerable informal teaching activities at times, sometimes under the direction and supervision of professionals, such as speech pathologists and occupational therapists, as well as teachers. Learning opportunities for students at home are usually aimed at providing short bursts of structured teaching to reinforce important skills or provide practice that complements professional intervention sessions. Parents can become experts in noticing when to reinforce or to correct their children's articulation or language, and in partnership with educational professionals can provide an invaluable continuation of professional intervention in everyday situations.

To reiterate, the people involved in any intervention are crucial. Not only the student who is the focus of the intervention and the classroom teacher, but also the family, fellow classmates, other support staff and educators in the school, and other professionals outside the school. The aligned efforts of all participants are needed to ensure the best possible process of intervention in order to make a sustainable change.

Learning environment for the intervention

The learning environment within which an intervention is implemented can have a significant influence on the effect of any intervention. This aspect of scoping learning intervention is about place and space, but it is also about how best to provide intervention that has a positive impact on classroom learning and school life.

Learning environment is influenced by many factors outside school. Although we are interested in all factors, in scoping learning intervention it is the factors within the school and classroom which are to be targets of change in learning intervention that are of most relevance. We consider these because learning is a function of students' interactions with their environments.

The key aspects of the learning environment are teachers and other adults; other students individually and as a group; the learning opportunities and teaching strategies used; the physical building, furniture and materials; the classroom culture, organisation and behavioural expectations. This is potentially a very complex dimension of learning intervention. It can be approached by seeking the perceptions of the student, family and teachers about what aspects of the environment support and hinder learning for a particular student. It is important to explore how the learner interacts with what is happening in their learning environment, and what effects are evident in relation to the referral focus.

Although learning intervention is initially scoped through identifying a targeted student and specific focus for intervention, it is vital to consider the connection between the intervention and the usual educational setting, and to keep returning to questions about relevance and application. Not only do we need to keep in mind how the targeted learning can be applied and practised in class, but also to consider how the intervention may be embedded into class learning activities, or whether there is a need for it to be parallel or separate. All these forms of connection with classroom learning will be appropriate at times and can be determined by asking the sorts of questions posed here:

- How do the learning needs of the learner align with those within the class?
- What is the appropriate level of difficulty of the activities and how does this align with the range of difficulty across the class?
- Is the intervention likely to be best implemented through embedding in class lessons, parallel to class lessons or separate from class lessons?
- How will opportunities to transfer learning from the intervention to class activities be provided and monitored?

All teaching is bound by the place and space within which it happens as determined by the facilities and resources available. Place and space are very pragmatic but important dimensions of intervention that can make or break its success. Spaces in schools are traditionally well separated to accommodate one class with a teacher, with walls and doors to contain that grouping. Other larger spaces are available for whole school gatherings, or for multiple classes in libraries or specifically designed art or technical domains. Architecture in schools is bound to the time in which it is built with contemporary architecture providing more open-plan options and flexibility of spaces, with movable walls and breakout rooms to allow the organisation of variably sized groups of learners.

One of the myths of inclusion is that all intervention needs to happen in the classroom where multiple teaching–learning interactions, for large groups, small groups and individuals, are already taking place. Many specialist teachers are encouraged to do their intervention work within such complex settings, in the name of inclusion. This tends to be a simplistic interpretation of inclusion that denies the practical impact of noise and distraction inherent in any classroom that has many learners engaged in a variety of learning activities. Decisions about implementing intervention solely in a classroom may in fact be contributing to compromising effectiveness.

The usual argument against withdrawing a small group or individual student for intervention is that the learners will feel alienated by being taken to another learning space for some of their teaching and will miss other class work as a consequence. However, if a very focused, intense teaching interaction is necessary for an individual learner or a small group, it is sensible to find a quiet, separate space within which that intervention can take place. If a general flexibility of group, space and place is considered usual and happens for all learners at some time, it is not seen as exclusionary, but as responsive teaching for effective learning. Students in flexible, responsive classrooms can even contribute to the management of their own learning opportunities by seeking small group intensive intervention at times.

Effective teachers have always used their learning spaces flexibly, typically arranging the desks and chairs to support a planned learning activity, and rearranging when the activity changes. This is the physical framework within which teaching and learning happens, and it needs as much consideration as all other frameworks. Struggling to make eye contact with students when doing an expository lesson, for example, is a barrier that can be removed easily by changing where the learners are in relation to the teacher. Similarly, trying to do group work in an inappropriate space is difficult when an alternative space would support such learning activities more effectively. Such basic factors that support or hinder teaching and learning are important to consider and plan around.

In terms of routines, teachers also set up expectations with their students about how their learning environment is to be arranged and rearranged safely, quietly and efficiently for different activities. These are the actions of responsible classroom citizens, who are actively engaged in establishing learning spaces, and who take care of furniture and work with their peers as they do this physical activity. Such practical organisation can be done following teacher instructions, or a set of graphics that indicate the arrangements needed, so fewer words are needed.

Though the focus of this book is on educational settings, we do need to consider other places for learning intervention outside schools, like homes, community halls, commercial premises and tutors' homes or offices. When intervention is about physical development it could be in a gymnasium or a physical therapy centre. If it is speech therapy intervention it may be in a community health centre or hospital. If intervention is focused on identity development for a cultural group it may be in a community hall or significant geographical site or a traditional meeting place. Each of these places provides a context for intervention.

One setting that is often a place for intervention, and where significant informal teaching takes place, is the student's home. Family members contribute to intervention across a full range of responsibilities. For example, young children engaging in speech and language intervention often participate in most learning opportunities at home. These are punctuated by more formal weekly or monthly sessions with a speech pathologist where modelling for the parents as well as assessment for monitoring purposes is carried out. Between these formal meetings families provide intervention either in formalised sessions or incidentally as part of their everyday living.

As described in Chapter 1, many settings are used in daily life for everyday learning and also for developing musical, dramatic and sporting interests. Learning particular expertise in music, for example, usually happens in individual, intensive teaching sessions, with immediate access to a responsive teacher or tutor. Opportunities to learn and collaborate in music are also provided in small group settings and larger groups where musicians apply the skills learnt in individual sessions and practised independently. This same notion of learning across a range of different settings is applicable to learning intervention and to the decision-making about learning settings.

Implementation of the intervention

The final aspect of scoping learning intervention is consideration of what will support the effective implementation of intervention, and what may be a hindrance. Things to consider under this aspect of scoping are drawn from research into the integrity of implementation, that is, the extent to which the implementation follows the plan and the intervention achieves its goals. The core elements of implementation are concerned with the expertise of the professionals and teaching assistants delivering the intervention; the explicit and deliberate support provided for these people throughout the intervention; and the use of assessment results to support decision-making (Fixsen, Naoom, Blasé, Friedman & Wallace, 2005; Fixsen, Blasé, Naoom & Wallace, 2009).

Much intervention involves considerable resourcing so it is important to make the most of this support while providing the best possible opportunities for the acceleration of learning for target students. By considering the following significant implementation factors it is possible to draw on the strengths of the intervention and compensate for any problems in order to optimise its effect. Essentially, all aspects of implementation need to be considered with respect to maintaining integrity.

It is common to take frameworks and programs that others have developed and to adapt them for different contexts. Contextual and cultural differences as well as pressures around resourcing can influence the type of adaptations trialled. However, the ways programs are adapted can mean the difference between the effectiveness of the approach and its failure. It is important for learning intervention professionals to know what needs to be maintained when making adaptations to a program, so that its published efficacy is still reliable. Aspects that are often changed include time frames, content, skills of personnel, size of the learning group and a space for the implementation.

In schools, pressure is often on to get the same effects in a shorter time, or with less time devoted to the intervention each week. Taking a 20-week intervention and making it fit ten weeks, because that is what is possible in the setting, will strain the integrity of the intervention, and would seriously call into doubt the possibilities of an effect. Similarly, reducing the length of time of each session may mean that important components may not be included in each lesson. Removing a section of an intervention procedure to reduce the time needed each session is common. This can reduce the integrity of the intervention considerably and needs to be carefully considered. On the other hand, experienced learning intervention teachers also report enriching the conversations in teaching by linking the content to real life experiences, using their teaching expertise to strengthen students' learning.

Using teachers/tutors/instructors who are less qualified or experienced than those who are meant to implement a program will also alter the integrity of any intervention. Intervention packages developed in research settings have determined how much training and experience is necessary for effective implementation and attempt to maintain that integrity through licensing access to programs and ensuring that professional education and supervision is available.

Increasing the reach of an intervention in its implementation is often a pressure. This can be attempted through using larger than recommended group sizes and can compromise the intensity of instruction and the instructor's ability to monitor student performance.

Finding an appropriate space is always challenging, and carrying out intervention in a noisy corridor instead of a research laboratory will obviously strain the intervention's integrity. However, lack of a dedicated space is a reality in many education settings. Advocating for an appropriate teaching space in order to optimise the effect of the intervention is often a part of the learning intervention professional's job.

Summary

Knowing what a student knows or can do is not enough for planning for appropriate intervention. Scoping of learning intervention involves consideration of many dimensions, starting with the primary purpose of the intervention. In clarifying the focus of the intervention it is vital to know how the targeted knowledge or skill fits into both the curriculum and also into a capabilities framework; both of which are developmental. These two contexts allow an understanding of what is next for a student's learning, and how to get there. It is important to know how the focus of the intervention fits into a bigger picture; how it is defined in terms of longer-term goals; is related to other aspects of learning; and is sustainable over contexts and time. In terms of scoping learning intervention, it is important to consider the context within which the learning will be applied; the time frame for the intervention; the people to be involved in the intervention; the learning environment; what layers of learning intervention are appropriate; and the factors that are likely to support and hinder intervention implementation.

References

Clay, M. M. (1979). *The early detection of reading difficulties* (3rd ed.). Portsmouth, NH: Heinemann.

Fixsen, D., Blasé, K., Naoom, S., & Wallace, F. (2009). Core implementation components, *Research on Social Work Practice,* 19(5), 531–540.

Fixsen, D., Naoom, S., Blasé, K., Friedman, R., & Wallace, F. (2005). *Implementation research: A synthesis of the literature.* Tampa, FL: Louis de la Parte Florida Mental Health Institute, University of South Florida.

Willingham, D. (2010). Have technology and multitasking rewired how students learn? *American Educator, 34*(2), 23.

5

EVIDENCE BASES FOR LEARNING INTERVENTION

The notion of cause and effect is one of the earliest cognitive constructs that humans develop. Babies seek to understand what causes changes in their world and build up a bank of links that are continually adapted as their experiences accumulate. The notion of cause and effect continues to drive meaning making throughout life, and is the basis of research and practice in learning intervention.

Evidence-based practice has grown out of professionals being considered to be scientist practitioners and began in the context of health care (Barlow, Hayes & Nelson, 1984). Evidence-based practice seeks to use what is known about the effectiveness of intervention from research that is rigorous to reduce the gap between research and practice (Barkham & Mellor-Clark, 2003; Broekkamp & van Hout-Wolters, 2007). However, the process of simply taking information from research and expecting it to inform practice is problematic. Because of this, practice-based evidence that combines the rigour of research with relevance in practice has come under the spotlight (Barkham & Mellor-Clark, 2003).

In this chapter, we explore the evidence that is used by learning intervention professionals in educational casework and responsive teaching based on a four-part model. First, the evidence that comes from scientific research is considered. We will look at how the evidence has been developed, the limits of this evidence and how to draw on it to make substantiated decisions about learning intervention. As published research evidence is not the only evidence that can support learning intervention practice, next we will look at evidence that comes from professional practice, that is, 'practice-based evidence'. We will then consider evidence that comes from the families and students who participate in casework as a vital component of any intervention. Finally, we will articulate how evidence is generated during educational casework, through carefully planned assessment, and how it can be used in conjunction with other types of evidence to justify educational decisions.

Sources of evidence for learning intervention

No one would argue against us practising in education in ways that have been shown to be most effective. The focus on evidence has therefore resulted in an expectation that teachers and psychologists will source research evidence to help make decisions about intervention and will thus have research-based justification for all they do. There are a few difficulties in taking this approach to evidence-based practice so literally, however, if it means we only take notice of published, peer-reviewed research. Instead, we need to base our educational decisions on a range of evidence, including scientific research, professional experience, reports of others' experiences and family testimonials, as well as the evidence we generate through assessment during responsive teaching and educational casework.

The consideration of multiple types of evidence in educational practice has been previously presented in health models where research evidence is considered with reference to clinical expertise, patient values and expectations (Sackett, Rosenberg, Gray, Haynes & Richardson, 1996). In the context of education a similar model for evidence-based practice includes three bodies of evidence: published research; professional knowledge; and the knowledge that resides with the family and student (Bourke, Holden & Curzon, 2005). Just using any one of these three bodies of evidence without cross-checking with the others will be less than adequate; triangulation of all three is needed for valid evidence in any particular situation. For example, use of a scientifically based intervention, without consideration of the evidence from the other two sources, can be inappropriate and, even worse than being ineffective, can be damaging. Using professional knowledge without checking with current published research can also be problematic. And, not sourcing evidence from professional and scientific research leaves student experience and family perception as the only lens within which any decisions are made, denying the value of research and professional insights. Professional practice, in fact, is the sophisticated drawing together of all of these types of evidence; seeking to optimise what we can do to accelerate learning for individuals and groups of learners for whom generally effective instruction is not working as well as anticipated.

In this book we are extending the established model of evidence to explicitly include a fourth type of evidence – that which is generated within learning intervention. In fact, this evidence of change and of what is supporting change for a particular learner is the most important evidence to collect once any intervention is in progress. In the model shown, we include evidence from within the responsive teaching or educational casework process, thus defining evidence-informed learning intervention. In Figure 5.1 we have used the notion of differing lenses through which additional light and clarity is brought to the learning intervention process. Each of these four types of evidence will be considered in the following sections.

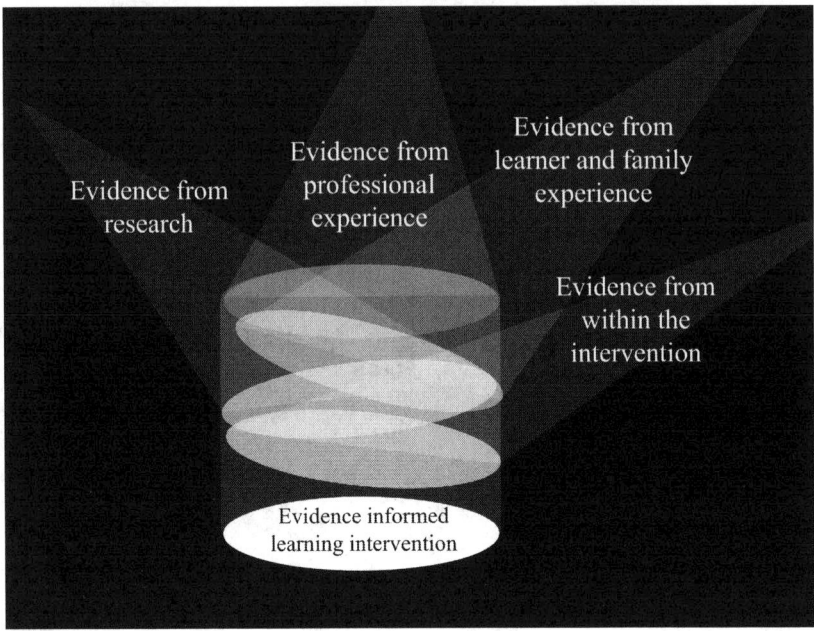

FIGURE 5.1   Evidence-informed learning intervention

Evidence from scientific research

Scientific research has sought to establish evidence in terms of cause and effect in educational intervention so that teachers and other professionals know what makes the most impact. We use a range of research to help us determine what caused what; and to compare the effect of different interventions. The consideration of evidence from scientific research is the starting point of hypotheses about what will make a difference.

There are many disciplines that contribute knowledge to help us understand the complexity of human development and of intervention for learning. There is research specifically into learning intervention, but research from related disciplines also informs our work. As we try to make more sense of the complexity of learners as dynamic systems, as physical, cognitive, emotional, social and cultural beings who function in highly complex environments, we draw on theoretical frameworks and research evidence from many strands of educational and developmental psychology as well as from the sciences related to all dimensions of human functioning and interaction.

Theoretical frameworks

Learning theories help us to make sense of the effectiveness of teaching strategies and other influences on learning. Teachers and learners, researchers and psychologists seek explanations for the complex processes of human development, learning and teaching. In response to that need to understand, many theories to help explain these processes have been developed. Such *ways of seeing* are embedded within cultures and only make complete sense within specific cultures. Yet, most of the theories upon which Australian and Aotearoa New Zealand educators rely are derived from North American or European contexts.

In the recent development of theory in education and educational psychology over the past 150 years, theorising around human development, learning and teaching has used a range of lenses. From behaviourism to social learning theory, to cognitive theories, to sociocultural theories, to dynamic systems theories, we have increasingly acknowledged the complexity of human experience. Throughout this time of increasing complexity, research and practice has focused on many separate aspects of human experience, usually defining problems that need treatment. Scientific research has deconstructed, very explicitly and formally, the complex human experience through experiments and by creating experts in the discipline as a system of legitimising what is known.

Recent theories are complex and sophisticated, recognising the interwoven dimensions of humans as they engage in their worlds, and the strengths that people bring to their engagement with life's challenges. These aspects of contemporary theory are increasingly compatible with Indigenous knowledge, which has remained focused on dynamic connections between people, place, past, meaning and responsibilities. At no time in educational and developmental theoretical history have Western and Indigenous *ways of seeing* been closer than they are now.

Increasingly, Indigenous ways of seeing are being combined with Western theory to make sure the explanations are applicable and relevant to the context within which they are being used. Aotearoa New Zealand has been grappling with the theories from Western educational psychology that do not resonate with locally developed ways of seeing, and therefore do not support culturally responsive research, teaching or educational casework practice. As there is a need for local Indigenous knowledge to be the lens through which to consider knowledge from elsewhere, ways to be able to draw on both sources of thinking are needed. In Aotearoa New Zealand this is being done through He Awa Whiria (a braided river) approach to reconciling Western and Kaupapa Māori perspectives (Fergusson, McNaughton, Hayne & Cunningham, 2011) and drawing from clinical (Western) and cultural (Te Ao Māori) streams of psychology. The outcome of this bicultural approach is "culturally reasoned epistemology" (Macfarlane, Blampied & Macfarlane, 2011). Thus, ancient Indigenous ways of seeing are becoming more accessible and prominent in contemporary theorising and research into learning and teaching. Since knowledge is created within culture, it is vital to know about these contexts and be able to evaluate the knowledge in terms of its relevance to our cultural context.

In Table 5.1 we have compiled a range of theoretical lenses that we can draw on in learning intervention. The table is a very simple representation that does not take into account the overlaps that are inevitable, nor the breadth and depth of explanation that is embodied in each theory. It is also important to consider how

TABLE 5.1 Learning theories and ways of seeing learning

Indigenous	Learning as cultural belonging and growth
Behaviourist	Learning as changes in behaviour
Social learning	Learning as changes in behaviour and thinking through social engagement or observation
Cognitive	Learning as changes in thinking
Information processing	Learning as changes of thinking through processing of information
Sociocultural	Learning as use of cultural tools (language) for social interaction and changes in thinking
Neurological	Learning as changing brain structure
Ecological	Learning as response to environment
Dynamic systems	Learning as transformation of multiple systems of human functioning

these theories can work together. They are not mutually exclusive, and although professionals tend to favour one default theory, they can fit other theories around it as needed. This summary is a starting point for each of us to use to further explore how we see learning and which theoretical bases support our explanations. Within these complex theories of development, learning and teaching are many lesser theories that have been developed to help make sense of fine-grained aspects of each of the capabilities that are the focus of teaching. The theories frame how responsive teachers and learning intervention professionals ask questions and set about intervening.

The list of ways of seeing learning in Table 5.1 can be used as a reference for learning intervention professionals when they consider the first two steps in both the Responsive Teaching and Educational Casework processes (see Chapter 2). These two questions, about frameworks and what learning intervention professionals understand about learning, are important for reflective practitioners: They help acknowledge and call to account individuals' implicit rules and assumptions of personal and professional engagement.

Every one of us relies on theoretical frameworks within which to create explanations of life experiences, and of learning and teaching. The theories that we use shape everything we do, and frame and filter the evidence we use to inform our practice. For example, if a behaviourist explanation of learning and teaching is used then responsive teaching and educational casework become focused on observed behaviours as indicators of learning, along with identification of the triggers and reinforcers that are operating to establish patterns of behaviour. In contrast, an information-processing lens will frame learning as attention, sensing and access to information, the processing of it (thinking) and the generation of language or action that demonstrates learning.

It is important for all learning intervention professionals to be conscious of the implicit assumptions that are inherent in any particular *way of seeing*, as that theoretical orientation influences what happens in responsive teaching and educational casework. As with all professional work in education, research in learning and teaching is based on theory and framed by theory. The theory affects the types of questions asked and the constructs studied, how learning is measured and what factors are noted when considering what has supported and hindered learning. Thus, evidence is created and framed differently in different theoretical contexts.

A perpetual issue for research is the question of context across research studies. There is tension given how artificial it is to separate factors in order to seek clarity of cause and effect, when it is the reality of the enormously complex interrelationships between multiple factors that needs to be understood. Scientific research is traditionally quantitative. It strives to clearly separate variables related to change so that their relative contributions can be more clearly measured. The aim is to find factors separated from contexts that can then be generalised across contexts. In contrast, Indigenous research, along with some other qualitative research approaches, leaves the complexity in place and attempts to explain the interweaving of multiple factors that support change. Under this paradigm, research that is carried out in particular communities is seen to be relevant to that community and may or may not be validly generalised to other contexts.

Published research

Published research in learning intervention provides a key source of evidence to support educational decision-making. This scientific research has produced vast amounts of quantitative research findings. Evidence-based practice in education has been supported by a wave of meta-analytical research that seeks to make accessible summary findings from the enormous number of research studies published across the world. By combining studies and carrying out statistical analyses across studies, meta-analytic researchers have made interpretations of the relative effectiveness of particular factors in education. Some researchers spend their careers analysing this field of research studies and making determinations about solid evidence of effect and impact. One such researcher is John Hattie. His development of a table of effective teaching strategies in relation to academic achievement, and the waves of professional development accompanying this work, have made his research accessible for educators. As Hattie explores additional domains of research his rankings are adapted to include these and to reflect the increased volume of published research. The focus of this work is a measure of effect, 'effect size', which is the difference between pre-test scores and post-test scores divided by the variability of those student scores. This algorithm takes into account the measures of change, as well as the range of scores. Hattie (2009, 2011, 2015) considers research in the broad context of educational achievement and has used the cut-off mark or 'hinge point' of 0.4 as the effect size at which a teaching strategy or intervention approach is deemed to have greater than average effect.

In order to carry out meta-analyses much of the context of each research study is necessarily discounted. Since combined effect sizes reflect effect across many different contexts, it is too simplistic to accept these figures as absolute. Instead they are guides to be taken as important starting points, directions for learning intervention professionals to consider when making decisions about components of effective intervention.

Another translator of evidence bases in the southern hemisphere is David Mitchell who has framed and filtered the research for professionals in inclusive and special education (Mitchell, 2014). Mitchell uses two categories of effect size in relation to learners with special educational needs:

- Convincing or strong evidence of effectiveness (0.7 or more)
- Good or preponderant effect (between 0.31 and 0.69).

A further consideration in evaluating research relates to the issue of whether there is evidence of 'no effect' or, instead, no evidence at all. Evidence of 'no effect' is really important, as it is evidence that this is not a worthwhile intervention (in the context within which the null effect was demonstrated). It is possible to explore those conditions and see whether there may be some other contexts within which this would potentially have a positive effect. In contrast, sometimes there is no published evidence of either a positive effect or null effect. The efficacy of the intervention is not discredited by this result. It simply indicates that it has not yet been adequately researched. All intervention begins without any evidence of effect, so this is not a reason to rule it out. Again, careful consideration of the design, the theory underpinning the intervention and the context within which it could be hypothesised to be effective is needed.

There are well-established frameworks for the process of testing the effectiveness of intervention. Such experimental research studies, with accepted parameters of statistical significance, can demonstrate cause and effect relationships that provide strong bases for making generalisations about the efficacy of particular intervention approaches and strategies. Within each one of these studies are many people, for each of whom the effects of the intervention are measured. These individual responses to intervention are then combined to come up with a single figure that represents the effect across all participants. That figure becomes the focus, alongside comparisons of intervention use that combine representation of effect. In experimental research, 'gold standard' randomised control trial (RCT) research is seen to be the most reliable and valid evidence of effect. Other research is seen to be less reliable or valid. This view of evidence is often cited to support decisions about which research studies to accept as evidence for the selection of intervention approaches or strategies, and which to discount.

A complication in this discussion is that for any effect size to be determined meaningfully there needs to be a substantial number of students in any group of participants. If there are less than around 20 then the statistics cannot be used meaningfully in this psychometric analysis. Underneath this process of trialling intervention with a large group of people is the inevitable variability of effect across participants. The intervention was probably highly effective for some, and less effective for others. Sometimes there are outliers who are totally removed from the research, since they do not fit the pattern (for some reason) and they are not included in the analysis. The findings are summed up as an average and the variability is deliberately lost by combining results.

In the field of learning intervention there are students for whom the effects will not necessarily follow what research suggests. These students who have not responded to classroom teaching as anticipated, may or may not respond to intensive intervention in the same way that average research results may suggest. Because of this, the statistically significant results that emerge from research are only ever a starting point. It takes a clever professional to match evidence with the particular learning needs of any learner, and make decisions to shape appropriate intervention.

This does not mean that large-scale scientific research is not extremely important as a key reference point. It remains the first port of call for learning intervention professionals who need to be able to engage with it and ask questions about the relevance of research to their particular contexts. Consideration of variability and context (e.g., Todd Rose, Rouhani & Fischer, 2013) are vital in taking any evidence from experimental research and using it in practice with individual learners.

Case studies and life stories

Case study research has been a constant in education. Often major breakthroughs in understanding start with one case that is shared widely, influencing others with whom it resonates. Published case study research is a valuable source of evidence to be considered by learning intervention professionals.

Such single subject research is often discounted because the focus was only on one student and therefore cannot be generalised to other students. This emphasis on generalisation originates from the large sample experimental research, which assumes that an intervention that is effective for a large enough group will be 'generally' effective. As we have already suggested, this is a false premise, particularly for learners who do not match the criteria of those for whom a particular intervention was effective. This is often the exact situation in learning intervention practice, since generally effective teaching has not worked for some learners and we need to find something else that may work. We need to look past the generally effective to find evidence that may be applicable in a particular case, and therefore case study research may provide valuable insights. If the situation and the factors influencing learning are similar to the focus case, then it may be just the right sort of research to consider. Inevitably, there is a 'trial and error', or rather, a 'trial and effect', approach in this situation.

An additional body of evidence for intervention comes from life stories, which are easily accessible. In this age of celebrity personalities there is a large market for interesting stories about the lived experiences of others. In fact, interesting life stories are marketed around the world and are the core of much media content.

To complicate matters of evidence, large research studies use the strategy of illustrating their research findings through real life stories of individual learners and their families, groups of learners and whole school change. For example, the

Australian Temperament study (Prior, Sanson & Oberklaid, 1989) is illustrated through a series of life stories of young children and their families, which can be considered cross-sectionally (at ages 1, 2, 3, 5, 7 and 9 so far) as well as through the developmental story of each of the children and their families (Peedom, n.d.). This blurring of lived reality and research, a phenomenon of our contemporary world, has implications for our ability to separate evidence into that which is credible, and that which is not to be relied on.

Evaluative research

Much current research is evaluative research, which aims to identify the effect of an intervention, often without any control group comparison. Evaluative research is often contracted work for education systems. As part of funded implementation, organisations put in place strategies to measure the effectiveness of intervention in order to inform future decisions about continuing funding and to justify grant support.

In these funding contexts, those who are managing the finances often determine the evaluative questions; and often want numbers that represent impact and can easily be compared. With such purposes and short time frames, the evidence about immediate effect is gathered and compiled to gain measures across a group of learners. Issues around how well a particular learner matches those described in the evaluation need to be considered as does evidence about lasting effects of the intervention under study.

There is also considerable research produced by the developers of particular intervention programs, which is done in order to gather evidence of the effect of an intervention, or to test the hypotheses that underpin the intervention in a systematic and credible way. Sometimes an argument is made that such evaluative research, if only done by the developers, discredits the intervention because the developers will want particular supportive outcomes. Other, more independent, evaluative studies carry more weight in this context. However, it is undeniable that all interventions will be first substantiated through this kind of internal evaluation, before external evaluation is practicable. It is therefore important to interrogate the evidence to see whether it has been established validly and reliably.

Evidence from professional experience

Research is not a fixed body of knowledge. It is an ever-expanding body of knowledge that is produced in many different ways. Humans are resourceful and are continually developing learning intervention that is applied without the benefit of any published research evidence. Intervention grows out of practice, from teachers shaping teaching to meet the needs of groups of learners or individuals. Teachers refine their practice over years so that much educational intervention is grounded in practice, rather than beginning with experimental research. Such experience is often captured in professional journals, at conferences and at other professional learning gatherings, or can be confined within schools.

While shared professional knowledge can be valuable, there is considerable evidence that professionals are not necessarily reliable and valid sources of evidence themselves (Madelaine & Wheldall, 2005). In fact, expert opinion can be problematic, as it is based on a relatively narrow band of experience, and may not necessarily be referenced to broader evidence. There are many instances of educational professionals using whole school intervention that does not have established evidence, or continuing to fund programs that have been shown to have less than optimum long-term outcomes. Such decisions are influenced by many factors including effective marketing, a need to be seen to be doing something substantive or new in response to a school need, loyalty to publishers or developers or community connections, and many other factors that are not necessarily related to efficacy of an intervention.

Inevitably professional practice will contain biases that may or may not be conscious. But that does not mean that we should discount professional evidence altogether. Instead, we seek to improve it and strengthen it so it can take its place as an important dimension of evidence and as an integral part of practice. It is imperative for learning intervention professionals to be aware of their own potential biases, and to constantly question their own opinions and interrogate decisions in reference to outside sources of evidence. It is also vital for professionals to gather evidence, as they practice, and then to interrogate that evidence to see if their perceptions are supported by more subjective assessment information. Of course, the type of assessment that is used can be influenced by the inherent biases of professionals so it is also important to have critical friends who assist in ensuring that all evidence gathering is reliable and valid. The process of assessment throughout intervention is central to intervention and is dealt with in much more depth in the following three chapters.

Evidence from learner and family experience

Considerable important evidence lies with the learner and family who are the focus of any learning intervention. The key purpose for gathering this evidence is to get to know each student as a learner. There are also outcomes in terms of meaningful relationships that will support future learning intervention. The resulting shared responsibility, and associated collective efficacy to support learning intervention, will strengthen the power of any intervention.

Student voice as evidence

It is a responsibility of all in education to access and take into account student voice. This responsibility derives from the United Nations Convention on the Rights of the Child (United Nations, 1989) through which children have a right to express a view about their lives, and adults have a responsibility to both facilitate that expression and to act on it. This responsibility extends into learning intervention, so that student voice should be built into both responsive teaching and educational casework.

Student voice sits squarely in assessment processes, which are embedded through-out both responsive teaching and educational casework. Assessment is not about doing things to students, it is about doing things *with* students and seeking their perceptions of their learning and of the factors that are influencing their learning. Considerable expertise is required to adequately access and interpret student voice. Often student voice is discounted because of issues around development, language and emotional and social factors. However, effective learning intervention profes-sionals can work towards building good relationships with students within which students feel comfortable sharing their perceptions and emotional responses to their learning experiences. The first two of the deliberate actions of teachers (see Chap-ter 10) are about establishing the intentions of the relationship between teacher and student, as well as expectations about sharing, which set the groundwork for honest expression of student voice as an integral part of the learning intervention process. In fact, each of the seven key teaching strategies discussed later in the book depends on the contribution of student voice to the learning intervention interac-tions, ensuring that student insights are accessed and become integral evidence that informs practice.

Families as keepers of evidence

Families can be a rich source of information about students since they have been constant participants in the full learning journey of the student and can provide insights into what has previously been effective and what has not. They also live with the developing complex learners and know them as much more than as school students. Many families keep meticulous records of their child's development and can find evidence of previous situations if asked. They have longitudinal perspec-tives that can be very important to take into account, since most learning interven-tion is but a small section of a much longer learning journey.

Often family perceptions are discounted as they can come with considerable emotional charge, which can distort the views in the eyes of the professionals. Years of frustration and anxiety around the learning and development of a child can affect how a family deals with the next set of well-meaning professionals. It is important to acknowledge this and to use the extent of expertise to work with the current set of circumstances for any family. The intervention is a part of the learning journey for each family, as well as for the target student, and perceptions will alter as changes occur for the learner.

Often the best ways to find out about a particular learner is through evidence that lies with that student and with the family. Particular expertise as well as uncon-ditional positive regard is required to be able to establish relationships with students and with families that allow the sharing and exploration of what is influencing learning. We cannot assume too much based on the age and previous achievement of a student. Instead we need to draw together our professional knowledge of learn-ing and development, and whatever else we can find out about the learner, into a full description of the learning needs at the time.

Evidence within the learning intervention

Once an intervention has started the focus is squarely on the evidence generated from within practice. Such evidence is vital to making sense of the effect of the intervention and what has contributed to that effect. On the basis of this evidence determinations of student learning are made, as well as identification of the factors that supported and hindered the learning. With the move towards embedding accountability through evidence explicitly in the professional practice of teachers and psychologists, there are increasing alignments between practice and research processes. Repeated cycles of responsive teaching and of educational casework are aligned with action research. Within these cycles of practice there is an expectation that seeking evidence from research, coupled with continual assessment to access evidence in practice, will inform and support decision-making. Evaluation based on such evidence will then inform future cycles of teaching or casework.

For learning intervention professionals, the intensive process of educational casework focusing on an individual learner aligns with *case study research*. The evidence and analysis is concerned with one learner in a particular situation. In this process evidence is gathered, through assessment, to establish the effects of intervention and to explore the factors that supported and hindered the intervention. Much of this evidence is not written up and so not published, but it remains a body of research that is drawn on in practice by those who know about it. When considering case study research as a basis for professional casework it is important to analyse it to see how well it aligns with or might be able to inform the current case. In fact, what you are doing is testing to see in what ways this case is replicable in your situation.

Not only is evidence about the changes for the student gathered during learning intervention, evidence is also collected about what it was about the intervention that made the difference as well as what factors supported and hindered the implementation. It is also important to explore what other learning opportunities – that may be happening synchronously with the learning intervention – may be working with the intervention to strengthen it or not.

A carefully developed assessment plan for the gathering of information about what the initial level of development or learning was, what changed, when, how much, at what points of time, or in response to what strategies or activities is essential. From this systematically collected evidence, subsequent hypotheses are generated and tested and decisions about the intervention are made. The focus has to be clearly on gathering evidence of effect in relation to the intended learning outcomes, identifying any unintended learning outcomes and also on any other information that may help shed light on what has happened and what contributed to that learning or development.

All interventions depend on multiple factors in implementation for them to reliably produce the intended outcomes. The notion of intervention integrity is increasingly important as a focus of research and learning intervention. Studies that have separated intervention strategies and demonstrated their effects are a starting point. However, it is quite a challenge to be able to replicate the intervention in a different context and maintain the published efficacy.

Intervention integrity is attained through following established procedures, specifically those that underpinned the research that demonstrated efficacy. Any variation from those procedures puts pressure on the integrity of the intervention and calls into doubt the anticipation of previously demonstrated effects. On the other hand, any intervention needs to be responsive to the particular contexts of its implementation. We cannot expect intervention to have the same effect for all learners, in all situations, and it is nearly impossible to match the conditions under which rigorous research is undertaken. This translation of contrived conditions for research into multiple realities is a perpetual challenge in learning intervention and evidence of how the intervention has been implemented as well as how that has affected it is essential for evaluation.

Wider influences on evidence-based practice

We conclude this chapter with a brief examination of the wider influences on evidence bases for learning intervention. Both business and politics are influential in the gathering and use of such evidence in educational practice.

The business of learning intervention

As in every dimension of our contemporary life, the business world has huge influence on research and development in learning and teaching, and on the availability of intervention approaches and packages. Intervention in education is big business. The boundaries between research, education and business have been blurred by a number of factors.

Education systems have considerable funds to purchase intervention packages or to provide professional development for teachers related to particular approaches to learning intervention. There is a considerable market in education. Families and communities also have considerable buying power, which is another dimension of the market. Additionally, some advocacy groups sponsor particular research or intervention approaches through their websites and events, and in the provision of professional development opportunities for teachers.

Research institutions have increasingly been required to be entrepreneurial, to make money out of their research. In that context, many researchers have become marketers of intervention approaches and packages. Increasingly, the release of research products (packaged intervention) has been controlled by universities or publishers, as researchers seek to retain control over the implementation of their research products to ensure the fidelity of implementation and to gather evidence of the effect of the intervention over time in order to make it more legitimate and also more marketable. For this reason there can be restrictions on the use of some intervention approaches and materials to those who are trained and supervised by the researchers as they gather evidence.

Many education systems align with research bodies and teacher education institutions as a way to gain access to current research and evidence-based teaching strategies. Such mutual relationships provide systems within which research can be carried out into the development and implementation of learning intervention frameworks or packages.

Other researchers have translated research into easy to read books or websites and struck a chord with the community. Some have become business successes based on their interpretation of research for a wider audience. Sometimes work has been translated into documentaries that extend its reach even further (*Revolution School*, ABC; *The Classroom Experiment*, BBC). Such researchers then become celebrities, a very influential role in our contemporary society. Attempting to present a less sensational voice in this market are some researchers who provide freely accessible brief summaries of research (MUSEC Briefings; What works clearinghouse).

Education professionals tend to find a particular source of evidence and then rely on it, since it is exhaustingly hard work to evaluate every new piece of research. In many instances learning intervention professionals need to trust the translation of research results by others for whom that is their career, while practice in learning intervention is then based on the best knowledge available. However, it is important to understand the influence of the market on the generation of research and on the translation of that research into commercial chunks for families and professionals in learning intervention. Perhaps the best approach is to be always vigilant and critical in receiving evidence, and to trace that evidence back to a source to check that it has been translated in a meaningful and relevant way. There is very little that is absolute, or context-free, in the complex world of human learning and the research conducted about that learning.

The politics of learning intervention

Politics and education system policy affect decisions around intervention in education. Changes in curriculum and funding make a difference for schools and learners, particularly for those with learning difficulties. As with the blurring of academic research and entrepreneurial pursuits, the politics and marketing of education has affected educational decisions. This means that not all decisions follow research evidence. Instead, they are made in order to meet community and media pressures, to respond to lobbying by advocacy groups and to work towards politicians' aims of re-election.

It is not possible to pursue this topic further in this volume, except to pose a few questions that can be kept in mind when evaluating evidence.

- What research in education is funded by governments?
- What evidence is used by education departments when setting education policy and provisions?
- What is the time lag between international comparative studies of education and when these are released in the media, and what implications does this

have on the relevance and importance of the results? Does the media coverage acknowledge this?

- How do the personal experiences of politicians influence educational legislative and funding decisions?
- What other contexts are drawn on by politicians who make educational legislative and funding decisions?
- What impact has school funding had on the provision of inclusive education in Australia in the past decade?

There will be many more questions that arise as you explore this topic, and even though we may see ourselves as professionals independent of politics, it is clear that everything we do is influenced by political decisions.

Accessing research evidence

The volume of research is enormous and is so variable that it is challenging to make sense of the many different outcomes that are provided in the thousands of studies published every year. There will be access to academic journals while studying and many education systems continue to provide this access for their teachers and other professionals. This means that it is possible to keep up with new research that is published. Requests in particular areas of interest can be set up through online search engines to activate notifications when a new study is published that includes particular keywords or is from particular authors. Professionals can then see the research in its peer-reviewed published form, consider how the conclusions were reached and whether this is a valid piece of new research evidence to inform, affirm or change practice.

There are ways to examine evidence from research and to build in processes for generating and evaluating evidence within practice. It is important to be critical in considering the evidence. The following questions are a useful guide for learning intervention professionals when exploring research.

- What are the learning needs this intervention aims to respond to?
- What is the theoretical basis for the intervention?
- What does the research say about effective intervention and about implementation factors?
- What is the context and process of the research?
- How does the evidence align with the learning needs and context within which this intervention is being considered?

If there is no research evidence, then the first two questions need to be used, and plans for gathering evidence put in place to check that the intervention is actually making the differences that have been hypothesised. The process of gathering evidence is achieved through the assessment embedded within the educational casework.

Summary

Professional decisions that meet the needs of any particular situation are made based on evidence, either outside evidence or evidence generated as part of the learning intervention processes. It is vital to systematically gather evidence as part of learning intervention and then to consider it in relation to the other evidence as a part of evaluation. The four types of evidence outlined in this chapter can be mapped against the steps of responsive teaching and of educational casework to clearly show that evidence supports learning intervention practice at every step (see Figure 5.2). For example, evidence from research and from professional experience can be used to make sense of the context of the case, while all four types of evidence are drawn on when making decisions about how best to intervene.

From these four types of evidence, it is possible to draw conclusions about what difference was made (the effect) and what made the difference (the cause). When doing this it is important to widen the lens again to take into account many factors that may have influenced the intervention. This includes not only those that were explicitly engineered in the intervention, but many others that were inherent in the context and in the implementation.

In evaluating and reflecting on practice, we will subsequently go back to evidence from published science to reference and gain perspective on the evidence gathered in practice. This is the ultimate outcome of evidence-based practice. These four bodies of evidence all underpin decision-making about the most appropriate

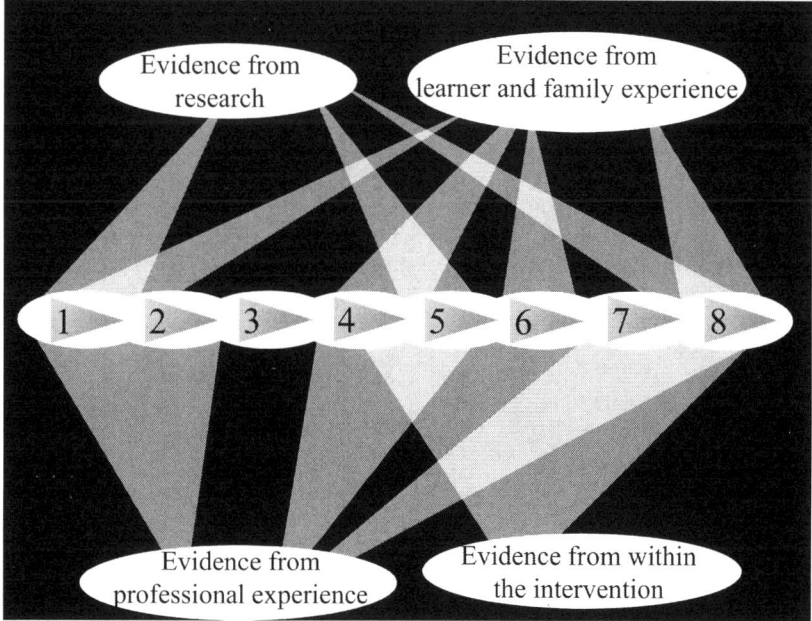

FIGURE 5.2   Evidence supporting each step of the Educational Casework Process

learning intervention for particular learners at a particular time in a particular context. To recap, these sources of evidence are considered by asking:

1 What is the evidence from scientific research about the effectiveness of particular learning opportunities or teaching strategies?
2 What evidence from professional practice do I bring in relation to this student's learning needs and the focus of intervention?
3 What is the evidence from the student and family about response to previous intervention, and current issues that will affect intervention? How can these three bodies of evidence be brought together to underpin learning opportunities and teaching strategies?
4 What evidence do I need to gather as the intervention is implemented?

References

Barkham, M. & Mellor-Clark, J. (2003). Bridging evidence-based practice and practice-based evidence: Developing a rigorous and relevant knowledge for the psychological therapies. *Clinical Psychology and Psychotherapy, 10*, 319–327.

Barlow, D., Hayes, S., & Nelson, R. (1984). *The scientist–practitioner.* New York, NY: Pergamon Press.

Bourke, R., Holden, B., & Curzon, J. (2005). *Using evidence to challenge practice. A discussion paper.* Wellington: Ministry of Education, New Zealand.

Broekkamp, H. & van Hout-Wolters, B. (2007). The gap between educational research and practice: A literature review, symposium, and questionnaire. *Educational Research and Evaluation, 13*(3), 203–220, DOI: 10.1080/13803610701626127

Fergusson, D., McNaughton, S., Hayne, H., & Cunningham, C. (2011). From evidence to policy, programmes and interventions. In Gluckman, P. D. (Ed.), *Improving the transition: Reducing social and psychological morbidity during adolescence.* Office of the Prime Minister's Science Advisory Committee, Auckland, NZ, 287–300.

Hattie, J. (2009). *Visible learning: A synthesis of over 800 meta-analyses relating to achievement.* Abingdon: Routledge.

Hattie, J. (2011). *Visible learning for teachers: Maximising impact on learning.* London: Routledge.

Hattie, J. (2015). The applicability of Visible Learning to higher education. *Scholarship of Teaching and Learning in Psychology, 1*(1), 79–91.

Macfarlane, A., Blampied, N., & Macfarlane, S. (2011). Blending the clinical and the cultural: A framework for conducting formal psychological assessment in bicultural settings. *New Zealand Journal of Psychology, 40*(2), 5–15.

Madelaine, A. & Wheldall, K. (2005). Identifying low progress readers: Comparing teacher judgement with a curriculum-based measurement procedure. *International Journal of Disability, Development and Education, 52*, 33–42.

Mitchell, D. (2014). *What really works in special and inclusive education: Using evidence-based teaching strategies* (2nd ed.). London: Routledge.

MUSEC Briefings (2005–2015). Issues 1–41. Sydney, NSW: Macquarie University Special Education Centre.

Peedom, J. (n.d.). *Life at series.* ABC TV and Heiress Films, www.abc.net.au/tv/life/about_the_series/default.htm

Prior, M., Sanson, A., & Oberklaid, F. (1989). The Australian Temperament Project. In Kohnstamm, G. A., Bates, J. E., & Rothbart, M. K. (Eds.), *Temperament in childhood.* New York, NY: Wiley, 537–556.

Revolution School (2016). [Television series]. Melbourne, VIC: Australian Broadcasting Company.

Sackett, D., Rosenberg, W., Gray, J., Haynes, R., & Richardson, W. (1996). Evidence-based medicine: What it is and what it isn't. *British Medical Journal, 312*, 71–72.

The Classroom Experiment (2010). [Television series]. London: British Broadcasting Corporation.

Todd Rose, L., Rouhani, P., & Fischer, K. (2013). The science of the individual. *Mind, Brain and Education, 7*(3), 152–158.

United Nations (1989). *The United Nations convention on the rights of the child.* Geneva: UN. Available: www.unicef.org/crc/fulltext.htm.

What works clearinghouse (2017). *What works clearinghouse: Find what works.* Retrieved 21 August 2017 from https://ies.ed.gov/ncee/wwc/

6

THE PURPOSES (WHY) OF ASSESSMENT IN LEARNING INTERVENTION

Everyone who intervenes in another's learning decides on the nature of the intervention based on an assessment of learning needs at the time. Parents make judgements about learning, and shape the next interactions with their children to build on that learning, informed by what they think or know to be the next step in learning. For example, young children's approximations in speech and language are often followed by an acknowledgement from the adult and a correct version of the word or phrase. Two-word utterances are often followed with full sentence models of the same meaning, so that the child's language is extended. As social beings, we do this instinctively and we do it constantly within our interactions to support the learning and development of the younger members of our families. The complex process of assessing learning needs and responding to them based on understanding of development can be unconscious and informal, as it is in families, or can be more deliberate, as it is in the formal practices of professional teaching.

When it comes to learning intervention casework, the process of gauging the learning needs of another person (or assessment for learning intervention) has become highly planned and formalised. Assessment is the way in which we gather evidence upon which teaching decisions are based: it informs responsive teaching. We extend this notion to assessment that supports learning intervention through educational casework. Teachers and psychologists can make better informed decisions about learning intervention if they have relevant information about the nature of students' current learning, which is acquired through assessment within the frameworks of responsive teaching and educational casework. In this chapter we consider assessment in each phase of educational casework and provide a template for planning and implementing assessment so that it is integral to effective learning intervention. In other words, we address the *why* of assessment. In the two following chapters, we then address the *what* and *how* of assessment decision-making.

A conceptual framework for decision-making in assessment

At each step of responsive teaching and educational casework we make decisions about assessment by carefully considering *what is to be assessed* and *for what purpose*. The clear delineation of these two dimensions supports the aligned choice of assessment strategies that will validly assess the target skills or knowledge to provide useful information for the required purpose.

The framework for assessment decision-making in Figure 6.1 has been previously placed in contexts of school psychology practice (Berman, 2001; Berman & Graham, 2002), special education (Wong, Graham, Hoskyn & Berman, 2008) and responsive teaching (Graham, Berman & Bellert, 2015). In the context of responsive teaching and educational casework, the model can be considered within all three layers of intervention (see Chapter 3).

One way of looking at the purposes of assessment is captured by the distinction between assessment OF, FOR and AS learning.

> Assessment OF learning – occurs when teachers use evidence of student learning to make judgements about student achievement against goals and standards.
> Assessment FOR learning – occurs when teachers use inferences about student progress to inform their teaching.
> Assessment AS learning – occurs when students reflect on and monitor their progress to inform their future learning goals or when the assessment task is also a learning task.

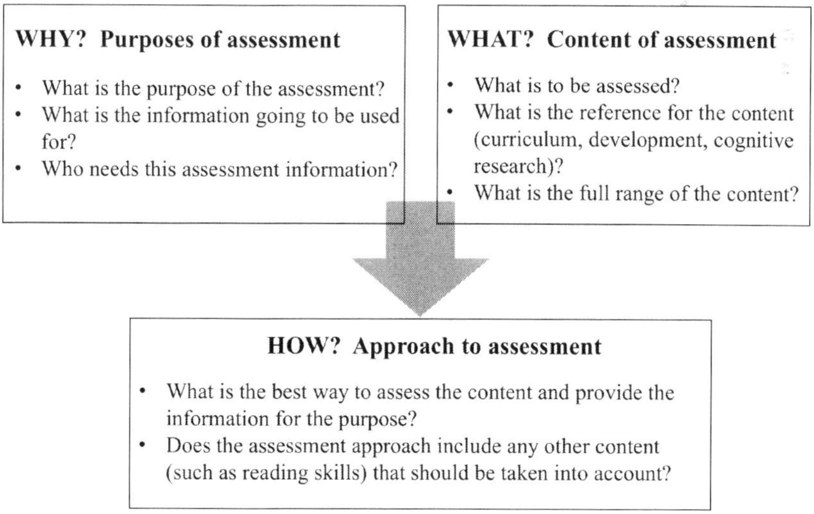

WHY? Purposes of assessment

- What is the purpose of the assessment?
- What is the information going to be used for?
- Who needs this assessment information?

WHAT? Content of assessment

- What is to be assessed?
- What is the reference for the content (curriculum, development, cognitive research)?
- What is the full range of the content?

HOW? Approach to assessment

- What is the best way to assess the content and provide the information for the purpose?
- Does the assessment approach include any other content (such as reading skills) that should be taken into account?

FIGURE 6.1   Conceptual framework for decision-making in assessment

Source: Berman, 2001.

It is important to understand these ideas since they are the basis of much discussion in schools. It is also important to develop a greater depth of understanding of the purposes of assessment in learning intervention, the limitations of assessment in meeting all or some of the purposes, and the potential for misuse of assessment information when it is used for purposes for which it is not designed. Traditionally, however, assessment in education has been seen as having four purposes: to determine the achievement of students (summative); to screen and select students (selective); to evaluate programs (evaluative); and to inform instruction (formative) (Berman, 2001).

A student referred for assessment at the beginning of casework is usually accompanied by a referral question about what is going on related to learning needs. Within that question are a number of dimensions: What is the current level of development and/or learning? What may be causing the current situation? and What can we do about it (which often includes questions about whether the current setting is the best place for this student)? These questions are summative, selective, evaluative and formative. In the next sections we will use these four assessment purposes to organise our consideration of actions based on assessment in the context of intervention for learners with learning difficulties and disabilities.

Assessment for summative purposes in learning intervention

Assessment that can tell us what a student has learnt, usually at the end of some teaching or some time period, is important. This type of assessment provides a picture of how well a learner has progressed in reference to the curriculum and to developmental expectations of the associated ATRiUM capabilities. Such summative assessment is a measure of students' previous learning of knowledge and skills, and is based on reference to both normative and criterion scales.

From criterion-referenced summative assessment information it is possible to write a description of what a student knows, understands and can do independently. These are the products of learning. Using normative assessment, it is also possible to state how a student's level of learning compares to other students of the same age or grade, as well as in comparison with other socioeconomic, geographical, developmental or cultural groupings. Such references provide a measure of the gaps that may be present between what is expected and what is actually achieved – a starting point for a number of selective decisions in learning intervention.

Assessment for selection purposes in learning intervention

Selection is a core use of summative assessment in learning intervention. Such assessment is aimed at screening, identifying and selecting students who may benefit from further assessment, placement in school programs, funding for 'special needs' or placement in 'special' settings. Some students are identified as in need of further assessment because of questions about progress or development that teachers or families have. Summative class or school assessment results are often the precipitator for a referral for further assessment for learners.

Students who are achieving below the rest of the class can be selected for referral to a learning intervention professional for further investigation of their learning needs. Sometimes this is a referral within a school, or sometimes it is outside the school. In any case, making referrals for further assessment is a decision that needs to be well informed and teachers and families need to be clear about what they are asking for and what will be done with the assessment information that is generated.

Again, based on class assessment information, some students are selected for in-school small group or individual programs, and for more formal special classes or different settings. Assessment in special education has traditionally been guided by the diagnostic processes of medical practice, as special education was originally set up to provide for learners with particular conditions or levels of functioning. This is still the case in inclusive education systems, in which limited resources need to be distributed to those who need them most.

To manage this situation, education systems develop criteria in order to allocate their resources, usually based on diagnostic labels from the medical and psychological sciences. Each education system provides information about which criteria and categories they accept in distributing their resources. A considerable amount of professional time is used in this type of assessment and in compiling the information to demonstrate how students meet the selection criteria for access to resources. The system requirements in this domain are an important framework that influences the work of learning intervention professionals.

Related to the selection for placement in special education is assessment that results in determination of a particular developmental condition, impairment, learning disorder or disability based on current established patterns of development and behaviours that have been grouped and named. Developmental science is used to frame assessment and identify learners who are progressing at rates or in ways that are not typical. Traditionally developmental psychology has focused on finding differences in patterns of development and behavioural responses that have then been described and given scientific Latin or Greek names (e.g. dyslexia), or named after the researcher who described the pattern that becomes a syndrome (e.g., Down, Asperger). Many referrals to educational psychologists are along the line of "Jane needs a test for dyslexia". These scientific labels are powerful, and can be helpful, but can also be inconsistent in meaning, and open to misuse (see Chapter 2).

The use of assessment to determine conditions or syndromes can help us understand possible developmental trajectories and the causes and contributing factors related to individual development. They can direct us towards what has been shown to be most effective in similar cases, and can be the basis on which selection for programs is made. Special schools have entry criteria that include the determination of particular developmental impairments, conditions, syndromes, disorders or disabilities. Each of these has specific criteria and rules about who can make these determinations, and how recent the assessment information must be.

Assessment for evaluative purposes in learning intervention

This type of assessment refers to the gathering of any evidence that helps learning intervention professionals make judgements about what worked and why it worked, and what did not work and why. Such assessment defines both the effect of the intervention, as well as assists in unpacking what it was about the intervention that supported or impeded the effect. Evaluative processes are forensic, in that they are carried out after at least some period of intervention with a view to understanding what effect has been made, and why that is happening. This kind of assessment is summative but with a focus on the intervention, not the student. As well, this type of assessment is instrumental in informing future decisions about intervention, so in a sense it can also have a formative purpose.

Assessment for formative purposes in learning intervention

Rather than just summing up past learning, information about student knowledge and skills can be used as a basis of planning intervention (assessment *for* learning). It is often the case that assessment *of* learning provides a measure of current development and learning as the foundation of any learning intervention. Such summative assessment information is used to establish a baseline of what a student knows, understands and can do, as a foundation for teaching what comes next.

The tenuous link that has been assumed between summative assessment and direction for future teaching is being challenged and has generated changes in the approaches and activity of teachers and other assessment professionals. Subsequently, the focus of contemporary assessment has turned more strongly to formative purposes for informing teaching so that every student's learning needs can be met. A focus on processes of learning (ATRiUM capabilities), responsiveness to teaching and the use of approaches such as Dynamic Assessment, all work together towards informing intervention decisions. To build on this important point, in the following sections we consider the specific purposes of assessment throughout learning intervention within the responsive teaching and educational casework processes.

Purposes of assessment in responsive teaching

Assessment is integral to responsive teaching. At each step of the Responsive Teaching Framework (RTF) (see Table 6.1) assessment is used to inform decision-making. Responsiveness in teaching is only possible based on what is known about the students as learners, and noticing what changes and growth are occurring. Teachers deliberately gather evidence about their students in order to be well informed about student learning needs; about what each student already knows; and also about what supports and hinders learning for that student.

TABLE 6.1 Assessment in the Responsive Teaching Framework

(1)	What frameworks do I need to consider?	
(2)	What do I bring as a teacher?	
(3)	What do my students bring as learners?	Assessment to gather information about: cultural contexts, needs, interests, experiences, capabilities, prior learning and achievements that the students bring to their learning; the nature of the learning group they create; what the students' families bring to each student's learning and our learning group.
(4)	What do I need to teach now?	Assessment specifically related to defining intended learning outcomes and ATRiUM capabilities.
(5)	How do I teach for all my learners?	Assessment embedded in learning activities to monitor learning.
(6)	What did my students learn?	Assessment of how each learner and the learning group responded to the instruction in relation to the intended learning outcomes, unintended learning outcomes, and factors that support and hinder learning.
(7)	What feedback supports my students' learning?	Assessment information is framed to provide feedback to students that best supports their learning.
(8)	How did my teaching support my students' learning?	Assessment information is used to evaluate the effect of the teaching on group and individual learning and to point to what the students are ready to learn next.

Source: Derived from Berman, Graham & Bellert, 2015.

Assessment is particularly relevant at Steps 3 and 6 of the RTF.

RTF Step 3: What do my students bring as learners?

In response to this question, responsive teachers seek to know about the cultural contexts, interests, capabilities, prior learning, achievements and lived experiences of the students who come together into a learning group or class.

The information about students as learners is not static, but will keep growing as the teacher gets to know the learners more deeply during their shared experiences in the class. Responsive teachers are open to constantly receiving new information about learners and to adapting their knowledge based on that new evidence about each learner. New knowledge about learners will constantly alter the focus and emphasis of teaching. Teachers need to ensure that they respond to these changes in the best possible ways, careful not to let such knowledge restrict what is to be expected of their learners.

Information about an individual learner is important within the context of the group of learners and also in reference to the family context of that learner. The relationship between teacher and families, and how each family connects with the teacher and the classroom and supports the learner in their engagement, is an important dimension of what needs to be considered in responsive teaching. When knowledge of the learners and their contexts is minimal, the curriculum content becomes the default driver for decisions about what is to be taught, what emphases are to be used and what is to be expected of the learners. In responsive teaching, where more is known about the learners, the curriculum is a reference for supporting the learning of a whole learner and groups of learners and is aligned with knowledge about the learners. Clarifying what the teacher brings (including cultural competence, understanding about learning, assumptions about disabilities and learning difficulties, and curriculum knowledge) and what the students bring is the aim of this phase of assessment. Without this information, the curriculum and system expectations drive teaching and make it more difficult to match current learning needs for many students.

A part of the assessment at Step 3 is gathering evidence of prior learning and achievement, which is usually referenced to the curriculum. It is also referenced to cross-curriculum capabilities. Teachers, therefore, need to know curriculum frameworks and the learning pathways within them well. They also need to acknowledge the full range of human functioning and the ATRiUM capabilities that support learners in accessing the curriculum; including dimensions such as motivation, engagement, self-efficacy and confidence, interest, effort and persistence, thinking skills, use of language, help seeking and collaborative skills, and so on.

RTF Step 6: What did my students learn?

The demonstration of learning, after being taught, is the traditional focus of assessment and is sometimes the only assessment that happens. It is the summing up of learning at some point in time. However, meaningful interpretation of such assessment can only be done in reference to what learners brought to their learning, and what factors affected learning. Information from the previous assessment needs to be robust enough to become a comparison at this point, so that student growth, or change, is clearly evident.

Not only do we want to know what has changed, or been learnt, we also want to know what contributed to that learning. We want to know about learning in relation to:

- the intended learning outcomes;
- any unintended learning outcomes; and
- factors that supported and hindered learning.

If we do not consider all this outcome information we only get a superficial picture of learning – a static description of outcomes, without reference to where the learner has come from, or what has contributed to the learning. Without this fuller understanding we do not have a strong basis upon which to make the next decisions about teaching and other ways to respond to a learner's current needs.

Purposes of assessment in educational casework

Having examined the assessment purposes within the Responsive Teaching Framework, using similar questions but extending and reframing them, we turn to a specific examination of assessment in the Educational Casework Process (see also Chapter 2). Assessment is integral and fundamental to our educational casework model. Assessment is linked explicitly to the purposes of both clarifying issues emerging from any referral for more intense instruction, and to planning the intervention. A strong alignment of assessment actions should be evident throughout the intervention, based on the intended learning outcomes and extending into outcome measures. Feedback and reporting, making sense of the intervention for the learner and for others, should also be based on the coherent information gathered throughout the intervention.

Assessment in educational casework has a number of different purposes, though at times the 'gatekeeping' function seems to override all others (that are actually much more important for effective learning intervention). Nevertheless, gatekeeping is central to many education systems as it is used to determine diagnoses, to establish evidence against criteria set by educational systems and to select students for placement into programs designed for particular groups of learners. The limited funding of education systems can be exhausted by this system-required assessment, while the much more important purpose of assessment, to inform intervention, can be sidelined financially and professionally. Some education systems have managed the expense related to assessment for establishing diagnoses by outsourcing it. This potentially removes decision-making further from the location of teaching and learning and the control of teachers and families in their schools.

There is, of course, more that assessment can offer to educational casework than access to funding and special placements. Formatively focused assessment practices used by learning intervention teachers and other professionals are crucial for clearly informing how an intervention may best meet the learning needs of a student. These professionals use developmental and educational tools to make determinations of current levels of student learning and development, as well as to generate hypotheses about responsiveness to teaching, thus informing intervention.

Assessment for Intervention (AFI) is a psychoeducational assessment process that aims to explicitly inform intervention and is considered best practice for psychologists in education in parts of Europe (Pameijer, 2016). It is assessment that explicitly provides directions for intervention, to bridge the gap between assessment information and personalised, contextualised intervention. Deciding on the intended learning outcomes (ILOs) for any intervention is based on assessment information, which allows learning intervention professionals to make sensible determinations of what may be achieved.

TABLE 6.2 Purposes of assessment within the Educational Casework Process

1 ▸	What frameworks do I need to consider?	
2 ▸	What do I bring as a learning intervention professional?	
3 ▸	What do we already know and what do we need to find out about this student's learning and development?	*Preliminary assessment* What is the nature of the student's development and learning and the influences on these? What is the context for this learner and for the learning intervention?
4 ▸	What are the priorities and parameters (scope) of the intervention?	
5 ▸	How do we intervene?	*Baseline assessment* What is the starting point of learning in the focus area (actual achievement)? What ATRiUM capabilities need to be emphasised? *Assessment for monitoring* What is the response to teaching as it is happening (actual and assisted achievement) and what factors are supporting and hindering learning?
6 ▸	What did this student learn?	*Outcomes assessment* What is the end point of learning in the focus area (actual achievement)? What transfer and maintenance is evident? What other learning is evident? What factors supported and hindered learning?
7 ▸	What reporting and feedback supports this student's learning?	*Feedback and reporting*
8 ▸	How did the intervention support the student's learning?	*Evaluating* Evidence of the effect of the intervention

Because there is a much closer lens on an individual learner in educational casework, there is a clearer definition of assessment throughout the process. This is demonstrated when the phases of assessment are aligned specifically with the Educational Casework Process as shown in Table 6.2.

The purposes of assessment within the Educational Casework Process are defined by the phases in casework, since different information is needed at different times. It is important to keep in mind the purpose when gathering information and to make sure that enough of the right type of information is gathered. Careful planning, with these phases in mind, supports robust assessment throughout casework.

Assessment is integral to the coherence of educational casework as it provides the evidence upon which important decisions are made about intervention. The process of gathering evidence also justifies future use of similar intervention, and of particular learning opportunities, or teaching strategies. Such assessment needs to be thorough and comprehensive in order to fulfil the demands of educational casework. Decisions about assessment are crucial, in particular about what assessment is needed and how it is best to administer or enact that assessment to get the best possible information to support learning intervention. In the remainder of this chapter we consider a number of aspects of assessment to be considered in casework, including preliminary, baseline, monitoring, outcomes, reporting and evaluation.

This analysis of assessment within educational casework will demonstrate that assessment is integral to every step of learning intervention, and meets many purposes during casework. The phases of assessment described in the following sections provide a scaffold for learning intervention professionals to use to systematically consider the purposes of the assessment practices that effectively support learning intervention.

Reliability of assessment

A key notion that underpins the effective use of assessment for making significant decisions across these phases of intervention is that the assessment information is reliable. When any results from assessment are gathered, it is assumed that these are reliable and that they have consistently assessed the focus level of knowledge, skill or capability at the time. Reliability is a vital dimension in the construction of conventional tests and is reported in detail in administration and technical manuals. The discipline of psychometrics provides techniques for measuring reliability that are necessary for learning intervention professionals to understand. It is also important, however, to use these notions more informally when making decisions about assessment approaches and strategies.

If an assessment measures skills or knowledge differently on different days or with different examiners, for example, then the assessment is not going to be very useful. This issue has implications for who administers particular tests that are used for selection decisions and to make diagnostic determinations. If anyone can use any test, then the reliability of the results could be called into question, particularly when access to resources is at stake. Instead, assessment professionals, who have undertaken more professional education in order to qualify them to administer, score and interpret assessment instruments as intended, are thus able to ensure the reliability of results.

Preliminary assessment

Preliminary assessment is related to Step 3 of the Educational Casework Process in response to the question: *What do we already know and what else do we need to find out about this student's learning and development?*

Considerable preliminary assessment has often happened before a learning intervention professional begins casework, sometimes over several years. Such information includes school and developmental records and previous psychoeducational assessment reports. Sometimes there are volumes of information recorded and available to consider in this phase and it is important to carefully evaluate what is useful and what else may need to be accessed to inform the clarification, scoping and prioritising of intervention that happens at this stage.

The aim of this phase of assessment is to understand the nature of the student's learning needs in order to define the scope (priorities and parameters) of the intervention and the conditions under which intervention can be anticipated (hypothesised) to be effective. In particular, the assessment information will inform the focus of the intervention and the context within which the intended learning outcomes will be applied.

Generally, the way that preliminary assessment works is to filter and funnel a large amount of information into a focused basis for making decisions about intervention. The assessment information gathering takes into account everything that influences this learner initially, and pares this down to be more manageable and useful for designing intervention.

There can be restrictions on this phase of assessment. Sometimes there is limited access to what may be important bodies of information that defines the limits of what can be considered. For example, many psychologists do not have access to school records to gather an historical picture of student performance, and can only do what they can with what they have. Sometimes schools do not have access to medical or psychoeducational information that may be pertinent. Sometimes there is limited access to all family members who are significant in this situation.

Baseline assessment

Baseline assessment derives from Step 5 of the Educational Casework Process in response to the question: *How do we intervene?* The name of this phase of assessment comes directly from experimental psychology. In the context of learning intervention, it has the same function: to clearly establish the starting point, prior to changing conditions or activating the intervention. This idea is also aligned to the Vygotskian theory of learning and the notion of actual achievement, as distinct from assisted achievement (that is the upper level of the learner's zone of proximal development). There is a specific baseline assessment sub-question that is relevant here: *What is the starting point of learning in the focus area (actual achievement)?*

The starting point for intervention needs to be defined clearly and provides a reference for assessing growth and learning. Sometimes the baseline will be derived from preliminary assessment, as part of one of the assessment processes used in that phase. For example, a young student beginning school whose assessment has included assessment of basic concepts through a standardised test will have not only standard scores, which have pointed to the decision to focus on basic concepts in intervention, but also a list of concepts that have been assessed. These concepts are everyday real concepts, and are comprehensive, so they provide a useful baseline of the student's demonstrated knowledge of basic concepts. In this case, the unknown words/concepts need to be the content of the intervention. When the content of the preliminary assessment aligns with the knowledge needed in the class, it is a straightforward process to provide the next step.

At other times, the baseline will need to be specifically assessed at the beginning of the intervention. This is the case when standardised tests have been used to identify and select students, but the information provided by these tests is not appropriate as a baseline measure. For example, picture vocabulary tests are often used to demonstrate student development of receptive vocabulary in comparison to others of the same age. However, the content of these tests are not generally appropriate as a baseline for two reasons. Since the concepts are selected to meet the needs of the test and do not represent a curriculum, it is not helpful to teach them as part of the intervention. Further, the test is not sensitive enough to be used as a measure of outcomes over a short period. It is unlikely that the learning during an intervention focusing on receptive vocabulary will transfer to knowledge of the particular test words.

It is much more appropriate for the baseline to be aligned to the content of the intervention and the context for using receptive vocabulary in real life. Demonstrated knowledge so far of the actual words to be focused on in an intervention will serve as the baseline, or the starting point. Similarly, when a structured intervention package is implemented it is likely that the baseline will be incorporated in the intervention. In fact, many packaged programs have baseline assessment built in, as well as procedures for collecting monitoring data.

Assessment for monitoring

Assessment for monitoring is also determined within Step 5 of educational casework in response to the question: *What is the response to teaching as it is happening (actual and assisted achievement) and what factors are supporting and hindering learning?* After establishing the baseline, monitoring is the assessment of changes in actual achievement during intervention. It is really frustrating to go out of a session with a student and realise that the learning has not been captured! Instead, having a system for assessing and recording achievement during an intervention will make this process an integral part of the intervention. Monitoring during assessment also provides evidence of the ongoing effect of the intervention and allows well-informed decisions about changes to be made as necessary. Additionally, it makes learning evident to the learner, and thus supports authentic student empowerment.

Some educational systems include procedures for baseline, monitoring and outcomes assessment to be recorded together, and to be consolidated as an intervention is implemented. Some intervention programs have measures built in, with checklists or tables to be completed during each session. Others use computer-assisted assessment to record daily achievement as part of an intervention session. Graphs or tables of achievement that gather and compile the evidence as the intervention progresses are thus created as part of the implementation of the intervention.

Another dimension of monitoring assessment that originates from research in dynamic assessment is termed *assisted achievement*. This term refers to what learners can do with assistance during intervention, as distinct from what they can achieve independently. Just as actual achievement can be noted, it is useful to know how responsive students are to certain methods of teaching through what learning they are able to demonstrate with assistance on each occasion. This provides a description of the zone of proximal development for learners, which is valuable information not only for the progress of the intervention but for understanding more about learners' general responsiveness to teaching.

Monitoring can also be something that is done outside the intervention. It can be appropriate to have assessment processes organised to happen in the students' classes, to see how the intervention is affecting learning. Linking the layers of intervention, that is, the classroom teaching with individual intervention, is vitally important. Such monitoring puts a focus on the *transfer of learning* from short-term individual intervention to classroom learning, and requires classroom teachers to focus on changes in motivation and learning. Systems for this to happen can be set up through negotiation as part of the implementation plan. Transfer is also an important part of developing the sustainability required for any intervention, unless it is intended that a learner is to be supported in this way indefinitely. This is particularly pertinent when considering what teaching assistants do to support learning and student independence.

Assessment underpins all decisions in responsive teaching and casework. It helps us know what should be the focus of intervention, and what effect the intervention had. Activities that are designed for learning can be the same, similar or distinct from assessment tasks. By embedding opportunities to demonstrate learning, or assessment tasks, in learning opportunities, teachers can gather information about what has been learned, how well it has been learned and what needs to be consolidated or extended. Assessment practice supports the gathering of evidence around the intervention and holds the intervention together. It is the process whereby determinations of change are made. Assessment is the start and the end of the intervention, and is embedded throughout, as changes are monitored.

It is much harder to ensure all teaching matches learning needs when teaching a group or class, and it is inevitable that there will be times when there is a mismatch, and some learners will be waiting and watching instead of being actively engaged in learning themselves. However, no precious individual teaching time should be wasted on learning activities that do not directly meet the learning needs of the student. Inclusion of a reflection at the end of an assessment task makes the learning explicit and ties it back to the intended learning outcomes of the lesson. It requires the learner to be aware of evidence of learning. Reflection can support metacognition and thus self-regulated learning for both learners and teachers.

Assessment of outcomes

Outcome assessment derives from Step 6 of educational casework in response to the question: *What did this student learn?* Its focus is on intended learning outcomes, unintended learning outcomes, and factors that support and hinder learning. The assessment questions included in this section of the educational casework model draw from the assessment of outcomes, and also the baseline, monitoring information and any assessment of transfer and maintenance. The combination and interpretation of this information will vary across cases.

The outcomes measures need to be appropriate for the intended learning outcomes of the intervention and valid and reliable for their purpose. Assessment of overall outcomes can be the natural extension of the monitoring that has been happening, or can be separate. When regular achievement has been recorded, the outcomes can be whatever is recorded in the last instructional session. In other situations, there may be a need for an assessment event to mark the end of the intervention and as a chance for students to demonstrate their learning and growth over the period of the intervention.

Outcomes assessment can involve the re-administration of one of the tests used at the beginning of the intervention. In the case of using a basic concept scale as a pre-test and baseline, and a focus on teaching the content in the test, it is possible to re-administer this test to see how the learning in the sessions translates into performance in test conditions. This may or may not be helpful, but it can be useful to show changes that have happened using standardised scores, if that is possible. Many test manuals, however, stipulate a minimum period of time before re-administration of the assessment is valid.

Reassessment can be done with a parallel form of a previously administered test to measure outcomes. Many academic achievement tests have multiple forms for this purpose. For example, commonly used reading and mathematics tests can have two forms and are often used as the standardised test for checking outcomes after reading intervention, providing age equivalents that can show gains in reading.

Sometimes demonstration of the improved knowledge or skills in a different context from that of the intervention is needed, perhaps in the classroom, or through a performance for the school or for the family, or some other product that demonstrates the learning that has been achieved. This may be appropriate when a student has been reluctant to perform in front of the class previously, but is now comfortable in doing so.

Unintended outcomes also need to be noticed and analysed in this phase of assessment. These can be capabilities that were not the focus of the intervention but which have been affected. For example, seeking help in the classroom, contributing to learning discussions or allowing family members to assist with homework may have improved. There can also be negative outcomes that become evident. All changes need to be noticed and examined as part of assessing the outcomes of intervention.

The sustainability of learning in terms of transfer and maintenance is a key consideration in the assessment of outcomes of intervention. The previous example, of performing in front of a group, may have been the intended outcome and focus of teaching in an intervention, but it could also be evidence of transfer from the setting of an individual intervention to a different context. For a student whose intervention was focused on expressive language, in particular sequenced retelling of a story, performance in the individual session may be the intended outcome, but it is important to consider where else this skill could be transferred and demonstrated.

Overall, it is also important to gather evidence of the maintenance of the outcomes of intervention over time. Sometimes this will be a part of the intervention or casework. At other times it will be separate, undertaken by classroom teachers and families after intense episodes of educational casework have been completed.

In the context of individual learners it is important to see effects of intervention over time so that decisions can be made about whether further short-term individual intervention is needed and how effective it may be for that learner. For some learners, particularly those with significant learning difficulties or disabilities, longer-term intervention or regular short-term interventions that complement classroom teaching may be required. In these cases it is important to know what transfer and what maintenance is achieved, and how to best support the ongoing sustainability of improvement for particular learners.

Assessment for feedback and reporting

Assessment for feedback and reporting derives from Step 7 of the Educational Casework Process in response to the question: *What reporting and feedback supports this student's learning?* Feedback and reporting on the assessment that has been a part of the Educational Casework Process will ideally have happened from the outset. In fact, these processes are integral to the initial clarification of the focus for the intervention. However, in Step 7 we are more interested in how findings from the baseline, monitoring and outcomes assessment are fed back to the learner and reported to other people. This is unlikely to be an end-on process, but instead part of the collaboration that is foundational to the intervention.

Assessment for evaluation

The final step in educational casework is the evaluation of the intervention, a response to the Step 8 question: *How did the intervention support the student's learning? What is the next step?* Assessment that helps us monitor and determine whether outcomes have been achieved is vital for gathering evidence about the effectiveness of intervention. We are interested in what aspects of the intervention were most effective, as well as the factors that supported and hindered its implementation. With a focus on evidence-based teaching and intervention, it is also important to gather evidence to test the effectiveness of every intervention, rather than making assumptions based on research studies that may or may not have been carried out in similar contexts.

Summary

In this chapter we have carefully considered the purposes of assessment, WHY assessment is used in responsive teaching and educational casework. We have established how assessment is integral to any intervention process, how it establishes a starting point, allows monitoring of the effects of intervention while it is happening, and measures outcomes. Assessment also underpins any evaluative judgements made about how an intervention may have contributed to learning. Planning all these components of assessment within a learning intervention is important to the success of any intervention, and is particularly vital in terms of being able to provide evidence of the effect of the intervention on student learning. The next dimension of decision-making in assessment is consideration of WHAT is being assessed (Chapter 7), since this will influence HOW assessment is done (Chapter 8).

References

Berman, J. (2001). *An application of dynamic assessment to school mathematical learning.* Unpublished PhD thesis, University of New England, Armidale, NSW, Australia.

Berman, J. & Graham, L. (2002). School counsellor use of curriculum-based dynamic assessment. *Australian Journal of Guidance and Counselling, 12*(1), 21–40.

Graham, L., Berman, J., & Bellert, A. (2015). *Sustainable learning: Inclusive practices for 21st century classrooms.* Melbourne, VIC: Cambridge University Press.

Pameijer, N. (2016). *Assessment for intervention: A practice-based model.* Keynote Address International School Psychology Association Conference, Amsterdam, July.

Wong, B., Graham, L., Hoskyn, M., & Berman, J. (2008). *The ABCs of learning disabilities* (2nd ed.). Burlington, MA: Elsevier.

7

THE CONTENT (WHAT) OF ASSESSMENT IN LEARNING INTERVENTION

The second foundation dimension for assessment decision-making is the content focus of the assessment: *what* it is that is to be assessed. It is easy to say that a particular assessment process or test is assessing literacy, or numeracy, or emotional status, or social skills, but as evidence-based practitioners using assessments to make decisions about student lives we need to be somewhat deeper in our consideration of what is really being assessed. This means we need to consider validity – unless there is validity in assessment, it is worthless and can even be dangerous.

Validity is the alignment between what we think we are assessing and what we are actually assessing. It is surprising that often these are not aligned. Many people, in practice and in research, use quick assessments to sum up learning, and then they talk as if what the assessment really did was to assess the true depth and breadth of their focus. An example is the use of a word reading test as a measure of reading. In fact this test is a measure of only one component of reading. It is not possible to talk about the complex multidimensional processes of reading based only on the results of this test.

There are many different types of validity that are important for us in learning intervention. However, the underlying principle is that learning intervention professionals need to be clear about the limits of the assessments that they use. They need to be able to select assessment aligned with the focus of intervention, to critically examine the assessment results provided in reports about learners and to understand the limits of assessment information reported in published research. To begin this chapter on the content of assessment, we consider validity in more depth.

Validity of assessment

Validity is crucially important when considering what assessment approaches and strategies to use in learning intervention. Validity is related to reliability (see

TABLE 7.1 Assessment validity in learning intervention

Content validity	How well does this assessment align with the content needed to be assessed?
Face validity	Does this assessment, on the face of it, assess the focus knowledge, skill or capability?
Construct validity	How well does this assessment cover the full depth and breadth of the knowledge, skill or capability?
Curriculum validity	How well does this assessment align with the curriculum?
Context validity	How well does this assessment match the context within which the knowledge, skill or capability is to be used?
Cultural validity	How well does this assessment match the culture of the student and/or of the context, curriculum or content?
Predictive validity	How well does this assessment predict future learning outcomes?
Concurrent validity	How well does this assessment match other assessments of the same construct/content/curriculum, etc.?

previous chapter). Once an assessment procedure is established to be reliable, then validity can be considered. Validity is the notion that an assessment is truly assessing what it claims to assess. This seems simple enough, but is in fact quite complex.

There are many ways of establishing test validity. Detailed information about it is provided in conventional test manuals, which use it to establish how well these tests have been developed. However, it is important to consider validity more broadly, because the statistically established, psychometric validity of a test does not necessarily translate into the other types of validity that are important for educational casework and responsive teaching. These types of validity are summarised in Table 7.1.

Content validity

Content validity is sometimes considered to include face validity and construct validity. To illuminate the notion of content validity, we will focus on the area of vocabulary. For example, a vocabulary test includes selected words. There will be a different range of content depending on the cultural context and purpose of the test. Each time such a test is selected, the content needs to be considered to see if it matches the content to be taught and that it is relevant to the particular cultural context of assessment. Some vocabulary tests will have overlap, but generally the content will be different and not comparable.

Tests may also not closely align with the particular curriculum content for students. This does not matter as long as the limits of the content are explicit. For example, picture vocabulary tests have been developed to measure receptive vocabulary development. The standard score (age normed) from these tests are often used as a quick measure of language and intellectual development, even though they do not measure the full construct of either of these capabilities. Often these tests have been developed in North America so there are terms that are not recognised by Australian and New Zealand students. Such tests can be useful to determine whether a student's vocabulary may be age appropriate, but are not useful for any other purpose in learning intervention. They are not an appropriate baseline or monitoring or outcomes measure because of their content. Many of the terms are not those we use in everyday learning and so would not be the focus of an intervention. Explicit teaching of a vocabulary bank in learning intervention should be aligned with the content needed by a particular student, so the words that are the focus of the intervention will be the baseline, monitoring and outcomes content for assessment. Content validity is thus achieved, and if these words are curriculum based, then evidence of curriculum validity is provided as well.

Face validity

Face validity is the easiest form of validity to establish; it is the lowest bar to reach. This term means that on the face of it the assessment is assessing what it claims. For example, a pencil and paper test of place value that asks students to match tens and ones to digits in multi-digit numbers, and to write the numbers to match drawings of base ten blocks, is assessing children's understanding of place value. So is a set of tasks that ask a student to first construct two-digit amounts using base ten blocks, and to explain why they selected those particular blocks, then to explain the values of the numbers in the tens and ones columns, and, finally, to explain the zero in a two-digit number (in the tens place). It is important to realise, however, that these tests may be assessing a significantly different depth of learning about place value. The second tool covers the full construct as defined in cognitive research, while the former is a surface exploration of the construct. This means that, although both tests seem to be assessing the same learning, in fact, only the second test has construct validity.

Similarly, there are many tests of reading that do not necessarily assess the same processes and yet provide reading age equivalents. But these tests do not assess reading in the same way and cannot be simply compared. One may be a test of word recognition – words are read separately and have no surrounding sentences or pictures. The other may consist of passages to read that are complemented by visual stimuli. Although these tests have face validity, the nature of the reading processes being assessed and the reading processes that they are examining are very different.

Construct validity

Construct validity is particularly important in situations when assessment leads to diagnostic labels like 'dyslexia' and 'dyscalculia' (see more later in this chapter). It is also important when assessing specific constructs within the curriculum. Notions of surface and deep learning are again relevant here. For example, it is possible to provide evidence of knowledge at a superficial level using some assessment, but when the test 'digs deeper' there may not be evidence of a student's more sophisticated and consolidated level of learning. If an assessment does not dig deep it can only provide evidence of surface learning which is not an adequate basis for inferring adequate deep learning. Instead assessment needs to cover the full depth and breadth of a construct and define how learning has been demonstrated. Assessment professionals need to be conscious of construct validity and discriminate between different assessment instruments and how they define particular constructs.

Curriculum validity

When we are assessing and reporting assessment information within a particular curriculum context, it is important to consider how well the assessment aligns with the curriculum. Curriculum is developed separately from assessment, particularly assessment that is used in educational casework, so it is important to check the alignment of assessment with curriculum in order to make valid interpretations and subsequently report assessment results.

Context validity

Context validity is also important to consider. For example, it is sometimes appropriate to teach specific skills or knowledge in small group or individual intervention settings and then support the application of skills and knowledge within a whole class activity. This is often done when pre-teaching particular concepts to an individual or small group of students before they are introduced in the whole class lesson. Small group monitoring may indicate that the target concepts are understood, but the only real test of this is when the skills and knowledge become the focus of class learning activities and it is noted how well students are able to use pre-taught concepts in the classroom.

Cultural validity

Cultural validity overlaps with some of the types of validity already discussed, but is significant enough to mention separately. All assessment is culturally framed by the culture of those who have developed it. The language used, the stimulus materials presented and the criteria for scoring are all culturally loaded and can hinder a student's opportunities to demonstrate knowledge and skills. It is vitally important to consider how well assessment matches the culture of students, and at the same time to consider this match or mismatch with regards to the culture of classrooms and of intervention.

Predictive validity

Predictive validity is relevant when we want to use the results of assessment to consider how well students are likely to learn in the future. We predict the future all the time from assessment results, yet we need to constantly check and question these predictions. Predicting, or hypothesising, is a key activity in science and in professional practice in education. Much research in learning intervention is about the predictive ability of particular tests. It is really useful when we can test at one age and predict the learning outcomes at a later age. On this basis we can make decisions about how much resourcing to put into the teaching of particular groups of learners.

The natural next step is to test those predictions, and to put in place everything we can to prevent less than optimum outcomes; to prove ourselves wrong when assessment predicts delays or disorders in learning. However, what often happens is that low scores on assessment indicate slow or disordered learning and so less energy is put into teaching. Sometimes students are placed in other settings based on these predictions, settings that provide lower expectations and lower stimulation, perhaps inadvertently fulfilling the expectations. The discussion here raises considerable ethical issues for learning intervention professionals and for the systems within which they work. Based on what assessment tells us and on what we know about learning trajectories we can predict learning and development.

Concurrent validity

Concurrent validity is a particular aspect of psychometrics, where assessment instruments are compared to other assessment instruments, usually to demonstrate that they are assessing the same thing. For example, when new versions of standardised tests are developed, they are compared to the previous version, and often to other tests that measure the same construct, as a way of demonstrating validity and the new test's capacity to be used in place of previous tools. An understanding of concurrent validity is important for professionals on the ground, as they often need to compare results from two different instruments that purport to measure the same thing.

Assessment of behaviour

Now that we have established the need to be clear about what is being assessed, we will explore some of the content areas for assessment in learning intervention. In this section we consider assessment of behaviour, and in the next section learning. These are common focus areas for assessment in educational casework. They are not mutually exclusive, however. In fact, they are integrally linked and overlap considerably. We will refer to ATRiUM capabilities to make sense of the assessment of these areas and their relationship.

Behaviours that are the focus of assessment in educational settings can be considered as those ATRiUM capabilities emphasised in active learning (A), relating to others (R) and managing self (M). Behaviours of children in their learning environments are a function of many factors including their age, knowledge of behavioural expectations, opportunities to learn the behaviours and to practise them successfully, and the complications related to emotional and social needs that can override academic learning as a priority at any time.

Assessment of behaviour is a very well-established activity in educational settings. Humans have been observing and judging behaviour for millennia, and over the past one hundred and fifty years have created principles and many strategies within behavioural psychology related to the assessment of behaviour. Considerable expertise is used in schools to make sense of what is happening for students in terms of the intensity and pervasiveness, and antecedents and consequences of their behaviour.

In responsive teaching and educational casework, assessment can provide snapshots of behaviour across a class, as well as of individuals across settings and contexts. Patterns of behaviour that are identified through classwide assessment provide teachers with evidence of behavioural learning needs of groups or individuals. These descriptions of learning needs support decisions about classroom organisation and management and highlight behaviours that may need to be taught or reinforced more explicitly, or practised more intensively.

In educational casework, assessment of the behaviour of an individual student can be undertaken in one or more settings or contexts. This is often done to help work out the function of the behaviours and what influences them. Understanding the nuances of behaviour that occur between different settings, and within settings, is achieved by most children as they develop and accumulate experiences, but for some children this is very difficult. Responsive teaching aims to ensure all students have opportunities to learn the appropriate behaviours that will not only be acceptable in the social settings of schools but will also support learning. Educational casework that aims to change behaviours responds to those behaviours that are not developmentally or contextually appropriate and sets out to make sense of the functions of those behaviours for students. It also intends to meet student needs in different ways so that their behaviours become more socially acceptable. ·

Many students who are referred for educational casework around behaviour concerns also have associated learning difficulties. For some students the behaviours that cause attention to be directed at them have been developed to avoid the frustrations of learning. For others the behaviours may be expressions of complex issues of social and emotional stress or distress caused by many aspects of life including frustration in learning, neglect, domestic violence, abuse and other trauma, and a sense of powerlessness.

Practice in behavioural psychology refers to clinical levels of externalised and internalised behaviours that are extreme and often dysfunctional ways of managing emotional distress. The externalised responses to these situations are what teachers and families experience as disruptive behaviour problems that can, if intense and pervasive enough, be determined to meet clinical behavioural conditions. Common externalising behavioural disorders that are identified in educational settings, and determined through psychological or psychiatric assessment, include oppositional defiant disorder and conduct disorder.

As well, extreme internalised responses to life circumstances or experiences can be seen in anxious and emotional behaviours, many of which are not ever identified as such in classrooms. Many withdrawn students manage their life circumstances by withdrawing, avoiding the eyes of teachers and staying out of focus in classrooms. Some students use persistent avoidance of school and social settings, which leads to significant absenteeism and subsequent lack of opportunity for learning. In extreme cases, these internalising behaviours also result in mental illnesses such as anxiety disorders, depression and personality disorders that can become debilitating and threaten the safety of the student.

Another psychological condition that is well known and relevant for some students is post-traumatic stress disorder (PTSD). As with other psychological or psychiatric conditions and mental illnesses, there are processes of assessment that psychologists and psychiatrists use to determine whether a young person meets the criteria for the condition, and then to put in place evidence-based therapeutic interventions. Trauma-informed frameworks can assist teachers in understanding how circumstances affect learners' engagement and success in academic learning and their development of capabilities. The mnemonic SPACE (staged, predictable, adaptive, connected, enabled) captures one trauma-informed instructional framework (Australian Childhood Foundation, 2010). It should be acknowledged that there is also a significant aspect of growth that can be a part of a life journey for such students. Teachers can understand and assist students, and support their recovery through the notion of post-traumatic growth (Calhoun & Tedeschi, 2014).

Both externalised and internalised behaviours can be considered as behaviours to be changed or as mental health conditions that may need psychological or psychiatric intervention. How these are dealt with in educational casework will depend on how established the behaviour patterns are for individual students and the elucidation of contributing factors as determined through assessment.

Assessment of learning

Teachers are experts in assessing learning. They do it all the time, and use assessment information to inform teaching as well as to report to students and their families about academic achievement. Teachers also pass on their curriculum-based assessment information as part of the referral process for educational casework. Other professionals who work in education are also experts in assessment within the curriculum, with a different range of tools that measure student learning. Such assessments of learning are often conducted in order to establish standardised measures of delays or differences in achievement (in comparison to others of the same age or grade) that become part of their casework evidence and, sometimes, the basis for access to resources for intervention. Educational professionals are also experts in gathering assessment information about the processes of learning that can complement the information that teachers gather in classroom settings, and that parents have about student learning outside school.

The full range of assessment across the curriculum is beyond the scope of this book. Instead, we will examine the assessment practices across key domains of learning that are generally the focus of educational casework assessment in schools, two of the ATRiUM capabilities – language, literacy, numeracy (U) and thinking skills (T).

Assessment of language

There is much known about how children develop language skills and considerable evidence about what is typical at different ages. Students learn the language of the educational setting in different ways. For some of them it is the language that is used every day in their homes, and for many children it is a variation of their home language, while for others it is a totally new language. For the first group, there is no need to switch dialects or codes when entering a classroom, just extending language as it is used within each of the curriculum domains. For others, the language of the classroom and of teaching is learnt at the same time as the curriculum content is provided. This adds an enormous additional learning demand to the classroom experiences of some students.

Components of language development and their use in learning which are the focus of assessment include:

- sound awareness and skills (phonology);
- the extent of vocabulary or word banks and meaning making (semantics);
- mechanisms for arranging words into sentences and including the nuances such as tense (morpho-syntactic structure); and
- the use of language in practical situations for communication and social interactions (pragmatics).

Based on considerable research evidence about learning and the development of language skills, there are robust assessment tools in this area that both define the age appropriateness of development and provide direction for intervention for individuals or group of learners. So, at any time, it is possible to gain a general picture of delay or disorder in development in terms of receptive and expressive language that can assist in determining how best to support language learning.

Assessment of literacy

The component skills of phonemic awareness and decoding, vocabulary and comprehension are brought together into fluency in reading. Each of these skills is extended throughout our lifetimes, contributing to the more sophisticated use of all components in the activity of making sense of written language and producing written language (spelling and writing), which are both essential capabilities for succeeding in academic learning.

There is considerable variability in learning to read and write, with some children coming to school already reading and others not yet ready to develop beginning reading skills. Some children come with very rich language bases on which to extend their understandings of the world into reading comprehension and writing. Some children are just beginning to learn the language of the classroom and are expected at the same time to establish component skills of reading and writing. Some children experience a considerable mismatch between the culture of their home and that of the classroom, which interferes with their engagement and learning. Some children have persistent or intermittent sensory impairments that will interfere with their ability to be literate. Some children have intermittent attendance at school that reduces the power of systematic teaching. Some children experience illness or family trauma that interferes with attendance or wellness. Social and emotional issues can also interfere with accessing systematic teaching. Obviously, there are many reasons why the long journey of learning to be literate is troublesome for some students, and these factors need to be taken into account in planning learning intervention.

Based on the developmental knowledge of literacy learning, there are many ways to assess each component skill, as well as to assess how well these are brought together in reading and writing. It is possible to get profiles of development and proficiency for each skill and also to make sense of how reading comes together and is used as a tool in learning. As well, assessment needs to consider all the factors that may be contributing to difficulties in learning.

Assessment of numeracy

Together with language and literacy, numeracy is a core symbol system that is central to effective learning across the curriculum and to functioning in our world. There is a solid research base that allows us to understand the learning trajectories within mathematical learning, from early counting, to understanding our place value number system, to applying this knowledge in arithmetic and problem solving. Other domains of mathematical learning, including algebra, chance and data, and geometry, are also well researched, so we know a lot about learning progressions in these numeracy strands.

Variability in learning within numeracy is influenced by many of the same things as literacy, and, similarly, there is an extreme range of success, including some learners who find mathematics difficult throughout life. The variability inherent in the population of learners is compounded by the dislike of mathematics that is reported by many people. In fact, mathematics anxiety is well documented as a key factor that hinders learning (Foley et al., 2017).

There are many ways to assess learning that are referenced to known learning progressions based on cognitive research. Traditionally assessment in mathematics used either arithmetic or word problems, but during the latter part of the 20th century, assessment has increasingly used developmental task-based interviews. Such interactions allow assessors to access student thinking and explanations for their arithmetic or problem-solving actions, which reveal their understanding of mathematical concepts, as well as their proficiency with the symbolic representations of those ideas. Assessment ranges from class pencil and paper tests, to small group problem solving, to individual interviews. There are also standardised tests that allow a determination of age equivalence and standard scores against age-appropriate, normed samples. Selection of an assessment tool will depend on the purpose of gathering the assessment information.

Assessment of thinking

The fourth core set of processes for learning are those related to thinking. Thinking is carried out using the language of the learner. It is developmental and alters in sophistication depending on the purpose of the thinking at any particular time. Much research has been used to explore human thinking, and there are a number of models that assist with making sense of this capability and that underpin assessment decisions.

Cognitive models of development and learning include Piaget's (1971) description of developmental stages of thinking which are tied to maturation of the thinker. In addition, Vygotsky's processes of internalisation are based on learning experiences using the sociocultural and psychological tool of language. Information processing models consider how we take in information, what we do to make sense of it, and then how we produce information to demonstrate our learning. Each of these frames provides ways of understanding thinking and the development of thinking that can underpin the assessment of thinking skills. Many aspects of these theoretical approaches are built into the classroom and specialist assessment that helps us make sense of the thinking of students, both embedded within curriculum disciplines and as used in everyday life.

A field of research that is relevant for the assessment of thinking is that of intelligence, from which comes the most controversial suite of tests used in education. These tests are controversial for good reason! Tests of intelligence have considerable theoretical and research foundations that make them robust in assessing what they assess. However, intelligence tests have a history of being used for purposes other than those for which they were designed, and for being the root of considerable problems in many contexts. They have been used to 'sort' people and because of their misuse, and misunderstandings of their limitations, they have become in some instances proxy for practices of discrimination in a range of contexts, including the eugenics movement of the early 20th century (Stephens & Cryle, 2017).

Traditionally, 'intelligence' was seen to be the only measure of quality of thinking and learning. People with higher measures of intellectual ability were assumed to be capable of higher-order thinking and deeper learning. There have been many students who seemed to have enormous capacity intellectually, but could not realise it for various reasons. In fact, many intellectually gifted students do not learn as well as anticipated in our schools. There are also many people who have achieved great things through their personal levels of persistence, drive and determination, rather than their natural intellectual talent as measured by intelligence tests. This complicated reality makes the focus on intelligence somewhat limited, since it needs to be considered from a wider perspective in order to really inform us about the nature of students as learners and what can be done to optimise their learning.

However, with a focus on thinking capabilities, at one end of the continuum there are students who are intellectually gifted, and whose thinking is deeper and more extended than most. At the other end are students who have been identified with a level of intellectual ability that is disabling for them in relation to the curriculum and everyday living. It is useful to use Sternberg's (1997) ideas around successful intelligence, in particular the notion of engagement with the environment, when thinking about the learning needs of students who have labels of either intellectual giftedness or intellectual disability. For all learners, it is important to understand the thinking skills that are developing and how to support students' next steps in that development.

Assessment of learning and behaviour in an ecological framework

The assessment of the dynamic systems of human functioning in a complex world calls on us to have a focus on how students interact with their learning environment and are affected by influences from family and community. The representation in Figure 7.1 helps us to keep this in mind when we are planning assessment and asking assessment-related questions.

It turns our assessment lens onto the relationship between each learner and their teacher and the activity that is the focus within learning and teaching interactions. What we need to explore and understand are learners' use of learning strategies to respond to teaching strategies and learning opportunities provided by teachers and their demonstration of achievement as a result of that learning. We are also interested in unpacking any factors in the learning environment, home and community that influence learning within the curriculum and the development of ATRiUM capabilities.

Assessment in reference to learning environment

As we have already highlighted, it is important to understand how a student engages with the learning environment. Families will have important perceptions that need to be accessed, and students will have experiences to report that will point to particular dimensions to be explored more systematically. Triangulating student and family perceptions is important, as these can align (sometimes through reporting from one to the other) or can be wildly different because they each see and hear different things. It is important to explore this alignment (or misalignment) and make sense of it.

Analysis of a student's schooling history can reveal a pattern of success at school linked inextricably to the classroom. For students who experience learning difficulties or disabilities, it is not unusual for some years to have been wonderful and some to be reported as terrible. Exploring what it was about different years is essential to

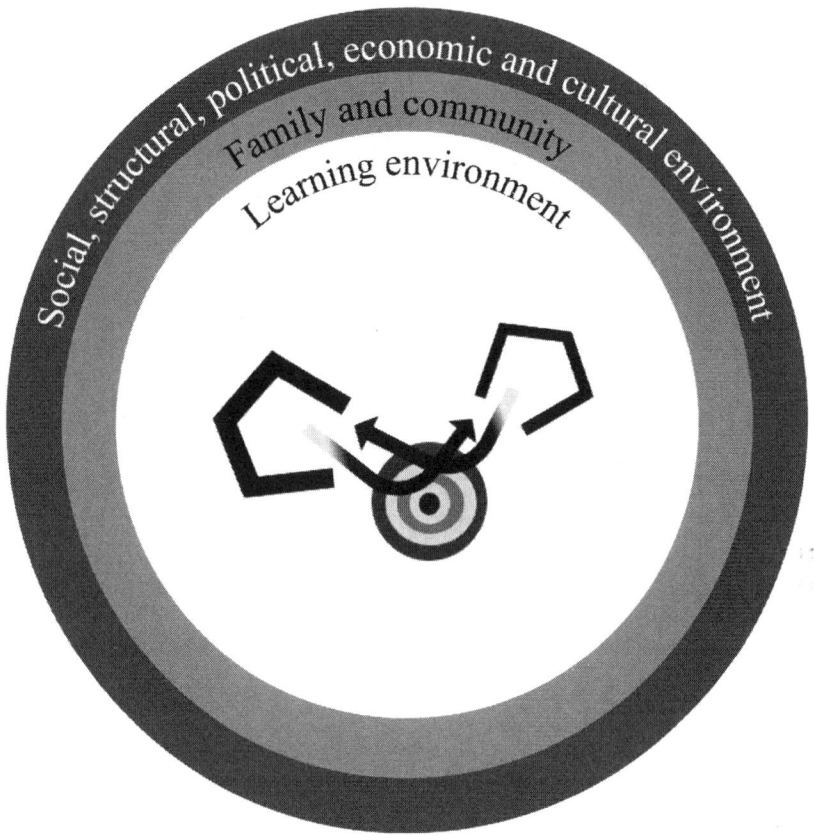

FIGURE 7.1   An ecological perspective on assessment

understanding how the environment is affecting students' school engagement and learning. It is vital to understand how students are influenced by teacher character- istics, classroom climate, style of feedback, student–teacher relationships, inclusive strategies, curriculum differentiation and home–school partnerships, all of which are managed by individual teachers. Such insights provide a valuable basis on which to work out what may be simple changes that will make big differences.

All teachers are professionals and therefore expected to have impact on their stu- dents' learning, but there can be resistance in schools to considering what it is that each teacher brings to their teaching. One of the first things initial teacher education students are asked is to recall a significant teacher, the one (or more) who made them want to be a teacher themselves, and to think about what it was about that teacher that had such an impact. We acknowledge that individual teachers make a difference in the Responsive Teaching Framework and the Educational Casework Process through the second question: *What do I bring as a teacher or learning interven- tion professional?*

It is important to understand how particular learners respond to different teachers and to use this as a basis for considering which teachers may be more successful in matching the learning needs of individual students. Triangulation of this evidence through asking teachers how they respond to particular learners is also important. Professionalism aside, it is always better if students can work with teachers who are responsive and open as this eliminates a very powerful, potentially negative aspect of the environment immediately.

If possible, it is also valuable to observe or experience the learning environment (the school and classroom) as part of assessment, to explore anecdotes provided by family members and other people, and to consider interactions and class climate. Some things we humans experience can be reduced to descriptions, checklists and numbers, but grasping a deeper sense of what is happening can only be experienced in real time. Evidence needs to be collected, particularly when different people describe the same situation in different ways.

Aspects of a learning environment that can be considered include the physical space, material and human resources, lighting, ventilation and temperature. Decisions about how important these are to particular cases need to be made, often based also on information from screening checklists or student or teacher reports. If a particular aspect of the learning environment is identified as being significant then a more systematic assessment of that aspect, and the response of the student to it, needs to be carried out.

For example, reports of low-level peer disruption or bullying that interfere with a student's in-class work may not be noticed in usual day to day teaching, but could become evident through other means. Videoing to check observations can be useful in exploring such embedded factors of learning environments. Similarly, teacher responses to a particular learner may need to be explored. Some students experiencing learning difficulties present as class clowns or are disruptive and take a lot of teacher management time. Understanding the function of the pattern of behaviour can be the key to changing it. This may need systematic exploration to really tap into how students' disruptive classroom behaviours are related to their academic learning.

In contrast, some students deliberately avoid being noticed to keep themselves safe so that, for example, they will not be asked a question to which they do not know the answer. Through using strategies like this, it is possible that some learners experience very little individual interaction with their teachers at all. As the learning environment also includes learning opportunities and teaching strategies, we need to consider how learners engage with and respond as part of this focus on assessment. Consideration of student access to the curriculum and ways for demonstrating learning provided by their teachers can be organised using the information processing theory of learning and the dimensions of the Universal Design for Learning model as outlined in Chapter 3 (Figures 3.3 and 3.4).

Assessment in reference to influences from family and community

Some students have been through multiple casework experiences. These students do not need to feel that this is another beginning, and this professional has the elusive answers to all their problems. Instead it is important to acknowledge previous casework, to learn from it and to seek families' insights into previous experiences. Families have a wealth of evidence about the development and learning of their children that needs to be part of the evidence base for any educational casework intervention. A partnership with families allows this to be included when it is pertinent, and also allows consideration of what influences may be relevant currently from the perspective of family and community. All casework has to build on what has already happened.

Sometimes it is enough to acknowledge what families know and give them opportunities to provide more information as they see fit. For example, if students have experienced trauma, this will most certainly be an influence on their experiences and learning. Understanding what caused the trauma is not always necessary in the educational domain, although it is vital that there is therapeutic treatment provided. It is sometimes enough to know that trauma is a part of the situation and, therefore, trauma-informed strategies can be trialled for these learners.

Assessment in reference to developmental and learning pathways

Meaningful assessment is based in solid knowledge of development and learning. It is not enough to know what current capabilities, skills and knowledge are, it is also vital to know how patterns of skills and knowledge fit into pathways of learning and development and, therefore, what is likely to happen next. The alignment between assessment and developmental pathways strengthens the contribution of assessment to effective learning intervention. Teachers and other professionals need sound knowledge about developmental pathways both related to the ATRiUM capabilities and to the academic curriculum.

Because we are focusing on learning intervention, we are particularly interested in assessment that most directly informs intervention, and explicitly references relevant learning pathways. There are a number of ways assessment can reference developmental and learning pathways that are pertinent to professionals in learning intervention, for example by arranging test items to reflect developmental pathways; by including levels of responses to items that reflect developmental pathways; by referring to theoretical frameworks that consider depth and quality of learning; and by using the notion of the Zone of Proximal Development and dynamic assessment.

There is considerable research evidence about typical patterns of development and learning, as well as the variability in those pathways. Developmental trajectories and learning pathways are not absolute. They are documented based on the development and learning patterns of many people, but there will always be those who do not follow the pathways at the same pace or meet milestones in the same order. Some students experience learning and development differently, in ways that we define as 'disordered'. Many of the students who are the focus of educational casework will be in the small group of people for whom development and learning are disordered, which is why learning intervention professionals become involved.

Teaching to basic levels of learning for students who have, for example, a diagnosis of twice exceptional giftedness and learning difficulties can lead to considerable frustration. An assumption that everyone develops in the same way is inappropriate, since some learners can jump to higher-order thinking and understand sophisticated concepts, although they may not have mastered what is considered lower-order knowledge. Trying to get these learners to demonstrate basic skills when their thinking is at a very high conceptual level is not helpful for their learning. Instead, complex ideas need to be acknowledged and supported, and workaround ways of ensuring lower-level skills can be provided to support this way of thinking.

Teachers can use practical and creative ways to support 'disordered' or different learning and to backfill the basic skills in some other way, including through cooperative tasks in which other learners manage some of the basics, while the twice exceptional student leads the higher-order problem solving. It is also possible to convince some learners that they do need the basic skills in order to realise the potential of their higher-order thinking, and to set up systematic development opportunities. Establishing the motivation and meaning needed to sustain the effort of the learner is the biggest challenge in this situation. The complications of development illustrated here are relevant to many conditions and disorders commonly found in schools.

Assessment of developmental and learning conditions and disorders

To date, many educational systems have relied on classification and diagnostic procedures from outside the field of education to decide how available resources are shared. In terms of disability, the primary reference for the conditions that attract funding is from the field of psychiatry in the form of the Diagnostic and Statistical Manual of Mental Disorders (DSM5) (American Psychiatric Association, 2013), or disease, with reference to the World Health Organisation's International Statistical Classification of Diseases (ICD10) (WHO, 2004).

As their titles suggest, both these references are medically oriented and seek to define students' exceptionalities in terms of their development and functioning. The key construct underlying diagnostic categories is that the development or behaviour of an individual is significantly outside what is considered to be 'typical' or 'normal'. Those who are noticed and classified are advanced or delayed in comparison to others of the same age, or their pattern of development is disordered. Tension arises in inclusive educational settings as this classification system frames difference in terms of deviation from the norm – primarily as deficit, disease or disorder – in comparison to other groups, and uses categories and degrees of difference, in terms of magnitude and pervasiveness, to determine access to resources.

One of the driving forces that underpin the use of diagnostic assessment and labels is the idea that there will be an intervention, 'treatment', or 'prescription' for teaching once a diagnosis has been determined. This is true to some extent, but can also be a distraction, since an enormous amount of heterogeneity exists amongst the people who meet criteria for any particular diagnosis. Overall, however, a diagnosis can be a useful starting point for exploring effective strategies for intervention and uncovering a great number of resources.

In recognition of the range of learning needs that exist within any one 'category' of learner, we advocate using diagnostic labels as a start, rather than focusing on these as the end point of the assessment process. Positioning differences along ATRiUM capability continua can encourage teachers and families, and the students themselves, to work out what any labels actually mean in terms of learning and the provision of appropriate instructional opportunities for individual learners. Assessing in order to ascertain learner profiles in terms of the ATRiUM capabilities encourages educators to go behind some of the commonly used labels to see what they might mean for individual learners and for their teachers.

The ATRiUM capabilities are used in all aspects of life and in learning across the curriculum. They can be the focus of assessment and intervention procedures; however, their use is usually with the aim of improving curriculum-related learning performance. For each of the ATRiUM capabilities in Figure 7.2 the following

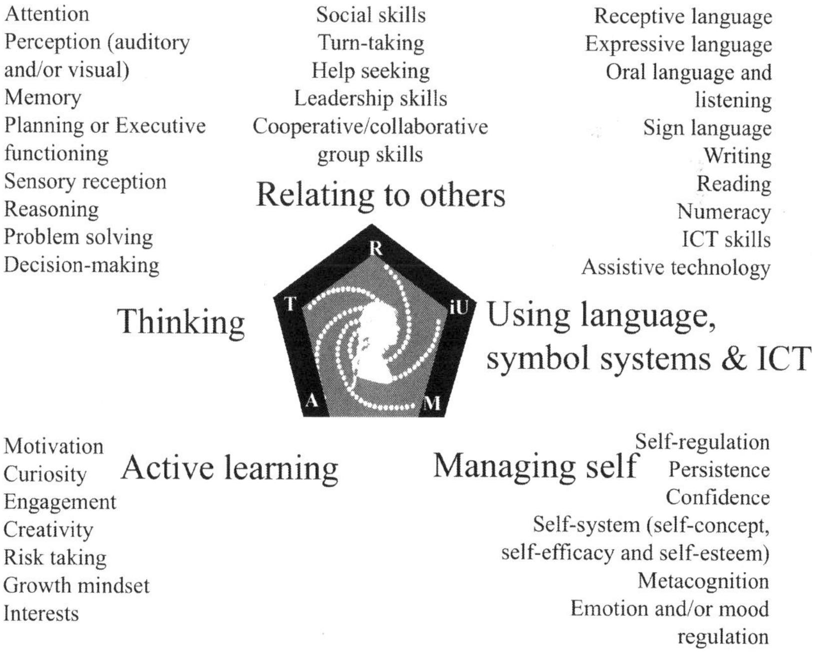

Attention
Perception (auditory and/or visual)
Memory
Planning or Executive functioning
Sensory reception
Reasoning
Problem solving
Decision-making

Social skills
Turn-taking
Help seeking
Leadership skills
Cooperative/collaborative group skills

Relating to others

Receptive language
Expressive language
Oral language and listening
Sign language
Writing
Reading
Numeracy
ICT skills
Assistive technology

Thinking

Using language, symbol systems & ICT

Motivation
Curiosity
Engagement
Creativity
Risk taking
Growth mindset
Interests

Active learning

Managing self

Self-regulation
Persistence
Confidence
Self-system (self-concept, self-efficacy and self-esteem)
Metacognition
Emotion and/or mood regulation

FIGURE 7.2 ATRiUM capabilities elaborated

question can be asked: How do these aspects of the learner's ATRiUM capabilities support and hinder learning at this time?

The complexity of learners and learning is evident in this simple elaboration of ATRiUM capabilities. As we have emphasised, all of these capabilities need to be considered in teaching, since they all come together to support learning. Education systems often simplify this complexity in assessment into two seemingly discrete but actually interrelated domains for intervention – behaviour and learning. We stress the vital importance of integrating behaviour and learning in your practice and of always considering students' learning needs across all ATRiUM capabilities.

Exploring assessment and developmental intervention related to each of the dimensions of the ATRiUM capabilities is outside the scope of this book. Many people spend their whole careers investigating just one of these dimensions and producing ways to think about them (i.e., theories) and ways to assess and intervene. However, it is useful to illustrate how learning intervention professionals can focus on one or more capabilities in educational casework.

A final way of thinking about assessment is through the notion of responsiveness to teaching. This approach is about understanding how students respond to particular learning opportunities and teaching strategies so that this information can inform decisions about future teaching through the consideration of ATRiUM capabilities. Assessment of responsiveness requires that questions be asked that always include an emphasis on student learning in relation to the teaching opportunity that has been provided. This kind of assessment information helps us to make sensible hypotheses about what will make the most difference in intervention.

Summary

Table 7.2 draws together the content of this chapter into a summary of the WHAT of assessment in educational casework for each phase of the process.

In this chapter we have explored WHAT it is that is assessed in response to the purposes of each phase of educational casework. Based on the notion of validity, and all the different types of validity, we have considered how best to support the phases of learning intervention through educational casework. As a culmination of such assessment, it is vital to understand what is supporting learning, as well as what is causing difficulties. Conclusions are informed by whatever focus has been taken with a view to using student strengths as a foundation for any changes. Traditionally, intervention in education focused on identifying deficits and intervening to fix or work around those deficits. In educational casework, we are interested in what supports learning and what hinders learning so we can construct a full understanding of how best to intervene. In the next chapter we examine, within the phases of assessment in educational casework, the approaches to assessment (the HOW) that can respond to the purposes and content of assessment already discussed.

TABLE 7.2 The content of assessment at each phase of the Educational Casework Process

	WHY (Purpose)	WHAT (Content)
3	Preliminary	*What do we already know and what do we need to find out?*
		Depends on the nature of the referral and the questions being asked. Development and learning and the factors that could be hindering and supporting that development and learning.
		• Curriculum referenced.
		• Capabilities referenced (the dimensions of human functioning; ATRiUM).
4		Learning environment referenced (including teaching).
5	Baseline	*What is the starting measure of learning in the focus area (actual achievement)?*
		The knowledge or skills that are the focus of the intervention.
		Demonstration under conditions defined in intervention, may include generalisation and transfer, if that is a dimension that needs to be included.
5	Monitoring	*What is the response to teaching as it is happening (actual and assisted achievement) and factors supporting and hindering learning?*
		As for baseline plus responsiveness to intervention and factors supporting and hindering learning.
6	Outcomes	*What did the student learn?*
		(i) the intended learning outcomes (actual and assisted achievement);
		(ii) any unintended learning outcomes; and
		(iii) factors that supported and hindered learning?
		As for baseline, plus responsiveness to intervention.
7	Feedback and reporting	*What feedback and reporting support this student's learning?*
		As for outcomes.
8	Evaluating	*How did the intervention support this student's learning?*
		Difference between baseline and outcomes assessment, evidence of transfer across contexts and maintenance over time.
		Factors that supported and hindered implementation.

References

American Psychiatric Association (APA) (2013). *Diagnostic and statistical manual of mental disorders.* Arlington, VA: APA.

Australian Childhood Foundation (2010). *Making SPACE for learning: Trauma informed practice in schools.* Ringwood, VIC: Australian Childhood Foundation.

Calhoun, L. G. & Tedeschi, R. G. (Eds.). (2014). *Handbook of posttraumatic growth: Research and practice.* London: Routledge.

Foley, A. E., Herts, J. B., Borgonovi, F., Guerriero, S., Levine, S. C., & Beilock, S. L. (2017). The math anxiety–performance link: A global phenomenon. *Current Directions in Psychological Science, 26*(1), 52–58.

Piaget, J. (1971). The theory of stages in cognitive development. In Green, D. (Ed.), *Measurement and Piaget.* New York, NY: McGraw-Hill, 1–11.

Stephens, E. & Cryle, P. (2017). Eugenics and the normal body: The role of visual images and intelligence testing in framing the treatment of people with disabilities in the early twentieth century. *Continuum, 31*(3), 365–376.

Sternberg, R. (1997). *Successful intelligence.* New York, NY: Simon & Schuster.

World Health Organisation (WHO) (2004). *International statistical classification of diseases and related health problems: Clinical descriptions and diagnostic guidelines* (10th Revision). Geneva: WHO.

8

APPROACHES AND STRATEGIES FOR ASSESSMENT IN LEARNING INTERVENTION

The HOW of assessment

There are conventional and alternative approaches to assessment that can be combined into a rich contemporary assessment framework that supports learning intervention. In terms of student learning, assessment is any opportunity that a learner has to demonstrate learning. There are many ways in which this is done in responsive teaching and educational casework. Generally, assessment is a response to questioning or some stimulus material through a range of processes, such as brief or extended oral or written language, graphic representations, creative products and performances, or selection from pre-prepared responses. Such activities can occur in class, in small groups, in large groups across multiple settings, or as part of individual interviews. Assessment can be an extended process perhaps taking place over a number of weeks for writing an essay or observation in class over a term, or can be short and sharp like an hour-long exam or a ten-minute performance.

Within conventional and alternative approaches to assessment there are multiple strategies that learning intervention professionals can use to find the information they want. Expertise in assessment is related to selecting the appropriate approach and strategies at any particular time that best fulfil the assessment purpose and validly assess the required content. Learning intervention professionals can use what is available around them, can purchase expensive commercially available tests and do intensive training, and/or can become skilled at alternative approaches to assessment.

Often the decision about what assessment strategy to use is determined by factors that are not pedagogical but logistical. Assessment strategies may be chosen because they are easy to administer, score and record, or because it is relatively easy to rank and order students against each other. However, much of what is needed to assess learning is complex and not the result of simple procedures. A mismatch between the approach chosen and the target of assessment means that assessment can be too removed from the authentic process of learning and will become invalid.

Learning intervention professionals need to be on the lookout for invalid assessments, and assessment that is not fit for its purpose. By first reviewing the WHAT and the WHY of assessment, we can make sensible decisions about HOW to do assessment.

Combining the WHAT with the WHY in educational casework

As we are exploring assessment more deeply, we have to consider the content of the assessment in tandem with the purposes of assessment in order to make the best decisions about each component. The purpose of assessment defines the way information is to be used and the decisions to be made, and also influences the nature of information about a particular content area to be gathered. Mapping the purpose and content decision-making against the main phases of assessment (preliminary, baseline, monitoring, outcomes, transfer and generalisation) allows us to consider how to assess in the best way to support educational casework.

Preliminary assessment

Preliminary assessment explores the nature of the student's learning needs. It responds to the question: *What do we already know and what else do we need to find out about this learner?* It helps define the scope of the intervention and the conditions under which intervention is anticipated to be effective.

The preliminary phase is when learning intervention professionals consider a range of assessment approaches, including document analysis and interviews, in order to explore a wide range of possibilities with families and teachers. The focus is on gathering developmental and contextual information regarding what has happened and what is happening now. The assessment explores the nature of family and community influence on learning, influences from the learning environment, as well as the learner's processes of learning and their responsiveness to different approaches to teaching. It is not just factors within the learner that are the focus of this stage of assessment. It is important to get an ecological picture that describes teacher factors, aspects of the learning environment and the complexity of family and community influences that may be vital to understanding the case.

There needs to be a strong focus on the learner during all assessment, not to find the inherent deficits that can explain all difficulties, but to understand the complex engagement interaction between the learner and the learning environment. Since learning difficulties are often the function of a mismatch between needs and teaching, it is important to clearly define student learning needs. Much of this type of assessment sets out to eliminate possible areas of focus, so that they do not need to be targeted in the scope of the intervention. Instead, factors that support learning and development need to be identified so they can be bolstered. It is also important to identify possible barriers that may be hindering learning and development that can be further explored. Many aspects of learner functioning are considered because one of the purposes of assessment is to screen for factors and provide direction for further in-depth assessment.

For example, hearing and vision are often checked in this phase. It is not unusual for investigations of learning difficulties, particularly in the early years of schooling, to identify significant hearing or vision difficulties that explain learning problems. By providing intervention, such as corrective glasses or hearing aids, the barriers for some learners are removed. Eliminating hearing or vision difficulties allows the process of exploring learning needs to continue once it is confirmed that the learner is hearing and seeing things as we would expect.

Interviews to explore multiple dimensions of learning can be done with different intensity by different professionals. For example, semi-structured interview schedules provide a guide for interviews by teachers or psychologists. More highly structured and systematic interview schedules are available for psychologists to use to gather information that can be translated into standardised measurements. These, in turn, may be needed for systemic purposes including referral for outside agency, education system or specialist assessment to determine eligibility for funding.

Preliminary assessment, the focus of making sense of what is known and exploring what else needs to be known and then defining the focus of intervention, is the most challenging phase of assessment. Clarifying the focus at this stage is essential to providing a clear coherence for what follows. It is not unusual for the presenting 'problem' in educational casework to be, in fact, not what needs intervention. Instead it may be masking or distracting from the true issue. It is also not unusual to find that the presenting issue cannot realistically be a target of intervention. Instead, some other focus, at times a smaller aim, needs to be defined. Such clarification and definition of shared understanding is important from the outset and needs to be a part of the preliminary assessment phase.

The framing that happens here is shaped by whatever conceptualisations and assessment tools are brought into play. All practitioners bring their own views of the world and these affect how they do the assessment, what questions they ask and what tools they use. These tools also have particular framing inherent in them. It is important for learning intervention professionals to be conscious of the power of their world views, and those of others, and to understand the biases that are inherent in what they bring to casework. This reflective aspect of assessment practice is articulated in Step 2 of the Educational Casework Process: *What do I bring as a learning intervention professional?*

For example, if you find yourself always seeing the same issues in multiple cases, it is time to get some new professional learning to challenge a possible default way of interpreting results and to ensure the most useful filtering of results from the preliminary assessment phase. When there is no set structure within which to make sense of what is going on, it can be more problematic and reliant on the insights and knowledge the professional brings to the case. The ATRiUM capabilities provide a structure within which to consider a vast amount of assessment information and to filter it into meaningful and usable factors that support and hinder learning.

Baseline, monitoring and outcomes assessment

Baseline, monitoring and outcomes assessment are all assessment of learning and closely linked in practice. They may often be the same assessment on multiple occasions. Assessment across these phases of intervention aims to define:

- the starting point of learning;
- the changes in the learning areas as they are happening and the factors that are supporting and hindering learning; and
- the end point of learning – what the student learning outcomes are.

For each phase, the assessment explicitly measures the skills or knowledge being taught in the intervention and the application of that learning in real life (i.e., the classroom or elsewhere). Its aim is to provide a clear indication of student knowledge or skills that are the focus of the intervention. Baseline and outcomes assessment information has to have intervention validity in order to provide a measure against which growth in learning can be determined. The content of the baseline and outcomes assessments is defined explicitly by the intended learning outcomes (ILOs), and thus results in "constructive alignment" between ILOs, teaching and assessment (Biggs & Tang, 2011).

Assessment for feedback, reporting and evaluation

All the previously collected evidence can support the phases of feedback, reporting, and evaluation. These are phases are focused on establishing the effect of the intervention and sharing that information. As an inherent part of the intervention, the feedback provided to students is vital, and it needs to be in terms of where their learning started and what has been subsequently achieved. Feedback also needs to be about what has made the difference for learners. In practice, feedback interactions occur between the teacher and the learner often as they note that learning has taken place and what has supported and hindered that learning. This process supports decision-making by both teachers and learners in subsequent sessions, and affects their emotional responses and levels of self-efficacy. Reporting to family members takes the same format, as they want to know what the student knows and understands and can do, as well as what has supported learning most effectively.

Sometimes it may also be necessary to gather additional assessment information in order to report to a funding body or other stakeholders. With this type of reporting, it is important to be able to say how much effect the intervention had in a form that is comparable and easily understood. For example, being able to say a student's reading age has gone from two years below chronological age to age appropriate is an important way to frame the acceleration effect of intervention.

Assessment approaches

Assessment approaches are derived from conventional testing as well as from alternative methods that have been developed to counter some of the problems identified with conventional testing approaches. Assessment approaches range from observational strategies within naturalistic settings, to more contrived assessment events like examinations and structured performances, and can include clinical assessment that comprises formal standardised tests, interviews and dynamic assessment to explore particular focus areas in greater depth. There is nothing absolute about assessment of any kind. Assessment always happens within contexts and is influenced by those contexts. The variables that can affect assessment include the framing of the purpose, the setting, the timing, the people involved, the nature of the items or tasks, and the type of scores and descriptors that are produced.

Conventional and alternative assessment

Conventional assessment takes the form of testing that is anchored in behaviourist theories of learning and supported by psychometric theories of measurement. There is much science behind this kind of assessment, yet it has not provided a complete answer to what we need to know about human development, experience and learning. In fact, assessment in the form of clinical testing or psychological analysis has acquired a bad name, and is rejected outright by many in the community, both lay and professional. It will therefore be useful to consider where conventional assessment comes from and what it tries to do.

The developers of conventional assessment tried to pare away the complications of human functioning and control as many variables as possible. The approach aims to remove any confounding variables to get to some 'pure' or 'true' measure of human functioning. In response to this relatively artificial and contrived way of looking at the complex nature of humans, there has been a move towards more realistic or authentic forms of assessment. The push for alternatives to conventional assessment has grown out of adaptations of conventional assessment, become performance focused, drawn on observations of naturalistic situations and samples of learning from everyday classroom activities, and extended into dynamic frameworks.

Alternative forms of assessment are supported by more contemporary theories of learning, teaching and assessment. In many cases these are sociocultural and ecological theories that recognise the position of the individual human learner within a complex ecology of social and cultural dimensions. Alternative assessment still draws on concepts from psychometrics and can meaningfully use fine-grained tests that are available as part of that approach. However, an ecological and dynamic systems lens, and the careful consideration of reliability and validity of any strategy, as well as a way of interpreting results that does not reduce learning and development to simple numbers recognises. The complexity and sophistication of learners and teachers in their environments. Numbers like reading ages, intelligence quotients and effect sizes can contribute to these understandings but they are not the best way to sum up real life experiences and the outcomes of learning intervention.

The language of assessment practice

The activity of assessment is often problematic, with some of the problems related to the assumptions underpinning the language of assessment. As with every domain of practice in learning intervention it is important to really know what is being talked about when we use words like *assessment* and *testing*, and the many other terms that are related to this area. The twelve pairs of terms in Figure 8.1 (adapted from Graham, Berman & Bellert, 2015) illustrate the end points of dimensions of assessment that are important when selecting and talking about assessment approaches that are most appropriate.

Assessment is not necessarily testing, but can include testing. It can be formal or informal. Each of the other dimensions provides options for assessment approaches or strategies. Traditional or conventional assessment tends to be at the left end of each of these dimensions, while alternative assessment can be placed at any point. In contemporary assessment practice, we draw from all points depending on the purpose and content of the assessment.

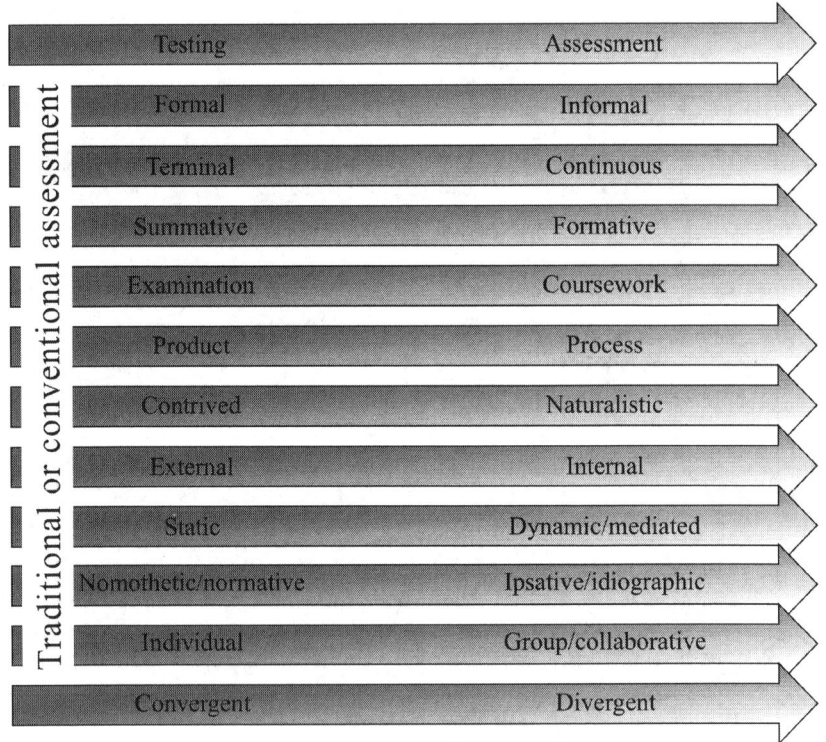

FIGURE 8.1 Dimensions of assessment

Source: Adapted from Graham, Berman & Bellert, 2015.

Assessment strategies

All the assessment strategies that teachers use can be applied in casework, as well as some other specialised strategies including interviewing and clinical evaluations that are drawn on, as appropriate. Much assessment is carried out in the classroom with teachers creating assessment activities regularly for different purposes. Classrooms are complex busy places within which teachers have traditionally used group-administered assessments, usually pencil and paper tests. These tests are still used in many contexts during students' school journeys. Such large group assessment of individual learning has its own limitations, largely related to the nature of the assessment and the extent to which it covers the full depth and breadth of the constructs it examines. However, such testing is an efficient way to quickly gain information about learning across a group of learners.

Individual assessment tools, including phonemic awareness screens, running records and task-based interviews in numeracy, are also often administered in classrooms. These assessments happen within the usual layers of classroom noise and activity. This raises questions about whether this setting is best for the assessment of learners who need to manage the distractions of the environment while responding to the assessment items.

Learning intervention teachers need to develop assessment activities for baseline and outcomes assessment that are targeted to the specific learning outcomes that have been agreed. As a consulting learning intervention teacher or other professional working in collaboration with a teacher, some contribution to developing teacher-administered assessment may also be appropriate. Classroom assessment practice is a good basis for learning intervention professionals, with Table 8.1 (based on Brady & Kennedy, 2012) providing an outline of the possible ways of assessing learning in this context.

TABLE 8.1 Types of classroom assessment

Tests	Performance assessment
Multiple choice tests	Anecdotal records
True–false tests	Checklists
Short answer tests	Rating scales
Matching tests	
Cloze tests	Product assessment
Interpretive tests	Portfolios
Concept maps	Exhibitions
Essays/extended writing	Projects
Interviews/conferences	

Source: Brady & Kennedy, 2012.

Observation in educational casework

Observation lets responsive teachers and educational casework professionals see what is happening for learners as they interact with their teachers and other learners. Observation in education is based on a long history that provides structure for systematic and valid procedures. A lot of information can be gathered through observation either informally and incidentally or formally and systematically. Student behaviour and learning can also be observed in standardised ways, thus allowing the derivation of standard scores or age equivalents and comparison of observations.

Interviews in educational casework

Interviewing skills are needed for educational casework as conversations with many significant people need to be carried out efficiently and professionally. Interviewing is in itself a specific skill set that needs to be developed and practised. Interviews are central to much assessment in educational psychology, as most types of assessment involve meeting and talking personally, either with the student, or with family members or teachers. Interviewing can also happen online, either through text, or face to face. We all have skills in these processes, which we use every day in all our interactions with other people. The difference for professionals is that these skills are more consciously developed and applied in alignment with the process and purpose of the interactions.

There are many reasons for conducting interviews throughout casework, in the preliminary assessment, goal setting, intervention planning, and monitoring and evaluation phases. These interviews may focus on:

- exploring and clarifying the current situation;
- compiling information on development, learning, behaviour, wellbeing, social relationships, motivation, interests, resilience;
- seeking insight into home and family circumstances;
- gathering insights into classroom and school relationships;
- accessing perceptions of family, student, teachers, other professionals and teaching assistants;
- administering formal assessment tools;
- providing feedback from formal assessment or other actions;
- developing goals, individual learning plans (IEPs) and similar documents;
- empowering family members and supporting change;
- sharing expectations of new settings or school organisation;
- introducing support people and establishing expectations;
- exploring the effects of teaching and evaluating intervention; and
- resolving crises.

Different approaches and skills may be needed in each situation, but generally interviews are considered along a dimension related to structure. Interviews can be unstructured, semi-structured or structured. Structured interviews are based on specified criteria, such as a formal test or checklist. They can be scripted by the test or sets of questions and there may or may not be room for exploring responses further. Semi-structured interviews are thematic, seeking to cover particular topics, in a flexible way, depending on what information is gleaned during the interview. Unstructured interviews allow the two participants to go in whatever direction the conversation takes them, but with a particular general focus in mind.

As learning intervention professionals become more practised at interviewing they can move between different levels of structure, depending on the phase of the interview, and become expert at blending different approaches in response to the comfort and engagement of the other person. Traditionally professional interviews have been one-way attempts to elicit information from students, family or teachers to feed into professional decision-making. However, any interaction is in fact a part of intervention and the people being interviewed do not go away unaffected by interviews. Such exchanges often frame the current situation and possible future situations. We must not underestimate the power of an interview in supporting or hindering change.

While interviews are a way to gather information, they are also a way to establish and strengthen, or weaken, relationships. The positive impact of interviews depends on the connections that are made and the match between the content and purpose of the interview as intended by the professional, and the content and purpose of the interview as perceived by the other person/people involved. If there is a shared understanding of these two dimensions then the interview will probably be useful and effective. If not, then there can be unintended outcomes that may not support the intended purpose.

Interactions between people are affected by everything that people bring to the session. Culture, perceptions, attitudes, values, knowledge, skills, self-concept, identity and expectations all contribute to the effectiveness of the interview in accessing the information needed for assessment and to nurture relationships. Effective professionals are aware of these interrelationships and work to make sure they are acknowledged and respected throughout the entire process. Potential mismatches of purpose and connection need to be anticipated and worked through whenever possible.

Many families who come to interviews in schools are not coming into what they see as a neutral setting. The school represents the culture of professionals and there is an immediate potential for a gap that will not support the effectiveness of the interview. This aspect may affect where the interviews are held. They can be done on steps of homes, in kitchens, under trees in playgrounds, or in a local café or library. They can also include support people or advocates for a parent who is unfamiliar with the professional educational context. Another key consideration is related to culture. Learning intervention professionals need to develop cultural competence to take their own culture and that of others into account in any interactions.

The skills applied in interviews are those of human interpersonal communication. Specific skills that support effective interactions include setting a time and venue, framing the purpose of the interview, making contact to set up the interview, organising the furniture, introducing people and the purpose of the interview, establishing rapport, observing, active listening (verbal and non-verbal), questioning (open--ended and closed) and asking for input, clarifying and reflecting, recalling and summing up, and providing follow-up information.

A common interview in educational casework is the introductory interview, which is an opportunity for teachers to get to know their students and set expectations of the relationship. 'Getting to know you' interviews also need to occur with families early in any casework. These interviews provide opportunities for the people involved to gain impressions about each other and establish shared understandings of what they are going to do together and why. Hopefully trust and mutual respect are created as a foundation for developing a partnership.

Administration of any test happens in a session that involves interpersonal interactions. It is important to use good interviewing skills and a set of strategies for establishing rapport and making sure a student is comfortable about engaging and taking risks. The interpersonal interactions around any test are opportunities for exploring how students see themselves as learners and to access student 'voice' to complement standardised information. Although tests are often quite structured and sometimes require the assessor to give no feedback, it is important to notice when a student is losing attention and interest, and note this down. This is important information that is complementary to the scores.

Many tests are designed to extend a student as far as possible (to their 'ceiling'), and as such end with a series of failed items. Even if the student does not know they failed these items, they most certainly will feel less confident in their answers. This is not a good way to end a session. It is important to do something else to make sure the session ends on a positive note. One possibility is to seek student perceptions of the tasks and ask which ones they enjoyed and which ones were hard. It can be useful to revisit some of the less threatening activities to close the session.

Commercially available standardised tests

A particular field of interest in assessment in learning intervention is the enormous bank of commercially available tests. There is big business in developing and selling standardised tests, many of which come from the US, where they are used to meet legislated processes of selection. However, many of these tests are also used in schools and education systems in other parts of the world.

It is important to understand as much as possible about the advantages and limitations of such tests for supporting learning intervention. Educational psychologists and speech pathologists, for example, undergo advanced study in assessment. They learn about the structure and construction of assessment tools, the benefits and limitations of them and the ways to use them appropriately and ethically. It is also important for learning intervention professionals to develop their knowledge and skills in using tests and analysing information derived from such tests.

Standardised tests are designed in such a way that the variation that accompanies different assessors is minimised, so that results of different students can be compared with validity. This means that anyone using these tests, and intending to compare results, needs to administer the test as it was administered when the normative data were collected. Scoring is also standardised, and interpretation and reporting must follow the guidelines provided in manuals. It is vital that the procedures for administration and scoring are followed.

Administration

Administration of standardised tests is guided by manuals that detail everything from how you set up the materials to how you score and interpret results. There are rules around how to fill in the test protocol or form; how to calculate the student's age (often to the day); how to score and record scores and how to calculate any cumulative scores or domain scores; and then how to translate those into meaningfully comparable measures.

There are many requirements for the administration of assessment instruments. Generally, there is a need to:

- find the most appropriate place for assessment considering noise, light, comfort and safety, size and placement of furniture;
- follow the explicit instructions for set up and placement of materials that go with any tool;
- be familiar with what you are supposed to say and when, the timing of any tasks, the basal and ceiling levels, and how you will record what is happening;
- be conscious of the feedback you are giving as you interact since valid assessment is built on interpersonal skills;
- be fluent in administration; and
- be able to manage when the response is not as anticipated.

It is not possible to just pick up a manual and walk through it while a student is there. Preparation is necessary in order to become familiar with the procedures, the script and how to manage responses from students. Preparation and practice are required in order to manage all of these. As well, professional skills will be needed to introduce and provide instructions for any screeners and checklists that we ask families and teachers to complete as part of gathering assessment information. How these are introduced and the instructions provided will affect how families complete them and the reliability of the information collected.

Scoring

Many assessment instruments, whether commercially produced or classroom developed, will require summarising of the results, usually in the form of numerical scoring. Learning intervention professionals need to know what to do with the responses to get raw scores, and then derived scores. They also need to know what these scores mean – and what kind of inferences can and cannot be validly drawn. The manuals for standardised tests clearly explain issues around scoring, such as how to establish basals and ceilings in subtests, how to score items, how to collate raw scores, how to transfer them to a summary page and how to derive statistically contrived scores that make the results comparable to those of other learners or other tests. This is where many errors can occur and it is vital to develop fail-proof checking mechanisms so that no errors get past the stage of scoring.

Each assessment instrument has a framework to guide how it is scored, analysed and interpreted. Usually there is a raw score that is then transformed using the psychometric structure of the test into a standard score. The scores generated by a sample of people in the norming group inform the fit of this model. Many derived scores are related to a mathematical structure where about 68 per cent of people are considered average, 14 per cent are considered above average and 14 per cent below average, with 2 per cent well below and 2 per cent well above average. These proportions are related to standard deviations, and are represented by a range of different derived scores such as percentiles, z scores, standard scores, t scores and stanines. Scores can be reported as a single number or in a range. Most test forms have a graph that can be used to share the derived scores and provides a useful way to discuss scores with teachers and parents and students. Sometimes it is not appropriate to do this. The assessment professional needs to decide the most appropriate way to report the assessment information collected.

There are some core psychometric constructs that are inherent in standardised norm referenced tests. It is important to know what they mean and to be able to interpret how they are used in any tests administered or any reports provided:

- Measures of central tendencies – mean, median and mode
- Measures of deviance – range, variance, normal distribution and standard deviation
- Scales – ordinal and equal-interval
- Normal curve
- Developmental equivalents – age equivalent and grade equivalent
- Scores – raw scores, derived scores
- Scores – percentiles, quartiles, deciles, stanines, rank scores
- Scores – T scores, normal curve equivalent (NCEs)
- Reliability – correlation (positive and negative), test–retest, equivalent forms, internal consistency, inter-rater, standard error of measurement, estimated true scores
- Validity – criterion-referenced, concurrent, predictive, content, construct.

Descriptors

Descriptors have been used as long as tests have been around. They are words and phrases that sum up the results of tests. These terms are linked to the time and culture within which they are used – and, subsequently, keep changing. For example, early descriptors in intellectual assessment included 'normal', 'moron', 'imbecile' and 'idiot', words we would never use to describe students now. More recently, descriptors for standardised tests refer to 'average', 'above average' and 'below average' and use a range of terms to describe the extent of the difference of a score to the mean, ranging from 'well-below average' to 'superior' or 'gifted'. Generally, the descriptors used in schools rely on the normal curve to define what is average (and above and below average), and age appropriate (and above or below age equivalent). It is possible to misinterpret and misuse these descriptors in the same way that full-scale scores can sum up someone's learning abilities in a less than useful way. Learning intervention professionals need to be aware of the use of such terms, and to be conscious in exploring how well such descriptors are appropriately used in any casework. Reframing these when they are used incorrectly is crucial to valid shared understanding of student learning needs.

This field of psychometrics is very complex and there is much more to learn beyond the scope of this book. It is up to learning intervention professionals to ensure they know what they need to know when dealing with scores and descriptors related to assessment of any sort.

Dynamic assessment

Educational professionals can build dynamic assessment into their usual assessment to better understand the learning of some students, and thus better inform future teaching or intervention. Dynamic assessment explicitly focuses on a student's responsiveness to teaching; to how much they can change their performance with the assistance of a teacher. Not only is it appropriate for teachers to use this form of assessment, it is also a useful part of the assessment repertoire of other assessment professionals.

Dynamic assessment is based on the idea that if teachers want to observe how their students learn, they should activate learning and be with them while it is happening. Dynamic assessment explores what occurs within the zone of proximal development (ZPD) (Vygotsky, 1978a) – the gap between what learners can do themselves and what they can do with the help of a more competent other who mediates a learning task with the aim of activating learning (see Figure 8.2).

Dynamic assessment actively explores how close the learner is to the next level of development or learning, which is evidenced through performance in an assisted or collaborative task. The zone of proximal development frames this notion of development, capturing the actual developmental level or achievement and the potential level of achievement at a particular time. In contrast to *static* assessment, *dynamic* assessment accesses two layers of development, what the learner can demonstrate independently (matured abilities) and what can be demonstrated with assistance (maturing abilities) (Vygotsky, 1978b).

Dynamic assessment deliberately incorporates a teaching phase so that learners' responses to instruction can be explored. It follows a pattern of a pre-test (to see what the learner can do unassisted), followed by some teaching or mediation, and

Assisted achievement, an indication of maturing abilities, is assessed in a **post-test** (dynamic assessment)

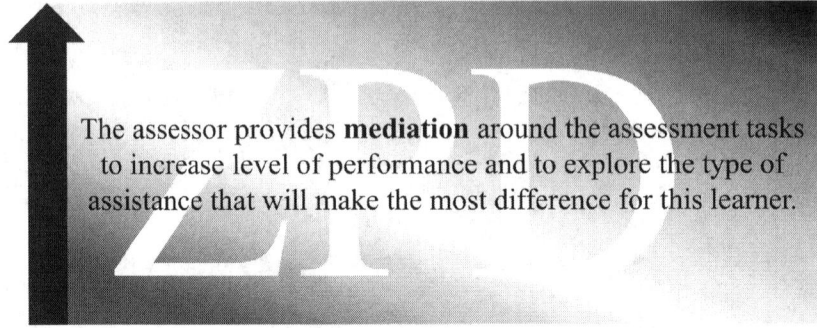

The assessor provides **mediation** around the assessment tasks to increase level of performance and to explore the type of assistance that will make the most difference for this learner.

Actual achievement as assessed in a **pre-test** (static assessment)

FIGURE 8.2   A representation of dynamic assessment

then a post-test to see what has been learnt in that session (Lidz & Elliott, 2000). Three types of information are accessed in this way: measures of actual (or unassisted) achievement; measures of assisted achievement; and information about factors that support and hinder individuals' learning. Not only is dynamic assessment appropriate for teachers to use, it is also a useful part of the assessment repertoire of other assessment professionals who want to understand learners' responsiveness to teaching. It has been applied to assessment of young children's capabilities (Tzuriel, 2000; Lidz, 2005), to understand language development (Poehner & Lantoff, 2005), to identify hidden gifted Aboriginal children (Chaffey, Bailey & Vine, 2003), to understand student use of reading skills (Cioffi & Carney, 1997) and mathematical understanding (Berman & Graham, 2002).

Dynamic assessment depends on the assessor being able to determine and explore the learner's ZPD in the assessment session. It also depends on the assessor's knowledge of the domain so that appropriate mediation can be provided to move a learner through the next steps in learning or development. With a focus on the processes of learning rather than only on the products of learning, there is a clear emphasis on cognitive processes, but also inclusion of affective or emotional and social capabilities (Lauchlan & Carrigan, 2013). All ATRiUM capabilities can be explored in dynamic assessment.

It is possible to develop curriculum-based dynamic assessment that is useful in educational casework and in responsive teaching (Berman & Graham, 2002; Haywood & Lidz, 2007). Such a process has curriculum validity, provides information about not only what a student can do unassisted but also with support, and describes what the nature of that support is. Such information can be fed directly into decision-making for classroom teaching, since it deliberately aims to match the student with the tasks they are asked to do (Haywood & Lidz, 2007), that is, to explicitly link assessment with intervention (Lidz, 2003).

Working with assessment specialists and within system assessment requirements

Educational casework often involves working with assessment specialists such as psychologists. One of the criticisms of assessment carried out by psychologists and other assessment professionals is that it is done in an artificial clinical environment and is not transferable to the usual classroom environment. However, administering assessments in a controlled environment is not a reason to discount the resulting test information. In fact, a lot of psychological research is done in such controlled conditions, and is not discounted for that reason. In fact, it can be illuminating to see what a learner can do in a controlled setting, in comparison to the much more complicated classroom setting. If we just assess in settings where a child is not achieving well, then we are likely to get confirmatory information, when we actually want to know what else or how much better a student can do under different conditions, and then take those conditions into account when designing intervention. It is important that this information be translated into usable information for teachers and families.

A particular issue around assessment in education systems and the students who are the focus of educational casework is the requirement to participate in system-wide assessment. Assessment within education systems includes large-scale system-wide testing that is used for multiple purposes that are political, financial, social and educational. Large-scale assessment is used to provide a summative assessment of learning at different points in a school journey. Such large-scale assessment can also be used to provide data for the comparison of schools and education systems.

Many students do not perform well in examination situations. When such assessment is used as a mechanism for determining how much resourcing will be provided to schools, dilemmas arise for schools and families. Special examination conditions are accessed within many education systems to try and make up for the negative effects that this type of assessment has on some learners. Essentially, some students are unable to demonstrate their learning under exam conditions, and so they will not be judged according to their learning, but according to how well they perform in an examination context.

Summary

In this chapter we have explored many assessment approaches used both by teachers and other professionals in order to support learning intervention. Conventional, psychometrically based tests and procedures, as well as alternative assessment approaches, have been considered, with a view that contemporary assessment requires the careful selection of appropriate assessment strategies that assess what needs to be investigated to meet the purposes of assessment. In the last three chapters (6, 7 and 8), we have framed the purpose, content and strategies of assessment within the educational casework process, and shown how assessment varies with the approach taken.

References

Berman, J. & Graham, L. (2002). School counsellor use of curriculum-based dynamic assessment. *Australian Journal of Guidance and Counselling, 12*(1), 21–40.

Biggs, J. & Tang, C. (2011). *Teaching for quality learning at university* (4th ed.). Maidenhead: McGraw Hill.

Brady, L. & Kennedy, K. (2012). *Assessment and reporting: Celebrating student achievement* (4th ed.). Frenchs Forest, NSW: Pearson.

Chaffey, G., Bailey, S., & Vine, K. (2003). Identifying high academic potential in Australian Aboriginal children using dynamic testing. *Australasian Journal of Gifted Education, 12*(1), 42–55.

Cioffi, G. & Carney, J. (1997). Dynamic assessment of composing abilities in children with learning disabilities. *Educational Assessment, 4*(3), 175–202.

Graham, L., Berman, J., & Bellert, A. (2015). *Sustainable learning: Inclusive practices for 21st century classrooms.* Melbourne, VIC: Cambridge University Press.

Haywood, C. & Lidz, C. (2007). *Dynamic assessment in practice: Clinical and educational applications.* Cambridge: Cambridge University Press.

Lauchlan, F. & Carrigan, D. (2013). *Improving learning through dynamic assessment: A practical classroom resource.* London: Jessica Kingsley.

Lidz, C. S. (2003). *Early childhood assessment.* Hoboken, NJ: John Wiley.

Lidz, C. S. (2005). Dynamic assessment with young children: We've come a long way baby! *Journal of Early Childhood and Infant Psychology, 1*, 99–112.

Lidz, C. S. & Elliott, J. (Eds.). (2000). *Dynamic assessment: Prevailing models and applications.* Amsterdam: Elsevier.

Poehner, M. & Lantoff, J. (2005). Dynamic assessment in the language classroom. *Language Teaching Research, 9*(3), 233–265.

Tzuriel, D. (2000). Dynamic assessment of young children: Educational and intervention perspectives. *Educational Psychology Review, 12*(4), 385–435.

Vygotsky, L. (1978a). *Mind in society: The development of higher psychological processes* (M. Cole, Trans.). Cambridge, MA: Harvard University Press.

Vygotsky, L. (1978b). Interaction between learning and development. *Readings on the development of children 23*(3), 34–41.

9

LEARNING OPPORTUNITIES

The aim of learning intervention is to provide optimum opportunities for learning that respond to students' identified learning needs. It is possible to learn one thing in many different activities, and responsive teachers strategically organise learning opportunities so that this can happen, based on what they know about student interests, their capabilities for learning, responsiveness to teaching and also the place of learning intervention in a student's learning journey. In the context of effective intervention for inclusive education 'opportunities to learn' has been framed as a meta-strategy that pulls together a range of behaviourist, cognitive and social evidence-based strategies (Mitchell, 2014, p.325).

Learning opportunities can be provided at any layer of learning intervention, from whole school or class activities to small group or individual activities, and can be amplified by the power of influences from the ecological context for a learner. Teacher action related to planning and providing learning opportunities becomes explicit teaching. Thus, we have conceptualised a clear distinction between the activity provided for the learner and the actions of the teacher, which continues through the separate discussion of learning opportunities and teaching strategies in Chapter 9 and Chapter 10, respectively. In this chapter, we consider the process of designing and selecting learning opportunities. We refer to packaged interventions as illustrations at times. Our coverage is not comprehensive, but aims to point to areas for further exploration by learning intervention professionals.

Once the focus of intervention has been defined through assessment, the next step is to investigate the research evidence base to see what has been previously shown to be effective. Following this, there is a need to consider how well available evidence relates to the present situation. This is the point in educational casework when learning intervention professionals draw together all relevant evidence (see Chapter 5) in order to construct the most responsive intervention.

The key questions around learning opportunities in intervention are:

- What learning opportunities (tasks, instructions and materials) are appropriate?
- What arrangement and intensity of learning opportunities is appropriate?
- Who should mediate the learning opportunities?
- What layers of learning intervention are appropriate?
- How are these learning opportunities to be resourced?

What learning opportunities are appropriate?

This first question cues consideration of what ways are best to teach the targeted skills and knowledge. This means deciding what tasks will be provided for students to participate in, and what instructions and materials will accompany these tasks. Based on what is known about the student as a learner and the focus for intervention, the research evidence is the place to look for initial responses to these questions. Much literature on learning intervention refers to diagnostic categories, for example, intervention for language delay, specific language impairment, ADHD, ASD, hearing impairment, vision impairment, intellectual disability, dyslexia, and so on. This approach is based on the assumption that there will be particular learning activities or teaching approaches that are distinctive, even mutually exclusive, for these groups of learners. That is often not the case, since there is much overlap of effective teaching for most learners. Thus, we have not referred to 'special education needs' or 'special needs' or 'special' learners in this book. Diagnostic labels can give a general direction for intervention, and certainly point to the literature base within which to begin identifying effective intervention strategies, but they convey only a small part of the information needed to design and select the best intervention for individual students at any particular time.

Instead, the point of reference for searching the research evidence is the clear identification of what needs to be learned next. Within the considerable research into effective teaching for students with learning difficulties and disabilities, direct instruction combined with strategy instruction are the components most consistently and convincingly identified (Hattie, 2009; Swanson, Harris & Graham, 2003) as important to consider in this discussion. The evidence is unequivocal in concluding that the most effective way to design learning opportunities for students in educational casework is through the lens of systematic, explicit instruction within specific content areas (Scruggs, 2012).

What arrangement and intensity of learning opportunities is appropriate?

How learning opportunities are arranged, both within sessions and across sessions, and in relation to their intensity, provides the conditions for systematic teaching. Learning intervention professionals need to match the arrangement and intensity of learning opportunities to the learning needs targeted in any intervention, and optimise engagement and active learning. To be systematic, learning opportunities should be arranged sequentially based on what is known about learning progressions.

Some pre-structured intervention programs have a sequenced arrangement of learning tasks that are based on what is known about learning pathways in certain domains or as a result of detailed task analyses. Research into the patterns and progress of students' learning discusses *learning trajectories* (e.g., Clements & Semmler, 2009), *learning progressions* (e.g., Alonzo & Gotwals, 2012; Wang, Ho & Cheng, 2015; Huynh, Solem & Bednarz, 2015; Meiers, 2004) and *developmental trajectories* (e.g., Thomas et al., 2009; Martinez-Castilla, Rodriguez & Campos, 2016). These references are a sample of the kind of developmental and educational research that strives to validly describe learning so teachers can know what their students are ready to learn, and what they need to learn next. This research also explores variability within development and learning in relation to physiological conditions or syndromes. Although the use of structures that underpin a systematic approach to learning is effective for most learners, it may not be appropriate for all learners.

A tension that arises when using developmental learning progressions as a reference for teaching is that they are based on the assumption that everyone has to go through the same progression, but this is not always the case. Some learners will step through a progression as it is written, at an even pace. All others will have their own individual ways of negotiating this learning. Some will be faster, though still growing evenly. Others will be inconsistent in their development, stopping on some steps for a period, before then breezing through several steps at once. Rigidly organised learning activities that may not match student learning needs are ineffective for learning, and can be detrimental to student motivation and engagement.

In particular, meeting the needs of learners who are gifted might mean discarding typical pathways of learning for others that have fewer or different steps. For very able students it may be best to start with higher-order thinking, and then follow up with lower-order thinking skills, as needed. In contrast, learners who have an intellectual disability experience learning progress at a slower pace and need numerous opportunities for practice and consolidation of ideas and skills. Explicit intensive support to transfer skills to unfamiliar situations will also be required for these learners. For another group of learners, those with specific learning difficulties, other less regular learning progressions may be needed that combine some aspects of giftedness with some functioning at disabling levels. In general, individual learning pathways need to be negotiated and navigated based on the responses of learners to the learning opportunities provided.

In light of this consideration, some intervention is designed from the ground up in response to individual learning needs, and is organised with the student always in mind. In such cases, the professionals' knowledge of a student's current learning and development, and relevant learning progressions that signpost what comes next in their learning and development, are crucial to appropriately arranging learning opportunities. Models to assist in arranging learning opportunities according to learning progressions include Dreyfus's (2004) model of skill acquisition and the

SOLO taxonomy of quality of student responses (Biggs & Collis, 1982) that are provided in a later section on intensity as increasing challenge.

The most appropriate arrangement of learning opportunities is also dependent on consideration of aspects of intensity. Intensity is a key dimension of the Response to Intervention framework, whereby intensity increases as the focus moves from whole class, to small group to individual learner. In operational terms, this determines how many learning opportunities are offered to each learner, and how many repetitions, or adaptations of activities at a particular level, are appropriate. Increasingly intense assessment, monitoring and feedback processes also support learning opportunities.

Often this is an *if–then* situation. If a learner demonstrates particular learning responses, then the teacher can move on to the next learning opportunity, but this can be much more complicated. To get a handle on this complexity, we can consider intensity in terms of the following modifiable features:

- intensity as repeated learning opportunities;
- intensity as increasingly explicit content and feedback;
- intensity as a smaller learning group;
- intensity as variation in time; and
- intensity as greater challenge.

Intensity as repeated learning opportunities

If the learner does not demonstrate responsiveness to a learning opportunity, the first consideration related to intensity is whether the learning need can be met by more of the same, that is, repetition of the same activity.

Instructional situations when repetition is important include when:

- a skill is not yet consistently demonstrated, and more opportunities to do so are needed;
- a skill is established and it is useful for that skill to become more automatic or fluent;
- domain specific concepts or vocabulary need to become established and remembered; and
- a student has an intellectual disability, specific cognitive difficulty or other condition that means more practice is needed for the skill or understanding to be established.

Many aspects of learning require repetition in order to develop skills. Some students like to do activities that require no new learning, and to aim for increased proficiency or fluency through practice. Other students find this really difficult, and need support to engage in tasks that they believe they know or can do already, and which they therefore see as having no meaning. The research evidence from Kang

(2017) about how best to use repeated tasks for practice and effective learning is useful in such a situation. The key message from Kang's work is that there can be a mismatch between what learners perceive to be the best way to practise, and what has been shown to most effective. This means that less effective choices may be made if left up to the learners, and therefore it is important for teachers to structure and support practice as an integral part of providing learning opportunities. Furthermore, the provision of practice opportunities should mix different kinds of activities, so that learners can get a sense of different requirements for the application of the same skill or knowledge. There is also a need to alter mental strategies, and to provide small bouts of practice rather than large blocks. By building in this complexity, as well as mixing in other skills to be practised, learned skills or knowledge are better established and more likely to be transferable to different situations and sustained in the future. As illustrated in this example, it is important to carefully plan the intensity and context of learning opportunities that are designed to practise skills and apply knowledge.

Intensity as increasingly explicit content and feedback

In some cases, instead of repeating the same learning activity, a student may benefit from increasingly explicit learning opportunities within which each component of the content within a systematic structure is taught and feedback from monitoring is directly related to the content. Such learning opportunities might be more targeted or focused on sub-skills or parts of a previous activity. In order to teach explicitly, there is a need for checking what is already known, what skills and knowledge are emerging, what has been established and consolidated, and what is transferred across contexts, so that explicit feedback can be provided.

To be explicit in content, the learning opportunities should be directly focused on specific skills, sub-skills and components of knowledge. Aspects of the arrangement and intensity of learning opportunities contribute to the development of systematic, explicit learning opportunities. A crucial context for increasingly explicit teaching is in relation to phonological awareness and processing, and, most specifically, the application of these skills to the sounds in words (phonemic awareness and processing) and then the building of more sophisticated skills in decoding (phonics). Many children learn these skills incidentally, and make good sense of the relationship between sounds and symbols, even when the sound/spelling correspondence is not close, as in English. However, children who are at risk of learning difficulties, and others who show early signs of other difficulties benefit from systematic explicit teaching of these skills (Allor, Mathes, Roberts, Jones & Champlin, 2010; Mitchell, 2014; National Reading Panel, 2000; Hattie, 2009).

There are many frameworks that provide a systematic way to both assess and intervene for the establishment of phonemic awareness skills. For example, in Table 9.1 the grid of skills from a phonemic awareness test shows that this student demonstrated established skills in rhyming, alliteration and blending (shaded), with the next steps for learning defined by the skills that were not as yet demonstrated.

TABLE 9.1 A student's phonemic awareness skills assessment results

Rhyming	Recognition of rhyme		Rhyme supply	
Alliteration (initial)	Sound to word matching	Supplying initial sound	Word to word matching	Supplying word with same initial sound	Supplying word with a given initial sound
Alliteration (final)	Sound to word matching	Supplying final sound	Word to word matching	Supplying word with a given final sound
Blending	CV and VC onset rime	CVC	CCVC	CVCC
Segmenting	Counting sounds in words	Segmenting words into component sounds	
Manipulating	Deleting initial sound	Deleting final sound	Deleting middle sound

Shaded skills established

Notes
C   Consonant
V   Vowel

Selection of learning opportunities can be accomplished in many ways, relying on many available resources. There are systematically structured programs that have activities available. There are also innumerable activities available in professional books and resources, as well as online. As teachers become more experienced, their repertoire of activities for teaching phonological skills will build and include those opportunities that are targeted and explicit, as well as those that are incidental teaching opportunities that occur within other activities.

Phonemic awareness and phoneme manipulation skills are part of a domain of learning that has a ceiling. That is, it is possible to make a claim that these skills are established. However, for many students who experience difficulties learning there will need to be follow-up to check on the maintenance and transfer of the skills, and perhaps, for some students, reinforcement teaching designed to strengthen the skills after they have been initially established. Once these foundation skills are established, however, it is appropriate to move on to the next level of skills in this domain, those related to phoneme–grapheme correspondence and word decoding.

Following on from phonological awareness and phoneme manipulation skills, the skills that are based in matching graphemes to phonemes (that is, phonics) are also taught through whole class lessons over considerable periods of time. For some students, early intervention, as soon as any difficulties are noticed, is vital, as is differentiating instruction to take into account students' different rates and patterns in learning (Tunmer & Arrow, 2013).

Often beginning reading skills represent an area of difficulty for students referred for learning intervention casework, since this domain of learning requires considerable exposure to written language. Often, these students have partially developed skills that need to be more consistently established. At the most basic single sound level, learning opportunities need to support the skills of naming, and making the sound of, every letter in the alphabet. Specific difficulties can be found for some students with the less common consonants (e.g., 'q' and 'y') and vowels that make so many different sounds depending on the words they build. Complicating this is knowledge of the many blends and digraphs that proficient readers need to be able to recognise and interpret. It is also often the case for students with learning difficulties that they have learned some strategies and may overuse them, even when they are not the most appropriate. Such misconceptions are addressed directly during explicit instruction.

Explicit feedback directly related to the fine-grained content including explicit cues or prompts also increases the intensity of learning opportunities. This way of thinking about an increase in intensity is related to the teaching strategies used within teaching/learning interactions. Again, a decision about whether to provide more intense instruction is based on frequent formative checking of learning, so that frequent prompts provide the next opportunity for learning. Effective teachers use graduated prompts and changes in intensity along many dimensions. In dynamic assessment, for example, the aim is to provide the least amount of support or assistance in order to gain a higher-level response from a student. When an implied prompt does not work, then a more direct or explicit one is provided. Following this, during learning teachers reduce the explicitness of prompts, and allow students to take more responsibility for their thinking and the activity of learning. On-the-spot teacher responses (Graham, Berman & Bellert, 2015) provide a range of intensity of feedback depending on what the teacher determines is appropriate at the time. If a student is likely to only need a hint or vague cue, then that is what is provided. Whereas, if a student needs more explicit support then the cue or prompt will accordingly be more explicit. An example of this increasing intensity or explicitness is shown in Table 9.2 where a teacher aims to focus on the difference between two multi-digit numbers.

The first example is the teacher asking a question that provided little direction, merely seeking comparison between two numbers. The second one is providing more guidance, focusing on a particular number, while the third one has an explicit direction to the number of digits as the reference for comparison. These excerpts have been pulled out of much richer sets of interactions, but they show different levels of explicitness and intensity (focused on explicit content and providing explicit feedback) that are used in teacher interactions as needed.

TABLE 9.2 Example of three levels of intensity as increasing explicitness

Level of intensity (explicitness) increases as needed →		
Seek focus on a particular aspect of the task or question	Guide focus	Direct focus
What is the same about these numbers?	*Think about this number here again*	*Look at how many digits are in this number*

Intensity as size of learning group

Built into the layers of learning intervention and the everyday flexibility of grouping in responsive classrooms is the consideration of the learning group size that best meets the needs of particular learners. A simple way to increase the intensity of instruction can, therefore, be by reducing the number of learners in a group so that each learner has more opportunity to respond and be heard, and to receive individual feedback. There is no doubt that one-on-one teaching provides focused interactions without distractions from other learners' needs and immediacy of response from the teacher. Such situations provide a context for the intense use of teaching strategies, constant opportunity to check for understanding, immediate feedback to the learner and the opportunity to make judgements about learning that may be less clear in a group situation.

However, not all learning is best done individually, and it is important to weigh up the benefits of learning in a group, with its richness of language and ideas and scaffolding from peers, compared to individual instruction where the student and the teacher are the only ones providing input. There will be times when a larger group provides a more intense learning opportunity than a small group. In a large group more people are expected to make a contribution and more complex interactions can happen. Learning in a large group and taking into account all members of the group can be more intense than engaging with one or two other individuals. Similarly, presenting work to a large group can be very intimidating, and more intense than presenting to a teacher alone. Learning intervention appropriate for a student who has difficulties with social interactions and finds groups stressful, or even distressing, may include gradually increasing the group size over time. A learning intervention professional's sensitivity to the intensity provided by group size is vital in arranging learning opportunities for students who are the focus of educational casework.

Intervention programs are designed for a range of group sizes, from whole class to pairs of learners or up to five students or individuals. In reality, it is nearly always the case that a mixture of learning groups is important. A student can receive intense, explicit teaching in an individual session, and then be supported to apply their learning within a small group or a whole class learning activity as well. The aim of any intervention is for the student to be able to demonstrate learning in the usual class setting, so this needs to be kept in mind. Not only is flexibility of group size supportive of successful transfer, but it also facilitates the close monitoring of learning in multiple contexts.

Intensity as variation in time

Aspects of time, such as the frequency of sessions as well as the length of sessions, are other dimensions of intensity that need to be considered. Often parameters around time are determined by factors other than the learning needs of students. Instead there can be pragmatic factors, such as funding, available staff, the school calendar

TABLE 9.3 Time intensity across a selection of literacy interventions

Intervention	Session time in minutes	Frequency of sessions per week
QuickSmart Literacy (Graham, Pegg & Alder, 2007)	30 minutes	3 times a week for 30 weeks
Quick60 Foundation and Intervention (Iversen, 2009)	40 minutes	Measured in hours rather than lessons (up to 60 hours)
Reading Recovery (Clay, 1979)	30 minutes	5 times a week for up to 20 weeks
MultiLit Reading Tutor Program (Ellis, Wheldall & Beaman, 2007)	15 (word attack and sight words)	At least 3 times a week
	20 (reinforced reading)	4–5
MiniLit (Reynolds, Wheldall & Madelaine, 2007)	60 minutes	5
Peer-assisted Learning Strategies (Fuchs, Fuchs, Mathes & Simmons, 1997)	20–30 minutes	2–3
RAVE-O (Wolf et al., 2009)	30 minutes (phonics) 30 minutes (RAVE-O)	5

and attendance of students that affect the amount of time available for intervention. Some research-based intervention programs provide guidelines for frequency of sessions per week, and length of sessions as well as group size, which has already been noted as an aspect of intensity.

In Table 9.3 features of a selection of structured literacy intervention programs are compared in terms of dimensions of intensity in relation to time. The programs include whole class, small group and individual intervention, and set expectations of sessions of at least 15 minutes duration to teach aspects of literacy such as fluency or word attack and sight words.

As is evident from Table 9.3, there is wide variation in the time expected for these intervention programs, and a range of expectations about how many sessions are to be offered each week. As a contrast, in order to account for the intermittent attendance at school of many students who are at risk of learning difficulties in reading, *Quick60* sets an expectation that students will complete the whole program rather than a number of weekly sessions. The progressive levels and close monitoring support built into this approach respond to the multiple factors that contribute to learning and learning difficulties. The bottom line is that intervention should be organised to make a difference to student learning and consideration of time is important in tailoring responses to student learning needs.

Intensity as increasing challenge

For teaching to be systematic, it needs to be structured with respect to the skills and knowledge of the curriculum content being taught and planned to provide enough opportunity for students to develop, consolidate and apply skills. Decisions about the intensity of learning opportunities should be based on how our students learn skills and develop knowledge. The following frameworks help us to make sense of student development of skills and assist in the design of learning opportunities that have the right amount of challenge. Dreyfus's (2004) model of skills acquisition (Figure 9.1) that was developed in the context of adult learning is a useful reference here.

The initial stage of Dreyfus's model reflects a process used often in teaching complex skills, that of task analysis, which refers to the deconstruction of a skill from any domain in order to break it into its component parts (Dreyfus, 2004). These parts are then sequenced so that by mastering each component in turn students progress towards the mastery of the entire skill or task. Task analysis has been the basis of much research and is fundamental to many teaching programs for learners who have impairments and disabilities (Johanssen, Hannum & Tessmer, 1989). Through the use of task analysis, the development of skills can be heavily scaffolded over longer than usual time periods. The danger with this approach is that the meaning that is needed for using complex skills can be lost along the way and, therefore, the drill and practice necessary for sub-skill development risks becoming meaningless and less motivating. Keeping meaning at the forefront of learning is crucial to activating emotional satisfaction, as defined in Stage 3 of Dreyfus's model.

The inclusion of a dimension of emotional involvement in this model emphasises that skill development is about more than just physical or motor skills (Dreyfus,

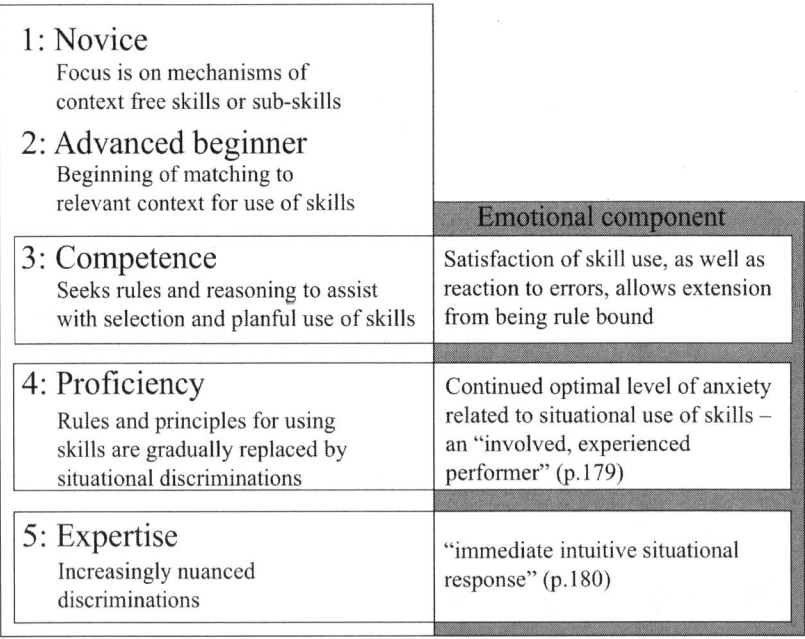

FIGURE 9.1 Summary of Dreyfus's (2004) model of skills acquisition

2004). The two examples Dreyfus uses in explaining his model are driving and playing chess, both of which involve activity (A), considerable perception, attention and reasoning (T), responding to others (R), using symbol systems (as inherent in chess pieces and the spatial arrangement of the board, and found in cars and on road systems) (U), managing emotional aspects of the skills and taking just enough time to support the best decisions for action at the time (M). In this model, skill development acknowledges all ATRiUM capabilities. There is an optimum level of emotional engagement that is needed in order to develop higher levels of expertise.

What is known about practice and about transfer are pertinent in understanding this model of learning progression, which explicitly includes steps of decontextualising a skill and then recontextualising it so that it can be expertly applied in relevant contexts. Intermittent, contextualised practice is inherent in both chess and driving. It is also important to explicitly consider transfer of learning, that is, sustainability across contexts. For transfer to new situations or problems, strategies for detecting similarities and differences are used so that students can learn to select appropriate strategies from their repertoires over time.

Another useful framework of knowledge development helps frame understanding of how higher-order thinking or increased 'depth of understanding' occurs for most individuals. Biggs & Collis (1982) formulated the Structure of Observed Learning Outcomes (SOLO) taxonomy, a theoretical model that makes sense of how we develop deep understanding of concepts. The SOLO learning cycle supports teacher determination of the sophistication of student learning through unpacking the five increasingly sophisticated levels of cognitive learning shown in Table 9.4. In SOLO terms, quantity of learning can be thought of as 'surface', while quality of learning is acknowledgement of 'deep' learning.

SOLO is a neo-Piagetian framework aligned with Piaget's stages of cognitive development (Table 9.4). The more complex version of SOLO depicted in Table 9.5 includes multiple cycles related to modes of functioning (Piaget's stages

TABLE 9.4 Levels of learning in the SOLO taxonomy

Quantity of learning (surface)			*Quality of learning (deep)*	
Prestructural	*Unistructural*	*Multistructural*	*Relational*	*Extended abstract*
Not knowing	Knowing one aspect	Knowing multiple aspects	Knowing how the multiple aspects relate to each other	Knowing how these aspects can be extended into different ideas or contexts
Pre-operational (4–6 years)	Early concrete (7–9 years)	Middle concrete (10–12 years)	Concrete generalisation (13–15 years)	Formal operations (16+ years)

Source: Adapted from Biggs & Collis, 1982, pp.24–25.

TABLE 9.5 SOLO learning cycles, mode of functioning and the course of cognitive development

Mode of functioning	Structure of response		Examples of extended abstract functioning by mode	
(Developmental stage)	Learning cycle		Conservation	Symbolism
Sensorimotor	Unistructural Multistructural Relational	= Prestructural		
Intuitive	Extended abstract	= Unistructural Multistructural = Relational	Objects	Words
Concrete	Unistructural Multistructural Relational	= Prestructural	Classes	Sentences
Formal – 1st order	Extended abstract	= Unistructural Multistructural = Relational	Systems	Propositions
Formal – 2nd order	Unistructural Multistructural Relational	= Prestructural	Theories (of increasingly higher order)	Propositions (of increasingly higher order)
Formal – 3rd order etc.	Extended abstract	= Unistructural Multistructural = Relational, etc.		

Source: Adapted from Biggs & Collis, 1982, p.216.

of cognitive development). In this model, extended abstract knowledge in one mode becomes the prestructural foundation for deeper learning within the next mode. Subsequently, deeper learning is reflected not only within one learning cycle, but through a multiplicity of cycles underpinning the development of conceptual sophistication.

The recognition of different levels of quality within content is useful as a way to think about how to build on to prior learning in a particular curriculum domain. Being able to establish that learning has been achieved in an earlier cycle or at a surface level can assist in designing subsequent opportunities to build understanding of that content. It also helps justify why content needs to be revisited to allow students time to reason with the knowledge they have in order to deepen learning.

The SOLO levels of quality of learning were originally derived from analysis of students' written explanations of their learning. Teachers have then used this framework to design instruction for increasing students' depth of understanding and cognitive development, as well as to facilitate their reflection on depth of learning. In particular, the SOLO framework has been used to ensure alignment between intended learning outcomes, assessment and explicit criteria for success in school science (Martin, 2011) and online learning (Hunt, Walton, Martin, Haigh & Irving, 2015), as well as in tertiary education (Biggs & Tang, 2011).

Further applications of SOLO have explored its use in analysing the marking of mathematical open-ended questions using rubrics (Çetin & İlhan, 2017), the evaluation of the depth of learning assessed in geography examinations in secondary schools (Bijsterbosch, van der Schee & Kuiper, 2017), and its application as a developmental model in the context of adult development and learning (Commons, Trudeau, Stein, Richards & Krause, 1998; Stålnea, Kjellströmb & Utriainenc, 2016). Overall, SOLO has been shown to be a robust theoretical framework that supports the distinction between lower or shallower levels of thinking and learning, and levels that are higher or deeper. Together Dreyfus's model of skill acquisition and the SOLO taxonomy provide examples of how the systematic sequencing of learning opportunities can enhance the effectiveness of teaching, and also what increased intensity in terms of depth of learning means in relation to knowledge and skill development.

Who should mediate the learning opportunities?

A key consideration in designing learning opportunities is who will engage with a student around the learning opportunities. At this point it is appropriate to reiterate that students who are the centre of educational casework definitely need good teaching in order to learn. Whatever teaching they have received to date has not produced learning as anticipated or in line with others of the same age. As already emphasised, any future teaching needs to be carefully tailored to respond to their learning needs. Often this means that teaching needs to be intensified in focus or become more systematic, in order to have impact on student achievement, and thus it is expert responsive teaching that is needed.

In this section the term *mediate* is used, since it is not always a teacher who provides the intervention, and we want to draw a distinction between the professional expertise of teaching and the activity of those who are not teachers, but who often assume responsibility within learning intervention. The term 'mediation' comes from sociocultural theory. It is the activity of any more competent other, within a social interaction that aims to lead development and learning of the younger or less competent participant. In formal education teachers are responsible for mediating learning opportunities, and expertly leading the learning of individuals.

Teachers mediating learning opportunities

The job of teachers is to not only provide learning opportunities, but also to mediate these activities for their students. Teaching can be provided in a number of ways that are reflected in the layers of learning intervention model. The default way for this to happen is through teaching a class of students, within which small group and individual teaching is carefully designed, as an integral part of the classroom program (Layer 1). Teaching starts with a universal design approach and becomes increasingly differentiated as student learning needs are more explicitly understood. In particular, quality differentiated classroom teaching is the foundation layer for students with disabilities (Commonwealth of Australia, 2014). Systematic, explicit teaching can also be provided through small group and individual short-term intervention in Layer 2 or longer-term intervention in Layer 3.

The teaching expertise applied within any of these layers is based on knowledge of children's learning and development, the curriculum content to be taught, appropriate learning activities and the most effective teaching strategies that will support students' activation of learning strategies. These foundational skills and knowledge allow teachers to expertly provide teaching for learning (see Chapter 10 for more on what it is that expert teachers do).

Based on evidence about the impact of systematic, explicit teaching, why would we ever do anything other than have a teacher implement all learning intervention? Unfortunately, resourcing has a lot to do with the consideration of other ways of providing intervention, as do the existing structures and expectations of education systems and schools. There are also theoretical bases and research evidence to support the inclusion of proxies for professional teachers as part of a flexible learning program. However, we reiterate that good teaching is based on an expert understanding of the learner, appropriate learning pathways or progressions (what is to be learnt next), and knowledge of how best to orchestrate appropriate instruction. So, it is vital that expert teachers manage any intervention, even if carried out by others. In the next sections, we will consider who else can effectively mediate learning opportunities in ways that complement the primary role of teachers.

Peer mediated learning opportunities

Two key approaches that rely on students as proxies for teachers are cooperative group learning and peer tutoring. These approaches also respond to the need to manage multiple students and the complexity of learning needs in classrooms. Both cooperative group teaching and peer tutoring have significant research evidence supporting their use with learners who experience disabilities or learning difficulties, as well as students progressing as anticipated in their academic learning (Gillies & Ashman, 2000; Hattie, 2009; Mitchell, 2014).

These approaches draw on carefully applied expertise and understandings of how cooperative group learning opportunities can be implemented successfully (Mitchell, 2014; Hennessy & Dionigi, 2013). In particular, the preparation of students is essential, both in terms of topic knowledge to participate meaningfully and competence with group process skills. As well, careful design of group tasks sets cooperative group learning up for success for all participants, and teacher use of careful monitoring strategies ensures that any problems can be dealt with quickly (Mitchell, 2014). Theoretical explanations for the positive impact of cooperative group learning include joint motivation, social cohesion, shared cognition and an inherent enjoyment of group interactions (Slavin, 2015). Cooperative group learning can usefully focus on academic skills and knowledge as well as on behaviour.

As with cooperative learning, peer tutoring is also an increasingly common classroom approach that can be valuable for all students – those who are receiving the tutoring and those providing it (Katz & Mirenda, 2002). Again, explicit teaching of the student behaviours needed to make these learning interactions more likely to work is essential, along with the assignment of appropriate activities and careful monitoring to provide support when needed. Class-wide and cross-age peer tutoring are approaches to providing learning opportunities that complement classroom teaching by consolidating or increasing depth of student learning (Mitchell, 2014).

Teaching assistant mediated learning opportunities

Another common situation that involves cross-age tutoring used in intervention in classrooms is the provision of instruction by teaching assistants. This school and system response to the identification of additional learning needs means that many teacher assistants may be assuming "direct pedagogical" responsibility in classrooms (Rubie-Davies, Blatchford, Webster, Koutsoubou & Bassett, 2010, p.445). Rubie-Davies et al. recommend changes to these current models of teaching effectiveness and the introduction of accountability for the 'teaching by proxy' that is a reality in many classrooms. Issues of appropriate preparation and the provision of consistent teacher supervision are very relevant to consider in supporting the work of teacher assistants (Shaddock, Giorcelli & Smith, 2007; Punch, 2015; Webster, Blatchford & Russell, 2013).

Parent mediated learning opportunities

Within learning intervention there are times when parents or family members take responsibility for mediating learning opportunities in consultation with teachers or allied health professionals. A common situation is when parents of a young child use strategies taught to them by a speech and language specialist to provide intervention to accelerate language development within everyday living. Families naturally teach language to young children, but with the support of specialist expertise they are able to provide more targeted responses to support their child's development of language. This can have significant impact on language development for children with language impairments and intellectual delays (see Meaden, Angell, Stoner & Daczewitz, 2014; Roberts & Kaiser, 2011) and within low socioeconomic contexts (Suskind et al., 2016). Although changes to parent interaction skills and accelerated language learning trajectories have been demonstrated, the longer-term impact of parent mediated intervention has not been firmly established. This suggests that sustained intervention is needed to produce continuing effects on young children's language development (McGillion, Pine, Herbert & Matthews, 2017; Suskind et al., 2016).

However, it is common for this approach to be taken with interventions, particularly with young children.

ICT mediated learning opportunities

Another form of mediation to be considered in this section is that provided through online learning opportunities. Prepared online learning opportunities, with built-in feedback, are increasingly being made available to students. Sometimes these complement face-to-face learning and teaching; at other times they are a substitute. There have always been anecdotes about teachers relying on textbooks, and regularly giving instructions such as: "Open your book to page 193 and work through the next two sections." There are many students for whom such structured learning, with consistent activities and feedback, is a comfortable way to work through curriculum content. Online learning opportunities can be similar, but much richer, with embedded multimedia material, live links to resources, and interactive quizzes that provide immediate feedback. Such resources can be all that textbooks are and more. There are also ways to interact with other learners online, through both synchronous and asynchronous platforms that alter how learning and teaching happen.

However, there is a shift of responsibility that is important to consider in both of these situations. It is crucial to think about the learning opportunities presented by both textbooks and online as also needing teacher expertise to be most effective. Responsiveness for online teaching can be built in, but it is only a teacher who can look beneath students' responses to understand what is supporting and hindering learning, and make judgements about whether more of the same or something totally different is needed.

By thinking of teaching as always requiring the input of a teacher, we retain the focus firmly on the teacher–student relationship within which teaching and learning happens, and on teacher expertise as a crucial factor underpinning the success of intervention. This way of thinking about teaching thus poses a question about whether the use of people other than teachers dilutes the effectiveness of teaching. The research evidence about the impact of cooperative group teaching or peer mediated learning suggests it has a much less powerful impact on learning than systematic explicit teaching by teachers. The research exploring the impact on learning of teaching assistants as proxies for teachers is even less convincing. In fact, there is evidence that teaching assistants can have a negative effect on student learning and independence (Webster et al., 2011). This is an instance that calls for the careful interpretation of research findings because it is clear that many teaching assistants have a positive effect on learners. A significant number of people employed in such roles are in fact teachers or allied health professionals who bring educational or therapeutic intervention expertise to the role. However, this is not always the case given the position, wage and qualification structures for paraprofessionals.

In short, given that the learners who are the focus of educational casework need more intensive and targeted teaching in order to learn, it is important to provide the most effective and focused teaching possible in the circumstances. This means that teachers need to carefully manage all learning opportunities for these students so that all teaching, including all teaching by proxies, is as intense as it needs to be to make a positive change.

What layers of learning intervention are appropriate?

The fact that a student is the focus of educational casework does not necessarily mean that the resulting intervention will be individually implemented: the best way to support learning and development for a student may be wholly within a planned class program with adjustments to increase intensity, or provide alternative learning opportunities or teaching strategies. Alternately, the intervention could be a mix of small group and whole class teaching, supplemented by some short-term individual intervention with a view to strengthening engagement and access to instruction in class. All of these possibilities within the layers of learning intervention need to be considered when decisions about the most appropriate context for providing learning opportunities are made.

Information generated by the previous questions will help determine what could be used within a class program to meet a student's specific learning needs, as well as what adjustments could be made. Then it is useful to consider how classroom learning opportunities, with or without adjustments, could meet identified learning needs. Often, they can, especially if universal design principles (Chapter 3) ensure access to the curriculum through the use of a range of modes that reduce barriers to learning.

School-wide and whole class intervention

Sometimes educational casework highlights whole school-wide and whole class changes that may support a particular student, but which also have the potential to better support many other students. For example, a student who requires explicit teaching of appropriate behaviours may be best served by a whole school positive behaviour framework that also provides more explicit and intense behavioural learning opportunities for all students, while school-wide evidence-based literacy teaching and a focus on explicit teaching of thinking skills will serve all students well.

Behaviour

Behaviour intervention in the context of whole school or classroom has traditionally been framed as 'management' or 'control'. However, educational settings have increasingly recognised that behaviour is also an aspect of functioning that needs to be taught and that many behaviour difficulties can be prevented through strong whole school and classroom approaches that teach behaviours that support learning, and provide clear expectations for behaviour that are acknowledged through systematic reward systems and consistent feedback from multiple teachers.

Just as families set up expectations about how to behave in home and social settings, so educational settings expect a particular set of behaviours and have increasingly focused on proactively teaching these behaviours. Much of this type of school-wide intervention that aims to prevent behaviour difficulties or problems is based on an approach developed by the US Department of Education's Positive Behavioral Interventions and Supports (PBIS) that is based on applied analysis of behaviour (Sugai & Horner, 2002). This approach is reframed in Australia and New Zealand as Positive Behaviour Support or Positive Behaviour for Learning (Mooney, Dobia, Barker, Power & Watson, 2008; Savage, Lewis & Colless, 2011). The approach has also been adopted as the basis of a culturally responsive, whole-school, strength-based, behavioural intervention for Māori in New Zealand (Savage, Macfarlane, Macfarlane, Fickel & Te Hemi, 2012). Such school-wide preventative behavioural interventions have considerable positive impact on the amount of time available for teaching and learning instead of for managing behaviour (Richmond, 2007).

Literacy

Similarly, the push for evidence-based teaching of reading and writing has prompted the use of school-wide systematic, evidence-based teaching. The adage 'learn to read so you can read to learn' is still absolutely relevant for classrooms of the 21st century. The largest area of focus in learning intervention is in relation to literacy, as literacy skills are the primary tool of accessing much of the curriculum, and also of demonstrating learning in our education systems. There is considerable research evidence of how children learn to read and write, as well as of intervention that is most effective, and it is generally accepted that foundational teaching of each component skill of reading and writing, on a strong foundation of language, is essential in all classrooms. The basis for systematic, explicit teaching of literacy is substantial. Such literacy-focused intervention involves assessment and teaching of phonemic awareness and decoding, vocabulary and comprehension, fluency, and spelling and writing as the basis of evidence-based literacy instruction and of intervention for struggling readers (Lane, Pullen, Hudson & Konold, 2009).

However, the field of reading is controversial with many teachers not necessarily understanding the evidence base of reading teaching and intervention. This situation has been presented as a dichotomy between 'whole language' and 'phonics' and is known as the Literacy Wars (Snyder, 2008). This is a simplistic and unhelpful battle that misses the point. Reading and writing are complex activities that draw on language for meaning, and on specific skills in phonemic awareness and decoding that are the mechanisms of written language. Therefore, learners need a rich language environment as well as explicit teaching in reading strategies. In particular, students who are at risk of learning difficulties can be supported most effectively by explicit teaching of reading strategies with considerable emphasis on the relation between the sounds we hear and how they are represented in written language (Moats, 2009).

If we know what is most effective for struggling learners, then we should be using it to prevent learning difficulties. And, we do know what is the most effective way to teach reading to students at risk of difficulties (e.g., National Reading Panel, 2000; Foorman, Francis, Fletcher, Schatschneider & Mehta, 1998; Torgesen, 2002) and students who still have difficulties after years at school (Parrila, McQuarrie, Klassen, Georgiou & Odishaw, 2010; Wanzek et al., 2013). It is never too late to focus on the skills of literacy because appropriate intervention will have an effect on reading competence.

Thinking

Development of thinking skills can also be fostered through school-wide or whole class systematic explicit teaching. At one time, we thought that thinking (cognitive) skills were fixed and that some people could just think 'better' than others. We now know that is not the case and that thinking, or cognitive, skills can be explicitly taught. Such cognitive education is about learning to learn or learning to think through developing cognitive, metacognitive and motivational processes.

Frameworks for the explicit teaching of thinking skills are informed by cognitive research. An example is the *PASS* framework (Naglieri & Das, 2005), which is easy to translate into classrooms and can help scaffold the teaching of thinking skills (see Table 9.6). This framework is a type of information processing model that fosters four types of thinking used extensively in learning.

Strategies focusing on these four types of thinking skills can be incorporated in general classroom conversation and used by all students to further strengthen their skills in planning. Planning is important to learning and has been associated explicitly with achievement in reading comprehension (Das & Georgiou, 2016) and mathematical learning, particularly with mathematical problem solving (Cai, Georgiou, Wen & Das, 2016).

Teachers need to see the value of teaching *strategies for learning* that are smarter, more strategic and more efficient, and of modelling these for their students. An explicit focus on what we do when we learn can be tied to curriculum learning and integrated within regular school activities. As well, transfer between contexts can be explicitly prepared for by deliberately practising learned processes, cognitive functions and strategies in other situations. Teachers

TABLE 9.6 PASS cognitive processing (thinking) skills

Planning	Strategic use of thinking and of actions in learning
Attention	Selective and sustained attention is needed in order to engage effectively in learning
Simultaneous processing	Making sense of separate pieces of information
Successive processing	Interpreting and providing information in a particular order

Source: Derived from Naglieri & Das, 2005.

can demonstrate a metacognitive style (e.g., utilising planning, monitoring and evaluating) in all domains and throughout the entire school day and emphasise good thinkers as:

- Patient (understanding and ideas do not always come right away)
- Curious (good thinkers ask questions about what they learn and look for more information)
- Focused (good thinkers concentrate on what is being learned)
- Open (good thinkers are receptive to other ideas and possibilities about information)
- Flexible (good thinkers are ready to change understanding through new learning)
- Relaxed (good thinkers know that they may not understand everything right away)

(Adapted from Naglieri & Pickering, 2010, p.74)

Making adjustments to class teaching

School-wide and whole class evidence-based teaching represents a good foundation within which to consider adjustments that may need to be made at times to ensure the most effective learning for individual students. This notion is central to the provision of responsive differentiation for students with disabilities, for whom education systems are legally obliged to make reasonable adjustments (Disability Standards, 2005; see Commonwealth of Australia, 2006). The definitions of levels of adjustment used in the Nationally Consistent Collection of Data for school students with disabilities (NCCD) (Commonwealth of Australia, 2014) is useful for decision-making. Specifically, the NCCD framework has been developed in response to the Disability Standards (2005), and was used to probe what teachers are doing in adjusting their teaching for students with disabilities. 'Quality differentiated teaching practice' is the foundation level of this framework, with adjustments possible at three additional levels (supplementary, substantial and extensive). This framework is aligned with the layers of intervention relevant for students receiving educational casework, and who may or may not have disabilities as defined by the NCCD.

TABLE 9.7 Level of adjustment for students with disabilities

Quality differentiated teaching practice	Supplementary adjustments	Substantial adjustments	Extensive adjustments
Responsive to the differential needs of all students with close monitoring and review	At specific times; modified or tailored programs, modified instruction; accessible materials	Frequent teacher-directed individual instruction; adapted instruction and materials	Personalised modifications at all times; assistive technology

Source: Commonwealth of Australia, 2014 (NCCD).

Classroom teachers and learning intervention professionals collaborate to make decisions about whether all of a student's learning needs can be met by the class program using the resources available, or whether supplementary, substantial or extensive adjustments are needed. Again, these adjustments are about reducing barriers to learning that are inherent in the interaction of a particular learner with the learning environment and the learning opportunities provided. A brief overview of the NCCD framework is shown in Table 9.7.

Behaviour

It is unarguable that learning depends on behaviours that support active learning (A) through relating to the teacher and others (R) and managing self in complex educational settings (M). If these behaviours are in place, then learning is more likely to be successful. As well, while thinking (T) and using language and symbol systems (U) are emphasised in learning, they are also integral to behaviour. Therefore, we stress the need to recognise the interconnectedness of learning and behaviour and always consider them together in educational casework.

Adjustments to aspects of whole class teaching are a common way to intervene for specific behaviour change that is integral to classroom learning for individual students. For example, teachers often alter the layout of the room, the availability of materials, the make-up of a table group or the amount of work provided in any one lesson in order to optimise student engagement and learning behaviours. Adjustment of any of these aspects of classroom activity may make a positive difference, but it is often the case that there is no systematic analysis of what happens and what effect any adjustments make.

In educational casework there can be a more systematic analysis of what is happening, as it happens, that can inform adjustments and can contribute to evaluation of an intervention. A key idea that can provide the basis for intervention is that behaviour serves purposes for us as social beings, and it is vital to make sense of the purpose or function of any behaviour in order to consider how to change it (Beavers, Iwata & Lerman, 2013). Teachers and other professionals can develop skills for functional behaviour analysis that will inform intervention (McCahill, Healy, Lydon & Ramey, 2014). Further, intervention based on functional analysis can be very effective in inclusive classrooms (Walker, Chung & Bonnet, 2016) and is the focus of much casework in education.

A framework for practice in educational casework with a focus on behaviour is used in New Zealand (see Johnson, 2016). This framework is an operationalisation of problem analysis (Monsen, 2008; Robinson, 1993) and situational analysis (Annan, 2005) approaches to educational psychology casework. In this model (shown in Figure 9.2), interventions are put in place after considerable data gathering and group consideration of the case in context. The interventions are then monitored and reviewed. This same framework is used less completely in practice in Australia, where specialist professionals (e.g., psychologists and psychiatrists) provide in-depth assessment information and write recommendations,

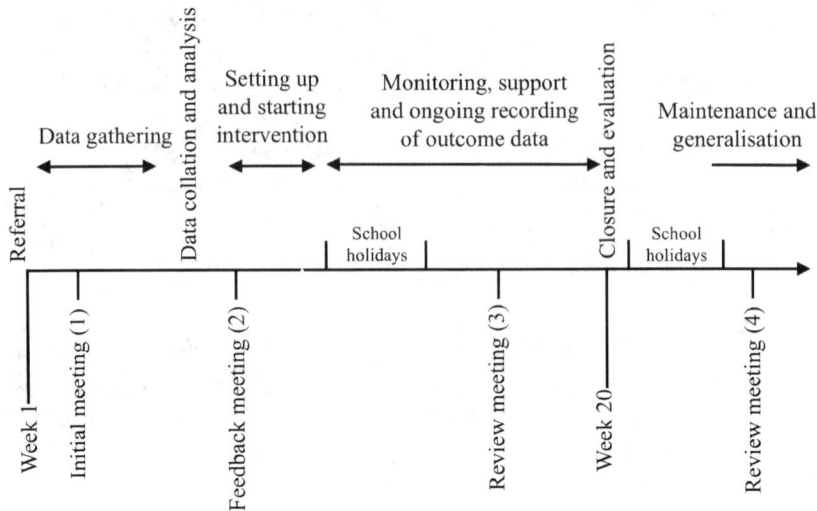

FIGURE 9.2   Framework for behavioural casework

Source: Johnson, 2016.

but may not be involved in the implementation and evaluation of any adjustments within schools.

Sensory reception

Adjustments are also the primary way to intervene for many aspects of sensory reception, thinking skills, and using language, literacy and numeracy. Learning environments are often busy places with considerable levels of noise and movement. Most learners can adapt and manage by filtering sensory information in ways that support their focus on what is important at any particular time. However, it may be appropriate to reduce sensory input for some students by managing levels of sound and light more responsively. The noise in classrooms can be significantly problematic for some students, particularly those with any level of intermittent or persistent hearing impairment. As well, lighting might need to be brighter, or subtler, for some students depending on their vision needs.

Thinking

Careful assessment of student learning, through educational casework, can point to particular aspects of thinking that may need to be fostered through more intensive teaching or instructional adjustment. These aspects can be anything from attention and perception, to memory, reasoning, problem solving and executive functioning. As an example, if sustained attention is a difficulty for a student, then decreasing distractors may support more sustained focus. As students mature, their self-awareness about what distracts them can be the basis for increased self-management of this difficulty.

The use of memory skills is another issue that can be adjusted in classrooms. Memory is vital to learning and those who have good memories are able to draw on disparate pieces of information in order to make links that others may not see, simply because they have forgotten some of the content. There is considerable research in the field of memory that makes distinctions between types of memory and profiles of development (Alloway & Copello, 2013; Alloway, Rajendran & Archibald, 2009). Some people remember fine details about experiences while others remember an overall sense of what has taken place, or even embed the experience within previous learning. Simple adjustments for learners experiencing difficulties with memory include building skills for using external memory aids (like taking notes or developing mnemonics) and exploring which types of external memory may best support learning needs at the moment. We all use external memory in our lives, from our shopping lists to the reminders on our phones. We also take notes, doodle, highlight text, construct concept maps and construct visual images, so we have access to the appropriate information at the right time. These actions are a mixture of external memory and memory strategies, which work together to make information accessible for all learners.

Effective strategies for storing and recalling facts include mnemonics, visual representations, rehearsal to store in longer-term memory and chunking (Mitchell, 2014; Naglieri & Pickering, 2010). We all use these strategies in our everyday lives; however, it is important to explicitly teach them so that all students, particularly those with learning difficulties become proficient at storing and retrieving important information.

Short-term small group or individual intervention (Layer 2)

Short-term individual or small group intervention tends to be much researched and fits into the second layer of learning intervention. These interventions use more intensive explicit teaching to address gaps in learning, and to help students catch up with their age peers academically or socially. In contrast, intervention in Layer 3 is more protracted, and usually focused on students with persistent learning difficulties, for whom educational casework is appropriate throughout their school years. We examine Layer 3 in the next section. Short-term small group and individual intervention occurs when effective teachers use small groups flexibly to mix and match students to learning opportunities in their everyday lessons, as well as when separate interventions outside the class are organised by the school or by families outside school. Such short-term interventions can range from a small number of structured sessions to as many as are needed to establish the skills that are the focus of the intervention. Small group or individual intervention can respond to academic learning needs through a focus on thinking skills development and using language, literacy and numeracy and ICT, both within bounded classroom curriculum content and outside it.

Thinking

Research with a focus on the construct of executive functioning emphasises the importance of planning in academic learning (Clements, Sarama & Germeroth, 2016). Intervention with a focus on executive functioning can set children up for more successful learning in all the basic academic skills including mathematics (Fuhs, Hornburg & McNeil, 2016). Executive functioning includes skills of goal setting, cognitive flexibility, organising, prioritising, accessing working memory and self-monitoring (Meltzer, 2014), all of which can be taught explicitly, as can their application to problem solving. Intervention to teach problem solving needs to consider multiple factors, including cognitive and metacognitive processes, the immediacy of feedback, and whether problems are meaningful and culturally appropriate (Taconis, 2013). Schema-based instruction for problem solving uses relevant conceptual cues and scaffolds the process of making sense of the problem, as well as deliberately working towards transfer of the process to other problems (Jitendra & Montague, 2013).

Literacy

There is a considerable tradition in small group or individual intervention for literacy development. *Reading Recovery* is a well-known structured individual intervention developed in New Zealand (Clay, 1979). Although Reading Recovery has been implemented around the world over the past few decades, it is now controversial because of a lack of evidence of sustained improvement (Iversen & Tunmer, 1993; Reynolds & Wheldall, 2007; Schwartz, Hobsbaum, Briggs & Scull, 2009). The considerable amount of published research evaluating this program and differing perspectives that authors take towards these findings illustrate how difficult it is to determine the relative effectiveness of any intervention, without taking into account the context of implementation and the learning needs of students. Since the selection of students to attend *Reading Recovery* sessions is purely based on achievement measures, the students included may not have had exposure to appropriate learning opportunities, or may have a general developmental delay. Without a clear match of intervention to learning needs progress will likely be very different for two students on the same program.

The *Quick60* program (Iversen, 2009) teaches all components of literacy at Layers 1 and 2 of learning intervention. The Foundation lessons (30 lessons) are structured for whole class presentation and small group preventative teaching. The later lessons related to a set of carefully sequenced non-fiction books are for small group intervention to support students with literacy delays after the first year of school.

Focusing on grapheme–phoneme relationships and decoding skills, the *MultiLit Reading Tutor Program* (Wheldall, & Wheldall, 2014) began as an individual intervention and has extended into a group intervention as *MacqLit*, and a more preventative approach within *MiniLit* (small group, early school) and *PreLit* (preschool class, small group or individual).

Similarly, the QuickSmart Literacy program (Graham, Pegg & Alder, 2007) focuses on the second layer of intervention and provides resources that support the word recognition and comprehension skills of middle school students. Thirty-minute lessons are structured consisting of six component parts that build students' proficiency and confidence in reading. Pairs of students work with a QuickSmart instructor three times a week for up to 30 weeks.

Numeracy

Our number system has taken centuries of human thought to develop, and is very sophisticated. However, we expect students to become competent with numbers early in life, and all subsequent curricula in mathematics and other subjects assume their understanding of this foundational capability with numbers. Unfortunately, many people find learning about numbers very difficult, for a variety of reasons. For many students a burst of intense, explicit teaching and enough opportunity to practise skills until they have established some level of automaticity is required to set them up for higher-order mathematical learning.

Automaticity with number facts is fundamental to the QuickSmart numeracy intervention (as it is for the word recognition in the literacy intervention as well). This program (Graham, Bellert, Thomas & Pegg, 2007; Graham, Bellert & Pegg, 2007; Pegg & Graham, 2013) is also applicable to the second layer of intervention. QuickSmart numeracy provides focus facts, flashcards, speedsheets, problem-solving activities and games, including a computer-based assessment system that monitors students' performance. The six component lessons are designed to build automaticity with basic number facts across the four operations and confidence with word problem solving. A number of evaluations have established the positive impact of this intervention for most students (Graham, 2017; Thomas & Lewis, 2010).

Social skills

Small group intervention can also focus on improving the skills needed for active learning in the social setting of schools and classrooms, that is, the social interaction skills necessary for relating to others and for managing oneself within the classroom. For example, student welfare staff, school counsellors and school psychologists are often involved in delivering intervention that focuses on developing skills to enable students to interact socially, to manage their anxiety or to grow through traumatic experiences. To this end, small group social skills interventions, within which specific interaction skills are taught and practised, are common. Because many different groups of students participate in these programs, and many different outcomes are intended, it is really difficult to compare social skills intervention across studies. For example, published effect sizes range from 0.2 (impact on academic learning) to 0.9 (enhanced peer relations) and the participants across studies are described as: being at risk of social exclusion; having special education needs; displaying depressive symptoms; labelled as autistic; or having an intellectual disability, emotional or behavioural disorder or delinquent profile (Mitchell, 2014). Combining results from such a diversity of studies into an average effect size is nonsensical. Instead, it is vital to go further into the research and to examine the purposes of intervention, the nature of the participants' social learning needs, and the way outcomes have been defined and assessed, in order to judge the usefulness of the evidence to particular instances of casework.

Social skills are considered 'academic enablers' (Di Perna & Elliott, 2002) that support students in active learning in the complex social settings of classrooms and schools. Within the considerable research in this domain of intervention there is evidence that the explicit systematic teaching of social skills in small groups can be complemented by whole class intervention (Gresham, 2016; Gresham, Vance & Chenier, 2013).

Emotional functioning

Small group or individual intervention to prevent or reduce anxiety has been developed in many contexts. Evidence related to school-based prevention and early intervention approaches to ameliorating the effects of anxiety show a wide range of effect sizes immediately upon completion of the intervention and during follow-up (from one to 30 months later) (Neil & Christensen, 2009). These interventions are often based on a cognitive behaviour therapy (CBT) approach that works by changing thinking and behaviour. CBT is recommended as an evidence-based intervention for psychologists to use, but the Australian Psychological Society stresses that the research evidence needs to be considered in light of the professional experience of the practitioner, the values of the clients and the resourcing available (APS, 2010).

As an example, eight structured sessions are used in Seasons for Growth, a short-term intervention that addresses the emotional issues around young children recognising and acknowledging their experiences of change and loss, and dealing with ways to adapt and move forward from these difficult experiences (Graham, 2002). The sessions are run with groups of four to seven primary students and have been shown to impact positively on the emotional development and social and behavioural functioning of a range of participants (Frydenberg, Muller & Ivens, 2006; Riley, 2012; Phillips, 2014).

Longer-term small group or individual intervention (Layer 3)

There are some students who need long-term or recurring individual or small group intervention. For example, children who have experienced significant trauma, abuse and neglect, or have a recurring mental illness, or have pervasive and severe difficulties in developing social skills, or intellectual disability may need consistent intervention over time. This third layer of intervention support is really made up of a series of shorter-term interventions or a set of pervasive adjustments that change as students develop and new teachers become part of a their learning journeys. A particular focus of intervention in numeracy, for example, for students who have some disabilities, involves determining what is needed in everyday life and explicitly teaching those skills. For example, learners who have an intellectual disability learn more slowly and benefit from more intense and frequent practice opportunities across the curriculum. The implication for these students' learning in mathematics is that these individuals will need carefully structured and intensive programs, particularly at transition times when moving from a known, comfortable setting to the next, unknown and often less structured setting.

Assistive technology, augmentative and alternative communication

Some students who are the focus of educational casework will have persistently distinctive needs in development that can only be met through long-term individual intervention in tandem with adapted classroom activities and assistive technology. In Layer 3, technology-based intervention can support the language and communication of students with some disabilities. These students, in turn, have specific learning needs related to the development of expertise with assistive technology and augmentative and alternative communication systems.

Specific issues around assistive, augmentative and alternative communication systems can be explored with families and technology professionals, who are the experts in this knowledge domain. There is also considerable literature to be explored in relation to students using assistive technology (e.g., Karlsson, Johnston & Barker, 2017; Peters, 2017) as well as processes used to make decisions about the usefulness of particular technologies for individual students (e.g., Zapf, Scherer, Baxter & Rintala, 2016). Much of this evidence is not in the education literature but is still important to explore when teaching a student who relies on such technology in the classroom.

Collaborative work between teachers and specialists in this situation is vital so that communication channels are efficient, and adjustments are seamlessly included as part of all learning opportunities. Sometimes it is valuable for teachers to develop particular expertise, such as with Auslan, in order to optimise the inclusion of a student who uses sign language as a primary form of communication. As well, teachers have to develop skills for managing assistive technology in order to support student learning most effectively. Sometimes these skills and expertise are delegated to others, such as a teaching assistant, who may have such specific responsibilities across the school.

Conceptual vocabulary

A key capability for learning is curriculum-based vocabulary, the language of concepts and ideas. Every domain of curriculum has its own bank of words and meanings that are necessary to know, but which also can be barriers to learning unless they are well understood. It is now accepted that all teachers need to teach the language of their topic, rather than assume it will be acquired or, even worse, assume it is known. Learning intervention teachers must check that the language being used is understood in the way it needs to be, and that any specific language is taught explicitly. The same applies to any symbol systems that are integral to learning activities and teaching strategies.

The development of a rich vocabulary bank in oral language is iteratively connected to conceptual understanding. Oral vocabulary and language, as well as conceptual understanding, are all associated with the development of vocabulary in written language. It is not enough to be able to sound out phonically regular words, since they will not mean anything if the word is not familiar. A barrier to learning for many students is that when reading is frustrating, there are fewer occasions of reading for meaning that can support the continued development of familiarity with written words and a meaningful vocabulary. A vicious cycle sets in, whereby less reading means less engagement with words. Even if words can be decoded they may not mean anything. Once students are turned off reading for pleasure, it is really difficult to keep their word banks building. In situations like this, it is important to keep access to written material happening, even if it is through being read to. The use of audio books is a way to ensure this access in families, so that children's oral language banks continue to grow to support written language learning.

Many children who stand out as not learning as well as anticipated in the first year of school have a much smaller vocabulary than others of their age. They may not have had the opportunity to be exposed to a rich bank of language, or they may find it difficult to learn vocabulary incidentally (Carlisle, Fleming & Gudbrandsen, 2000). Along with explicit teaching of vocabulary within topics in class, there can be pre-teaching of vocabulary for some students to help establish their familiarity with important words that will be used in whole class learning activities. Such pre-teaching can also include explicit teaching of strategies for learning new words so that the students become increasingly proficient in learning words independently (Wilson, Jesson & McNaughton, 2013).

Such explicit teaching of content through intense, explicit small group or individual teaching, complements class lessons and can support many students to engage successfully with the curriculum (Scruggs, 2012). Such systematic Layer 3 intervention can target the vocabulary and comprehension of content, the spelling of the content-based vocabulary and writing for specific purposes – all of which are directly related to the curriculum content. The principles of evidence-based intervention for vocabulary development, comprehension, spelling and writing can also become part of this Layer 3 intervention.

Enriching and extending learning opportunities for gifted learners

Before we leave this discussion of the consideration of layers of intervention, we need to consider students whose learning needs mean that they should have access to extended or deeper learning opportunities in some or all domains of the curriculum. The increase in intensity that gifted or talented learners need is likely to be in terms of higher-order conceptual understanding, or advanced skills development within content areas. While it is easy to only consider intellectual giftedness in this section, we stress the need to consider advanced development across all of the ATRiUM capabilities, and to provide appropriate learning opportunities to continue the development of students' strengths, as well as any areas of difficulty that they may experience.

Thinking

Traditionally, giftedness is assumed to relate to thinking or cognitive skills. This is still an important focus, and schools are charged with the responsibility of providing learning opportunities that fit the current levels of learning of each of their students, including those who do have faster developing or deeper levels of thinking in comparison to age peers. Careful use of rich classroom tasks, with expectations for a range of intellectual engagement, will provide what is needed most of the time for gifted learners. The SOLO framework, dealt with earlier in this chapter, provides sound structure for considering how to deepen the intellectual challenges for some students, in fact, to provide a range of levels of challenge to meet a range of learning needs at once (Hook, 2006; Martin, 2011). At other times learning needs can best be met through complementary small group or individual alternative learning opportunities, either within the class program or in other contexts. Sometimes access to classes at higher grades or even in the next educational setting can be appropriate. There is not room to explore this controversial issue here, but if ability groupings and acceleration are aspects of educational casework their effectiveness and relevance will need to be carefully explored as part of the process.

Relating to others

There are students who are gifted in how they relate to others, showing exceptional social skills, sensitivity and caring toward others. This domain of giftedness is valued highly in our society, with such children often channelled into leadership roles. It is important that these skills are developed as well as possible throughout schooling. The research into how best to provide education for gifted learners is worth exploring, starting with the effect sizes provided by Hattie's meta-analyses (2009, 2011, 2015) that show that grouping by ability is not an effective way to enhance learning for these students. As well, further food for thought is to be found in other literature (e.g., Steenbergen-Hu, Makel, & Olszewski-Kubilius, 2016).

Twice exceptional learners

A complex situation that may be the focus of educational casework occurs when a gifted learner also has significant difficulties learning in one or more domains of the curriculum, or in developing and applying one or more of the ATRiUM capabilities. It is possible to be gifted in literacy and to have profound difficulties in mathematics, for example, or to show other extreme variation in development and learning. For example, while students who have determinations of high-functioning ASD may show deep knowledge and understanding of some specific domains of learning, they may need explicit systematic teaching in other areas of development, usually using language and relating to others. Such students, who have a really wide range of atypical development, with some aspects being in the gifted range and others perhaps in the disability range, are referred to as being twice exceptional and there is considerable research evidence and professional resources to support intervention for academic and developmental success. Issues around academic self-concept and self-belief are the focus of some of that research (e.g., Townend & Brown, 2016; Wang & Neihart, 2015) since this is a primary issue for students who struggle to understand why some learning is so easy and some is so difficult. Further elaboration on this complex topic is beyond the scope of this book, and we emphasise the need for teachers and learning intervention professionals to consider all learners as having their own unique profiles of capabilities for learning, achievement within the curriculum, and learning needs.

How are these learning opportunities to be resourced?

To complete this chapter's consideration of the most appropriate learning opportunities to provide as part of educational casework, we consider the issue of resourcing. Resources are both human and material.

Human resources

The most important resource in any intervention is the 'more competent other', the teacher. However, others are involved in intervention, particularly when it is the implementation of a pre-packaged program. It is important to be clear about what responsibilities personnel have in the design and implementation, assessment and reporting phases of intervention. It is also vital to ensure each member of an intervention team has had the appropriate preparation to be able to implement the intervention as intended.

What are their responsibilities? There is always a need for a teacher to act as the key professional in any intervention, and, as we reiterate in this book, not just any teacher, but one who is tuned into learner needs, who knows the domains of learning well and knows how to facilitate development in those domains. Even if someone who is not a teacher runs the learning intervention session, a teacher must supervise the intervention as a whole – a teacher who has the capacity to determine students' responsiveness to intervention and to assist in decision-making based on educational evidence.

Material resources

The material resources or equipment needed are also important. These can range from pencils and paper to desks and chairs, computer and printer, specialist equipment and record books. Much time is lost in classrooms by students looking around for the right resources, and many discouraged learners have learned to use the search for such materials as a way to delay or avoid engaging in learning activities. It is hard to manage such situations in a class, but much easier in individualised instruction settings. Given the importance of learning opportunities to students who struggle, there is no excuse for any time to be spent on finding resources during precious teaching and learning time. Instead, all materials need to be organised, ready and accessible. The responsibility for this can be negotiated between teacher and learner with the learner taking increasing responsibility as the routine and requirements become familiar.

Summary

In this chapter we have considered the learning opportunities that teachers develop and arrange in order to meet the learning needs of students. The consideration of whether the whole class teaching program can meet individual student needs, or if it requires adjustments, or needs to be complemented with small group or individual intervention, is core business for teachers and educational casework professionals. The general principle embedded in this chapter is to start with the class program, and then to think about adjustments, and then consider alternatives outside the class program. Of course, any long-term supports, such as assistive technology and any specific skill development required by the student, need to be considered from the outset. Pulling together these two perspectives will result in learning intervention that is positioned within the most appropriate layers of support. Our consideration in this chapter of issues around the variability of learners, and within each learner, and the variability of development across the ATRiUM capabilities has highlighted the need for an inclusive approach to learning intervention to be taken with all learners, not just those who have identified disabilities.

References

Allor, J., Mathes, P., Roberts, K., Jones, F., & Champlin, T. (2010). Teaching students with moderate intellectual disabilities to read: An experimental examination of a comprehensive reading intervention. *Education and Training in Autism and Developmental Disabilities*, (45), 3–22.

Alloway, T. P. & Copello, E. (2013). Working memory: The what, the why, and the how. *Australian Educational and Developmental Psychologist, 30*(2), 105–118. doi:http://dx.doi.org.ezp.lib.unimelb.edu.au/10.1017/edp.2013.13

Alloway, T. P., Rajendran, G., & Archibald, L. M. D. (2009). Working memory in children with developmental disorders. *Journal of Learning Disabilities, 42*(4), 372–82. doi: http://dx.doi.org.ezp.lib.unimelb.edu.au/10.1177/0022219409335214

Alonzo, A. C. & Gotwals, A. W. (2012). *Learning progressions in science: Current challenges and future directions.* Rotterdam: Springer.

Annan, J. (2005). Situational analysis: A framework for evidence-based practice. *School Psychology International, 26*(2), 131–146.

Australian Psychological Society (APS) (2010). *Evidence-based psychological interventions in the treatment of mental disorders: A literature review* (3rd ed.). Melbourne, VIC: APS.

Beavers, G. A., Iwata, B. A., & Lerman, D. C. (2013). Thirty years of research on the functional analysis of problem behavior. *Journal of Applied Behavior Analysis, 46*(1), 1–21.

Biggs, J. & Collis, K. (1982). *Evaluating the quality of learning: The SOLO taxonomy (structure of the observed learning outcome).* New York, NY: Academic Press.

Biggs, J. & Tang, C. (2011). *Teaching for quality learning at university* (4th ed.). Maidenhead: McGraw Hill.

Bijsterbosch, E., van der Schee, J., & Kuiper, W. (2017). Meaningful learning and summative assessment in geography education: An analysis in secondary education in the Netherlands. *International Research in Geographical and Environmental Education, 26*(1), 17–35, DOI: 10.1080/10382046.2016.1217076

Cai, D., Georgiou, G. K., Wen, M., & Das, J. P. (2016). The role of planning in different mathematical skills. *Journal of Cognitive Psychology, 28*(2), 234–241.

Carlisle, J. F., Fleming, J. E., & Gudbrandsen, B. (2000). Incidental word learning in science classes. *Contemporary Educational Psychology, 25*(2), 184–211.

Çetin, B. & Mustafa İlhan, M. (2017). An analysis of rater severity and leniency in open-ended mathematic questions rated through standard rubrics and rubrics based on the SOLO taxonomy. *Education and Science, 42*(189), 217–247.

Clay, M. M. (1979). *The early detection of reading difficulties* (3d ed.). Portsmouth, NH: Heinemann.

Clements, D. & Semmler, J. (2009). *Learning and teaching early math[s]: The learning trajectories approach.* New York, NY: Routledge.

Clements, D., Sarama, J., & Germeroth, C. (2016). Learning executive function and early mathematics: Directions of causal relations. *Early Childhood Research Quarterly, 36*(3), 79–90, https://doi.org/10.1016/j.ecresq.2015.12.009

Commons, M. L., Trudeau, E. J., Stein, S. A., Richards, F. A., & Krause, S. R. (1998). The existence of developmental stages as shown by the hierarchical complexity of tasks. *Developmental Review, 18,* 237–278.

Commonwealth of Australia (2006). Disability standards for education 2005 plus guidance notes. Barton, ACT: Australian Government.

Commonwealth of Australia (2014). Nationally consistent collection of data: School students with disability. Australian Government Department of Education and Training. www.schooldisabilitydatapl.edu.au/about/introduction

Das, J. & Georgiou, G. (2016). Levels of planning predict different reading comprehension outcomes. *Learning and Individual Differences, 48,* 24–28. https://doi.org/10.1016/j.lindif.2016.04.004

DiPerna, J. & Elliott, S. (2002). Promoting academic enablers to improve student achievement: An introduction to the mini-series. *School Psychology Review, 31*(3), 293–297.

Dreyfus, S. (2004). The five-stage model of adult skill acquisition. *Bulletin of Science, Technology & Society, 24*(3), 177–181.

Ellis, L. A., Wheldall, K., & Beaman, R. (2007). The research locus and conceptual basis for MultiLit: Why we do what we do. *Australian Journal of Learning Disabilities, 12*(20), 61–65.

Foorman, B. R., Francis, D. J., Fletcher, J. M., Schatschneider, C., & Mehta, P. (1998). The role of instruction in learning to read: Preventing reading failure in at-risk children. *Journal of Educational Psychology, 90*(1), 37–50.

Frydenberg, E., Muller, D., & Ivens, C. (2006). The experience of loss: Coping and the seasons for growth program. *Australian Educational and Development Psychologist, 23*(1), 45–67.

Fuchs, D., Fuchs, L. S., Mathes, P. G., & Simmons, D. C. (1997). Peer-assisted learning strategies: Making classrooms more responsive to diversity. *American Educational Research Journal, 34*(1), 174–206.

Fuhs, M., Hornburg, C., & McNeil, N. (2016). Specific early number skills mediate the association between executive functioning skills and mathematics achievement. *Developmental Psychology, 52*(8), 1217–1235.

Gillies, R. & Ashman, A. (2000). The effects of cooperative learning on students with learning difficulties in the lower elementary school. *Journal of Special Education, 34*(1), 19–27.

Graham, A. (1996, 2002). *Seasons for growth; Loss and grief education program.* Sydney, NSW: MacKillop Foundation.

Graham, L. (2017). *Learning about learning intervention.* William Cruickshank Memorial Lecture at the International Academy for Research in Learning Disabilities. Brisbane, QLD.

Graham, L., Berman, J., & Bellert, A. (2015). *Sustainable learning: Inclusive practices for 21st century classrooms.* Melbourne, VIC: Cambridge University Press.

Graham, L., Bellert, A. & Pegg, J. (2007). Supporting students in the middle school years with learning difficulties in mathematics: Research into classroom practice. *Australasian Journal of Special Education, 31* (2), 171–182.

Graham, L., Bellert, A., Thomas, J., & Pegg, J. (2007). *QuickSmart*: A basic skills intervention for middle school students with learning difficulties. *Journal of Learning Disabilities, 40* (5), 410–419.

Graham, L., Pegg, J., & Alder, L. (2007). Improving the reading achievement of middle-years students with learning difficulties. *Australian Journal of Language and Literacy, 30*(3), 221–234.

Gresham, F. (2016). Social skills assessment and intervention for children and youth. *Cambridge Journal of Education, 46*(3), 319–332, DOI: 10.1080/0305764X.2016.1195788

Gresham, F., Vance, M., & Chenier, J. (2013). Improving academic achievement with social skills. In Hattie, J. & Anderman, E. (Eds.), *International guide to student achievement.* New York, NY: Routledge, 327–328.

Hattie, J. (2009). *Visible learning: A synthesis of over 800 meta-analyses relating to achievement.* Abingdon: Routledge.

Hattie, J. (2011). *Visible learning for teachers: Maximising impact on learning.* London: Routledge.

Hattie, J. (2015). The applicability of Visible Learning to higher education. *Scholarship of Teaching and Learning in Psychology, 1*(1), 79–91.

Hennessy, A. & Dionigi, R. (2013). Implementing cooperative learning in Australian primary schools: Generalist teachers' perspectives. *Issues in Educational Research, 23*(1), 52–67.

Hook, P. (2006). A thinking curriculum. *Curriculum Matters, 2,* 81–104.

Hunt, A., Walton, F., Martin, S., Haigh, M., & Irving, E. (2015). *Moving a school: Higher order thinking through SOLO and e-Learning.* Auckland, NZ: University of Auckland.

Huynh, N., Solem, M., & Bednarz, S. (2015). A road map for learning progressions research in geography, *Journal of Geography, 114*(2), 69–79.

Iversen, S. (2009). *Quick60 foundation program and small group intervention.* Auckland, NZ: Iversen Publishing.

Iversen, S. & Tunmer, W. (1993). Phonological processing skill and the Reading Recovery program. *Journal of Educational Psychology, 85,* 112–125.

Jitendra, A. & Montague, M. (2013). Strategies for improving student outcomes in mathematical reasoning. In Cook, B. & Tankersley, M. (Eds.), *Research-based practices in special education.* Upper Saddle River, NJ: Pearson, 73–85.

Johanssen, D., Hannum, W., & Tessmer, M. (1989). *Handbook of task analysis procedures.* New York, NY: Praeger.

Johnson, J. (2016). *Casework in education: Planning and decision-making for specialist practitioners.* Auckland, NZ: Dunmore.

Kang, S. (2017). The benefits of interleaved practice for learning. In Horvath, J., Lodge, J., & Hattie, J. (Eds.), *From the laboratory to the classroom: Translating science of learning for teachers.* Abingdon: Routledge, 79–93.

Karlsson, P., Johnston, C., & Barker, K. (2017). Stakeholders' views of the introduction of assistive technology in the classroom: How family-centred is Australian practice for students with cerebral palsy? *Child: Care, Health and Development, 43*(4), 598–607.

Katz, J. & Mirenda, P. (2002). Including students with developmental disabilities in general education classrooms: Educational benefits. *International Journal of Special Education, 17*(2), 14–24.

Lane, H. B., Pullen, P. C., Hudson, R. F., & Konold, T. R. (2009). Identifying essential instructional components of literacy tutoring for struggling beginning readers. *Literacy Research and Instruction, 48*(4), 277–297.

McCahill, J., Healy, O., Lydon, S., & Ramey, D. (2014). Training educational staff in functional behavioral assessment: A systematic review. *Journal of Developmental and Physical Disabilities, 26*(4), 479–505.

McGillion, M., Pine, J. M., Herbert, J. S., & Matthews, D. (2017). A randomised controlled trial to test the effect of promoting caregiver contingent talk on language development in infants from diverse socioeconomic status backgrounds. *Journal of Child Psychology and Psychiatry.* doi:10.1111/jcpp.12725

Martin, S. (2011). *Using SOLO as a framework for teaching: A case study in maximizing achievement in science.* Invercargill, NZ: Essential Resources.

Martinez-Castilla, P., Rodriguez, M. & Campos, R. (2016). Developmental trajectories of pitch-related music skills in children with Williams syndrome, *Research in Developmental Disabilities, 51–52*, 23–39.

Meadan, H., Angell, M., Stoner, J., & Daczewitz, M. (2014). Parent-implemented social–pragmatic communication intervention, *Focus on Autism and Other Developmental Disabilities, 29*(2), 95–110.

Meiers, M. (2004). *Managing longitudinal research: An account of the first six years of the longitudinal literacy and numeracy study.* Paper presented at the Australian Association for Research in Education Conference, Melbourne, VIC. November.

Meltzer, L. (2014). Teaching executive functioning process: Promoting metacognition, strategy use, and effort. In Goldstein, S. & Naglieri, J. (Eds.), *Handbook of Executive Functioning.* New York, NY: Springer-Verlag, 445–473.

Mitchell, D. (2014). *What really works in special and inclusive education: Using evidence-based teaching strategies* (2nd Ed.). London: Routledge.

Moats, L. (2009). Knowledge foundations for teaching reading and spelling. *Reading and Writing, 22*(4), 379–399.

Monsen, J. (2008). The Monsen et al. problem solving model ten years on. In Kelly, B., Woolfson, L., & Boyle, J. (Eds.), *Frameworks for practice in educational psychology: A textbook for trainees and practitioners.* London: Jessica Kingsley.

Mooney, M., Dobia, B., Barker, K., Power, A., & Watson, K. (2008). Positive behaviour for learning: Investigating the transfer of a United States system into the NSW Department of Education and Training Western Sydney Region schools. *Curriculum Leadership Journal, 6*(20), 17–33.

Naglieri, J. & Das, J. (2005). Planning, attention, simultaneous, successive (PASS) theory: A revision of the concept of intelligence. In Flanagan, D. & Harrison, P. (Eds.), *Contemporary intellectual assessment: Theories, tests, and issues.* New York, NY: Guilford Press, 120–135.

Naglieri, J. & Pickering, E. (2010). *Helping children learn: Intervention handouts for use in school and at home* (2nd Ed.). Baltimore, MA: Paul H Brookes.

National Reading Panel (2000). *Teaching children to read: An evidence-based assessment of the scientific research literature on reading and its implications for reading instruction.* Washington, DC: National Institute of Child Health and Human Development.

Neil, A. & Christensen, H. (2009). Efficacy and effectiveness of school-based prevention and early intervention programs for anxiety, *Clinical Psychology Review, 29*(3), 208–215.

Parrila, R., McQuarrie, L., Klassen, R., Georgiou, G., & Odishaw, J. (2010). *Effective interventions for adolescent struggling readers: A research review with implications for practice.* Edmonton, Canada: J. P. Das Centre, University of Alberta.

Pegg, J. & Graham, L. (2013). A three-level intervention pedagogy to enhance the academic achievement of Indigenous students: Evidence from *QuickSmart* Mathematics research relevant to Indigenous populations: Evidence-based practice. In Jorgenson, R., Sullivan, P., & Grootenboer, P. (Eds.), *Pedagogies to enhance learning for Indigenous students.* Singapore: Springer, 123–138.

Peters, K. (2017). Considering the classroom: Educational access for children fitted with hearing assistive technology. *Audiology Today, 29*(1), 20–30.

Phillips, M. (2014). Children and young people with refugee backgrounds: Their experiences of change, loss and grief and the Seasons for Growth program. *Grief Matters: Australian Journal of Grief and Bereavement, 17*(3), 80–84.

Punch, R. (2015). Use and efficacy of paraprofessionals in special education. An internal report commissioned by the Program for Students with Disabilities Review Unit, Department of Education and Training, Victoria, Australia. www.education.vic.gov.au/Documents/about/department/psdlitreview_IntegrationAides.pdf

Reynolds, M. & Wheldall, K. (2007). Reading Recovery 20 years down the track: Looking forward, looking back. *International Journal of Disability, Development and Education, 54*(2), 199–223.

Reynolds, M., Wheldall, K., & Madelaine, A. (2007). Meeting initial needs in literacy (MiniLit): Why we need it, how it works, and the results of pilot studies. *Australasian Journal of Special Education, 31*(2), 147–158.

Richmond, C. (2007). *Teach more, manage less: A minimalist approach to behaviour management.* Lindfield, NSW: Scholastic Australia.

Riley, A. (2012). Exploring the effects of the 'Seasons for Growth' intervention for pupils experiencing change and loss. *Educational & Child Psychology, 29*(3), 38–53.

Roberts, M. & Kaiser, M. (2011). The effectiveness of parent-implemented language interventions: A meta-analysis. *American Journal of Speech-Language Pathology, 20*, 180–199.

Robinson, V. (1993). A problem-analysis approach to decision-making and reporting for complex cases. *Journal of the New Zealand Psychological Service Association, 8*, 35–48.

Rubie-Davies, C. M., Blatchford, P., Webster, R., Koutsoubou, M., & Bassett, P. (2010). Enhancing learning? A comparison of teacher and teaching assistant interactions with pupils. *School Effectiveness and School Improvement, 21*(4), 429–449.

Savage, C., Lewis, J., & Colless, N. (2011). Essentials for implementation: Six years of school wide positive behaviour support in New Zealand. *New Zealand Journal of Psychology, 40*(1), 29–37.

Savage, C., Macfarlane, A., Macfarlane, S., Fickel, L., & Te Hemi, H. (2012). Huakina Mai: A whole school strength based behavioural intervention for Maori. Christchurch, NZ: Te Tapuae o Rehua.

Schwartz, R., Hobsbaum, A., Briggs, C., & Scull, J. (2009). Reading Recovery and Evidence-based Practice: A response to Reynolds and Wheldall (2007). *International Journal of Disability, Development and Education, 56*(1), 5–15, DOI: 10.1080/10349120802681564

Scruggs, T. E. (2012). Differential facilitation of learning outcomes: What does it tell us about learning disabilities and instructional programming? *International Journal for Research in Learning Disabilities, 1*(1), 4–20.

Shaddock, A., Giorcelli, L., & Smith, S. (2007). *Students with disabilities in mainstream classrooms: A resource for teachers.* Canberra, ACT: Commonwealth of Australia.

Slavin, R. (2015). Cooperative learning in elementary schools. *Education 3–13, 43*(1), 5–14, DOI: 10.1080/03004279.2015.963370

Snyder, I. (2008). *The literacy wars: Why teaching children to read and write is a battleground in Australia.* Sydney, NSW: Allen & Unwin.

Stålnea, K., Kjellströmb, S., & Utriainenc, J. (2016). Assessing complexity in learning outcomes – a comparison between the SOLO taxonomy and the model of hierarchical complexity. *Assessment & Evaluation in Higher Education, 41*(7), 1033–1048, http://dx.doi.org/10.1080/02602938.2015.1047319

Steenbergen-Hu, S., Makel, M. C., & Olszewski-Kubilius, P. (2016). What one hundred years of research says about the effects of ability grouping and acceleration on K–12 students' academic achievement: Findings of two second-order meta-analyses. *Review of Educational Research, 86*(4), 849–899.

Sugai, G. & Horner, R. (2002). The evolution of discipline practices: School-wide positive behavior supports. *Child and Family Behavior Therapy, 24*(1–2), 23–50.

Suskind, D., Leffel, K., Graf, E., Hernandez, M., Gunderson, E., Sapolich, S., et al. (2016). A parent-directed language intervention for children of low socioeconomic status: A randomized controlled pilot study. *Journal of Child Language, 43*(2), 366–406. doi:10.1017/S0305000915000033

Swanson, L., Harris, K., & Graham, S. (Eds.). (2003). *Handbook of learning disabilities.* New York, NY: Guilford Press.

Taconis, R. (2013). Problem solving. In Hattie, J. & Anderman, E. (Eds.), *International guide to student achievement.* New York, NY: Routledge, 379–381.

Thomas, A. R. & Lewis, R. (2010). *Evaluation of the QuickSmart program in the New England Region.* Armidale, NSW: University of New England.

Thomas, M., Annaz, D., Ansari, D., Scerif, G, Jarrold, C., & Karmiloff-Smith, A. (2009). Using developmental trajectories to understand developmental disorders. *Journal of Speech, Language and Hearing Research, 52*, 336–358.

Torgesen, J. K. (2002). The prevention of reading difficulties. *Journal of School Psychology, 40*(1), 7–26.

Townend, G. & Brown, R. (2016). Exploring a sociocultural approach to understanding academic self-concept in twice-exceptional students. *International Journal of Educational Research, 80*, 15–24.

Tunmer, W. & Arrow, A. (2013). Reading: Phonics instruction. In Hattie, J. & Anderman, E. (Eds.), *International guide to student achievement.* New York, NY: Routledge, 316–319.

Walker, V. L., Chung, Y. C., & Bonnet, L. K. (2016). Function-based intervention in inclusive school settings: A meta-analysis. *Journal of Positive Behavior Interventions,* DOI:1098300717718350.

Wang, C. W. & Neihart, M. (2015). Academic self-concept and academic self-efficacy: Self-beliefs enable academic achievement of twice-exceptional students. *Roeper Review, 37*(2), 63–73.

Wang, C., Ho, H., & Cheng, Y. (2015). Building a learning progression for scientific imagination: A measurement approach. *Thinking Skills and Creativity, 17*, 1–14.

Wanzek, J., Vaughn, S., Scammacca, N. K., Metz, K., Murray, C. S., Roberts, G., & Danielson, L. (2013). Extensive reading interventions for students with reading difficulties after grade 3. *Review of Educational Research, 83*(2), 163–195.

Webster, R., Blatchford, P., Bassett, P., Brown, P., Martin, C., & Russell, A. (2011). The wider pedagogical role of teaching assistants. *School Leadership & Management, 31*(1), 3–20, http://dx.doi.org/10.1080/13632434.2010.540562

Webster, R., Blatchford, P., & Russell, A. (2013). Challenging and changing how schools use teaching assistants: Findings from the Effective Deployment of Teaching Assistants project,. *School Leadership and Management, 33*(1) 78–96.

Wheldall, K. & Wheldall, R. (2014). The story of MultiLit: Effective instruction for low-progress readers. *Perspectives on Language and Literacy, 40*(3), 32.

Wilson, A., Jesson, R. & McNaughton, S. (2013). Reading: Vocabulary programs. In Hattie, J. & Anderman, E. (Eds.), *International guide to student achievement.* New York, NY: Routledge, 332–334.

Wolf, M., Barzillai, M., Gottwald, S., Miller, L., Spencer, K., Norton, E., et al. (2009). The RAVE-O intervention: Connecting neuroscience to the classroom. *Mind, Brain and Education, 3*(2), 84–93.

Zapf, S., Scherer, M., Baxter, M., & Rintala, D. (2016). Validating a measure to assess factors that affect assistive technology use by students with disabilities in elementary and secondary education. *Disability and Rehabilitation: Assistive Technology, 11*(1), 38–49.

10

TEACHING STRATEGIES

There is no guarantee that learning opportunities will produce learning: it takes a combination of skill and will, and the right balance of teaching and learning strategies, for that to happen. In this chapter, we turn to what happens within teaching–learning interactions, specifically what it is that teachers do that activates learning when mediating learning opportunities. Anybody can interact with learners while they are engaged in learning tasks, and many people do, but it is strategic teaching actions that make the difference to learning for many students. Through strategic intentional engagement with learners, teachers can ensure that a learning opportunity becomes a learning experience. So, what do teachers do to make this happen? Teaching strategies are the actions of a teacher in responding to the engagement and activity of the learner. Together, the student's learning strategies and the teacher's instructional strategies become a dynamic set of interactions, some of which may be predictable, while others are spontaneous and unplanned. The responsiveness of teaching in matching the learning needs of the students is what makes the difference in effective teaching.

In order to meet the needs of the readers of this book – those who will be responsible for educational casework for students experiencing disabilities or learning difficulties – we will elaborate further here about the teaching strategies used in individual teaching. Not all educational casework, of course, will involve individual teaching; many learning needs can be better met in classroom settings or through small group instruction. However, it is not uncommon for students with learning difficulties or disabilities to experience short-term intervention that includes individual teaching: it is important that this precious time is used to best effect. The opportunity cost for learners is too great otherwise.

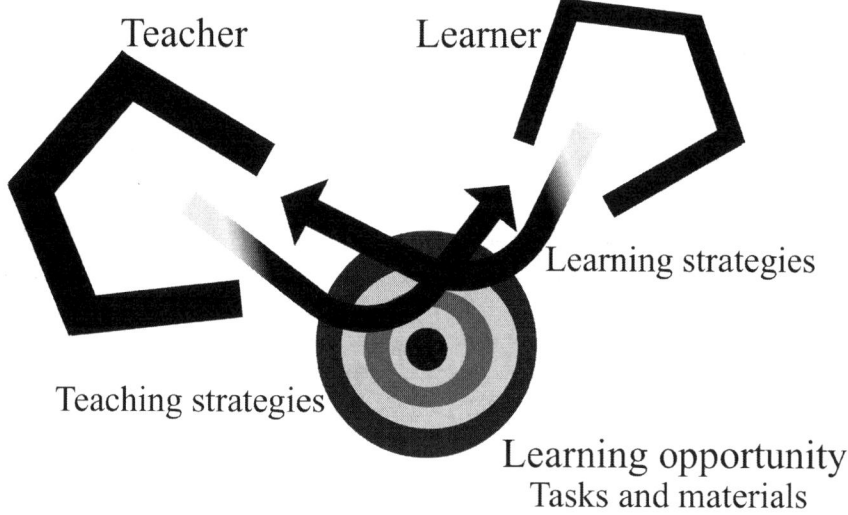

Teacher Learner

Learning strategies

Teaching strategies

Learning opportunity
Tasks and materials

FIGURE 10.1   Teacher–student interactions around a learning opportunity

Teaching strategies around learning opportunities

Every set of interactions between teacher and learner is a complex interplay between teaching strategies and learning strategies; between what the teacher does and says and what the student does and says. Teaching strategies are selected to activate learning strategies, and then are chosen again in response to the learning strategies that are evident. The teacher expertly interacts with the student with the aim of activating and maintaining learning, and in doing so reinforces strategies for learning.

All teaching uses representations of information as the focus of the teaching–learning interaction. This information is shared through talking, written text, illustrations or concrete materials. In individual teaching there is a clear set-up for the interactions, as shown in Figure 10.1, which is an elaboration of Figure 1.7.

In individual teaching, the teacher presents a learning opportunity and then interacts with the learner who engages with the activity. In an individual intervention session the teacher is able to provide immediate responses without interruption. This concentrated and uninterrupted set of interactions allows for a connected, coherent, continuing dialogue focused on learning that is not always possible in group learning situations. In a classroom, the dialogue between teacher and learners is mostly fragmented, as the teacher moves around multiple learners, the teacher is, through necessity, less responsive to individual learners.

Focus on teaching–learning relationships and interactions allows us to pull apart what it is that expert teachers do and say to activate and facilitate learning. Focusing on a single relationship is artificial in a way, but it reduces the complexity that is inherent in a teacher's relationship with a group of learners and lets us explore what is happening in detail.

Evidence base for effective teaching strategies

There is much research about effective teaching strategies from which to draw insights. Often these strategies are mixed up with the processes of designing or selecting learning opportunities. For example, cooperative learning and reciprocal teaching are both included as teaching strategies in many texts though students take the lead in these approaches. Similarly, summaries of research routinely include a mixture of learning opportunities and teaching strategies in their analyses. However, having addressed learning opportunities in the previous chapter, our focus in this chapter is firmly upon teaching strategies

Mitchell (2014) has organised a discussion of evidence-based *teaching strategies* that support inclusive classroom teachers and special educators, with the caveat that these strategies are separated for the purposes of research and interpretation but in reality are usually combined in some ways. This stance reminds us of the artificial nature of certain types of research that try to understand mechanisms of teaching and learning, and, conversely, the process that teachers follow when they take the findings of such studies and put them into the reality of everyday teaching and learning interactions.

Mitchell has included many aspects of designing instruction or learning opportunities in his analysis and has also included the specific actions of teachers, or teaching strategies. A simple organisation of Mitchell's evidence-based teaching strategies plotted against family and community, learning environment, learning opportunities and teaching strategies is shown in Figure 10.2. It is not possible to map across the categories of this framework exactly, since there is definitional blurring for many of entries, but the resulting figure unpacks important features of key teaching strategies and where they are broadly applicable.

Hattie's (2009, 2011, 2015) meta-analyses of influences on student achievement also include factors relevant to the many layers of the ecology of schools and classrooms, family and community, learning environment, as well as learning opportunities and teaching strategies. However, since describing expert teachers as having "elevated sensitivity to the academic learning needs" of students (Hattie & Yates, 2014, p.109), the focus of Hattie's analyses has turned increasingly to teacher expertise. There are strong themes in this evidence that support the framework provided in this chapter, about what it is that teachers do to greatest effect. These are brought together into Figure 10.3. This figure organises influences with at least a 0.6 effect size (Hattie, 2009, 2011, 2015, 2017). We have excluded consideration of the two outer layers of the ecological model in this representation, instead zooming in to the factors that are related to teacher expertise. There is overflow from teaching strategies into learning opportunities in this organisation, and we emphasise that it is not useful to see these categories as mutually exclusive, but instead to explore how they work together to provide instances of effective teaching.

These two bodies of evidence arranged in Figures 10.2 and 10.3 highlight two important dimensions of teaching. The first dimension is teacher expertise in knowing about conceptual learning, pathways for cognitive development and how to teach for continuing learning. The second is the embedding of assessment in instructional decision-making as the basis for both teacher and learner

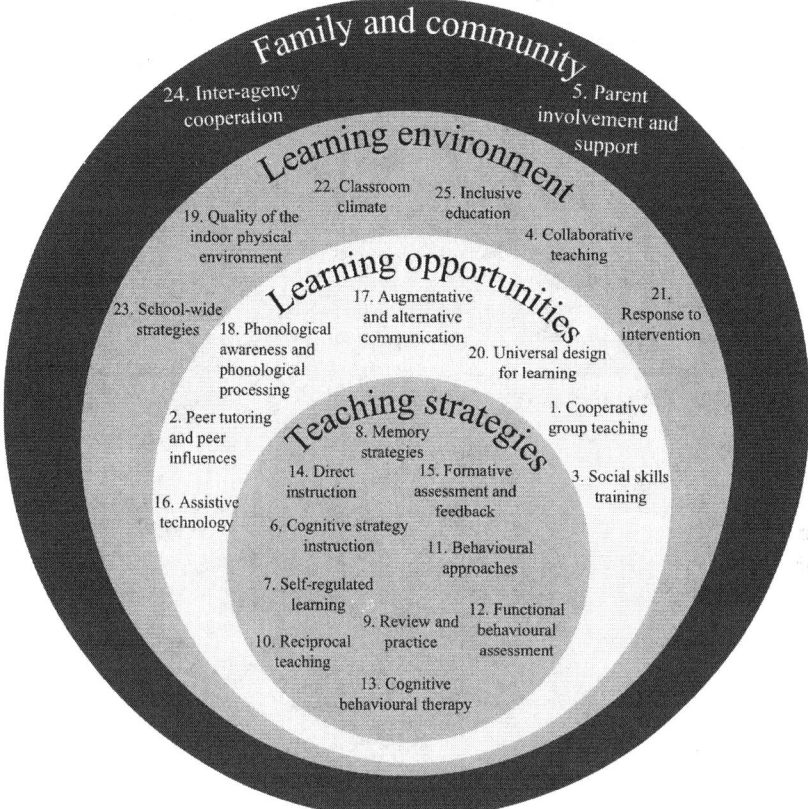

FIGURE 10.2 Evidence-based teaching strategies for inclusive and special education
Source: Authors' image; Mitchell, 2014.

to work jointly towards shared goals. In addition, research into explicit teaching, often for students with learning difficulties, has contributed to our knowledge about what factors within teaching interactions have the greatest impact on student learning. Liem and Martin's (2013) summary of teaching strategies for direct instruction contributes to this consideration of what it is that effective teachers do in teaching–learning interactions, and reflects much of what is also prominent in Hattie's work:

- the goal of learning is shared and there is optimism about learning, with the student seeing the task as achievable;
- teaching is carefully prepared, sequenced and thought-out;
- questions are posed and processes and strategies are modelled;
- there are opportunities to deliberately and purposefully practice skills and knowledge; and
- learning is continually assessed within the activity, and feedback is provided to the student.

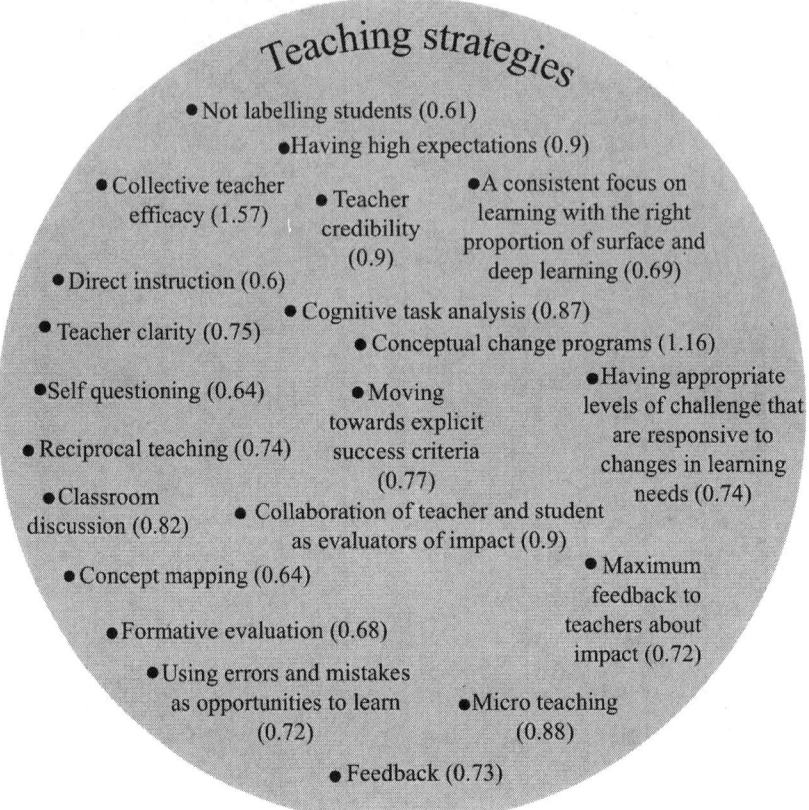

FIGURE 10.3 Effect sizes (> 0.6) for teaching strategies

Source: Authors' image; Hattie, 2009, 2011, 2015, 2017.

It is imperative to make sense of these frameworks and this evidence in considering what it is that teachers do to activate learning, particularly for students who are experiencing difficulties.

Deliberate actions of responsive teachers in intervention

Although teacher decision-making in interactions is often unconscious, it is useful to make it conscious and deliberate. This can be done through a meta-strategic approach that supports awareness and conscious deliberation about expertise in teaching interactions. Much is negotiated within the teacher–student relationship, where the teacher as the more competent other takes the lead in shaping the negotiation from that point of competence.

It is extremely difficult to script what goes on in an intervention session since everything teachers do in interaction with learners is also based on who they are and what direction the interaction takes. Our personalities as teachers come through, even when the same words and strategies are used. Teachers' choices of strategies are also affected by what they perceive the learner needs at any moment. Sometimes that perception is not conscious at the time, but is nevertheless influential. Keeping this in mind we explore teaching strategies in this chapter with a view to providing a framework against which each of us can reflect on and continue to develop our own skills as teachers.

The approach in this section is derived from very close examination of mediated learning (Feuerstein & Rand, 1974; Feuerstein & Feuerstein, 1991; Lidz, 2002) which has generated a bank of teaching strategies that work towards effective learning, guided by a focus on the whole learner and on developing processes of learning. The intent and reciprocity that is inherent in mediated learning deliberately provides opportunities for the learner to take increasing responsibility for initiating interactions and for learning. There is evidence that mediation using this model produces "higher levels of functioning in learning, differentiate[s] responsiveness of learners to intervention and connect[s] assessment with instruction" (Lidz, 2002, p.82) since the intent is to find meaning and to extend that meaning to contexts outside those in the initial interactions and thus make learning transferable. There is a clear intent for teaching and learning interactions to produce meaningful higher-order learning useful to the learner in contexts other than the session. Features of skilful mediation include:

1   Setting and maintaining expectations about the intention of the intervention.
2   Establishing expectations of sharing that will be needed to reveal the unique differences of the learner and make learning explicit or evident.
3   Defining goals for learning and processes for noticing growth and change through learning.
4   Explicitly tuning into current competence as well as providing challenge for developing competence.
5   Interpreting and sharing meaning.
6   Highlighting the relevance of the learning for other times and in other situations (particularly for learning in the classroom).
7   Developing consciousness and self-regulation of thinking and behaviour in learning.

These seven deliberate actions of responsive teachers (DARTs) are based on the key dimensions of effective mediated learning (Skuy, 1997). Further, they align with evidence-based teaching strategies for inclusive and special education (Mitchell, 2014), as well as with high impact aspects of teacher expertise (Hattie, 2017), and with teaching strategies derived from direct instruction (Liem & Martin, 2013). These actions are described in more detail in the remainder of this chapter.

1.   *Setting and maintaining expectations about the intention of the intervention*

The impact of intervention will depend not only on the efficacy of the learning opportunities and the teaching strategies employed but also on the expectations of the learner in relation to learning. Therefore, it is important to consider how the intervention is framed, and to establish expectations and a shared understanding of the purpose of the sessions, to secure the foundation for the active participation of the learner.

Every learning opportunity designed for learning intervention includes instructions that are related to the intent of the teaching. It is important to establish expectations around each activity and the anticipated learning. Instructions can be given in many different ways – verbally or in writing, or through demonstration. It is important to check that the instructions have been understood and that the learner knows what to do. There are many ways to confirm this including asking, for example, "Do you know what you need to do?" However, such questions that can be easily answered in the affirmative even if the student does not understand. Effective interventionists need to also pick up other cues about whether a learner understands the expectations of a task well enough to get the most out of it.

In situations when it is clear the student does not understand the requirements, it is important to use increasingly intensive strategies to achieve that understanding. Depending on what was hypothesised as blocking the understanding of instructions, the strategy may be to repeat the instructions, based on the premise that they were not heard, or they were partially heard or attended to; to paraphrase the instructions, if language was seen to be the barrier; or to elaborate if there seems to be a need for further information or more finely grained explanation. Elaboration could also include gesture, demonstration, sketching or some other representation to support the language-based instructions.

Teaching and learning in all intervention depends on the relationship between the teacher and the learner. Proficiency in the ATRiUM capability of relating to others (R) is necessary for both the teacher and the learner to establish a positive teacher–student relationship – one of the high ranking factors of academic achievement in Hattie's synthesis of meta-analyses (2009, 2015). An individual intervention that involves a series of one-to-one sessions depends profoundly on this relationship. In contrast to the teacher–student relationship in a class, in which there is one teacher and many students, intervention is a highly concentrated teacher–student relationship, that requires more contribution from the student and a reciprocity of interactions (Feuerstein & Feuerstein, 1991; Lidz, 2002).

The situation requires a clear explanation of the teacher's credibility and responsibility as well as the reason that the student is participating in individual intervention. In the words of the Responsive Teaching Framework, this is about what the teacher brings (RTF 2) to the relationship and also what the student brings (RTF 3). Many teachers in this situation use euphemisms for describing what is intended, when in fact it is vital to frame this in the best possible way to support engagement of the student in the process. This first deliberate action of teachers in learning intervention is the basis of shared intention between teacher and student and is foundational for all other actions.

2. *Establishing expectations of sharing that will be needed to reveal the unique differences of the learner and make the learning visible*

This second deliberate action of teachers builds on the previous one, and focuses on the responsibilities of both the teacher and learner. Traditionally teaching is a mixture of teachers telling and then questioning, or demonstrating and asking students to do the same thing. Teachers tell students something presumed to be new and then question them to see if they can repeat or retell it. The students' response is then used as evidence of learning. Teachers also model or demonstrate a particular skill and then ask students to demonstrate that they can do it too. While there are still parts of teaching and learning that are reliant on telling and questioning, we now understand teaching and learning to be much more sophisticated, and need to explore teaching strategies in more breadth and depth. For example, good teachers are experts at using the language of telling, and they are also expert at knowing when *not* to tell, but to ask or guide instead. In each of these following sections, we will position the notion of telling at one end and less direct options along a continuum towards the other end. *Telling* represents directive strategies, teacher control, teacher responsibility and explicitness. Moving towards the other end increases examples and episodes of student contribution and active learning.

Consideration of what is known about engaging young people in therapeutic relationships in psychological practice can inform our roles in establishing and maintaining good teacher–student relationships. In therapeutic counselling the aim is to build a therapeutic alliance within which trust and freedom to be honest and open are integral, so that the client is receptive and responsive to therapy. The focus of the therapy, or intervention, is often extremely sensitive and compounded by the ways the young person has previously managed difficult situations, often coloured by a string of failures and frustrating experiences in relationships and reactions to their emotional responses to the world.

Similarly, many students who find themselves in individual learning intervention are discouraged learners who have experienced considerable failures and frustrations and may believe they are not good at learning. Many of them have well-developed strategies for avoiding engagement with learning in order to protect themselves from the anticipated failures. Many of these strategies are unconscious and expert and will continue to be default responses to learning activities and to teachers putting the spotlight on their capabilities. In an individual intervention there is only one spotlight and it is consistently on one learner: there are no shadows in which to hide. This situation will create considerable stress for some learners and needs to be acknowledged as an important aspect of the intervention.

There are parallels in individual educational intervention not only with regard to the aspects of reluctance and discouragement that the learner brings into the relationship, but also in what the teacher does to establish relationships that encourage growth and transformation. In both situations, trust needs to be established; otherwise learners will put effort into protecting themselves from exposure or threat, rather than into partnering for change and achievement. It is important for the learner to perceive the teacher as credible, which involves a mix of not only trust, but also competence, dynamism and immediacy (Hattie, 2016).

In contemporary education the balance is tipped somewhat so that teachers and learners share responsibility for being active in learning situations. Effective teachers know when to direct and when to share that direction with the learner, so that over time the learner becomes self-regulated and seeks learning rather than being a passive recipient of teaching. A useful way to think about the sharing of control throughout an intervention session is as a see-saw of active and passive engagement by both teacher and learner. At one end is the expert teacher who knows and can do what is being taught and does so as part of the teaching. At the other end is the learner who has an opportunity to demonstrate what is known and what can be done at the prompting of the teacher. In the middle is where the learning happens; in the partnership between teacher and learner, with as much or as little support or guidance as is needed to achieve learning tasks. There is room for student voice and for negotiated learning experiences in such intervention sessions.

In contrast to the linear model of graduated release of responsibility (I do, we do, you do; Fisher & Frey, 2008) that was developed for classroom teaching, the reality is that teaching and learning in intervention is a see-sawing of responsibility and activity between teacher and student, with joint responsibility along the way. It is *I do, you do, we do, I do, we do, you do, we do,* and so on, in whatever order is most appropriate to respond to learning needs at the time. Effective teachers know how much assistance or contribution to provide, so that the learner is supported to take increasing responsibility and to demonstrate learning independently.

There is an inherent authority in the teacher role that needs to be managed carefully in individualised instruction. Power in relationships can be useful but can also be oppressive. Effective learning intervention teachers get the balance right to allow the learner room to take responsibility, while at the same time using expertise to shape the session most effectively. Teaching aims to empower learners. This is a complex notion that has to be negotiated and renegotiated and balanced throughout learning.

Relating to others in individualised intervention is facilitated by the use of the social tools of language, both verbal and non-verbal. Language and other symbol systems are the vehicles for teaching in the social plane and for learning in the individual plane. This means that not only are we using language as the social mechanism for the intervention session, but also as the means of transforming cognition within the learner. Learning intervention depends on the use of appropriate language and symbol systems to support learning. It is vital that the teacher is able to determine when such tools of learning are in themselves becoming barriers to learning and teaching and is able to adapt them to make the teaching and learning flow.

Thinking is the hidden capability that needs to become more visible during individualised instruction, so that the teacher has a good idea of what is happening on the learner's individual plane and can build on it with the next teaching strategy. Thinking also needs to be visible to the learner as the basis of metacognitive development. Thinking is accessed through the language and actions of the learner and interpreted by the teacher. Thinking out loud by both the teacher and learner are often part of effective learning intervention sessions. It is possible in individualised intervention to be very flexible in offering opportunities to think out loud and to try things with immediate feedback from the teacher. In classes or groups the teacher is not as available to provide immediate feedback or assist with the outcome of the activity if it was not as expected.

Effective learning intervention, in the simplest of terms, is about passing responsibility from the teacher to the learner, so that the learner becomes increasingly self-regulated and sustaining. This can be thought of in terms of passing the baton between teacher and learner within each learning activity, as well as in the longer term having the baton totally in the learner's control.

At times learners need only vague direction, cues and prompts, while at other times they need very direct, explicit teaching strategies. Teachers and learners have their own responsibilities within their relationship and in the activity of each learning opportunity. These responsibilities vary depending on the nature of the learning opportunity and the learning needs of the student. Effective teachers can judge how much learner responsibility is most effective at any particular time and vary it accordingly. Effective teachers also vary this in order to assess the effect of the teaching by letting the learner demonstrate what has been learnt.

In individual learning intervention the responsibility in teaching and learning needs to be renegotiated in a complicated context. For many students there is a context of academic failure, and along with the experience of unsuccessful learning is a history of unsuccessful negotiations of responsibility for learning. An outcome can be that many students have a sense that they are not able to be responsible in any way for their learning: they are hopeless and helpless. They have not been able to take advantage of the teaching offered in a successful way, and they have not been able to alter the teaching offered to make learning more successful. They have been doubly disempowered and present as discouraged learners who have expectations about the responsibility for learning that need to be reshaped to make them open to learning and growth.

3. Defining goals for learning and processes for noticing growth and monitoring learning

The third deliberate action of teachers is a more explicit articulation of goals for the intended learning and the setting up of processes and expectations around how both the teacher and learner will know when it has happened. This is usually accomplished through the use of intended learning outcomes (ILOs). The most important aspect of ILOs is that there is a shared understanding of what is being targeted and that everyone involved is actually talking about and intervening for the same thing. If there is agreement about this, then effort is aligned towards the same outcome. However, this is easier said than done.

Different systems require the definition of ILOs or goals in particular ways, and there are a number of scaffolds that learning intervention professionals can use for this task. The generic one is captured by the mnemonic SMART, but there are variations within this acronym. Mostly the 'T' refers to 'time', but in the context of routines-based assessment (McWilliam, Casey & Sims, 2009) in early childhood intervention, the 'T' stands for 'tied to routines' (Jung, 2007).

Much framing about SMART goals is focused on objectively measuring the intended outcome. This emphasis has grown out of behavioural psychology and psychometrics, and aims to make the process reliable, so that there is a clear understanding of what is being taught and how everyone will know that it has been learnt. Another version of SMART goals from the European practice of educational psychology includes an 'I' for 'inspiring'. This inclusion recognises the importance of the motivational factors involved in learning intervention. The third version originates from Vygotskian-based Mediated Learning Experiences (Skuy, 1997), which includes joint (teacher and student) goal setting as an integral part of the intervention. These three versions are summarised in Table 10.1.

The SMART and SMARTI goals are defined by learning intervention professionals' need to measure the outcomes, and are thus anchored in behaviourist learning theory. In contrast, the ML goals are designed to be engaged within a teaching–learning relationship and emphasise the learner increasingly taking the initiative, in collaboration with the teacher, and working towards accomplishing the goals.

We add a new dimension to this process of goal definition in Table 10.1 by making explicit the intention to activate learning that is *sustainable*, by which we mean learning that can be transferred to new situations and will be maintained over time (see Chapter 1). These two constructs, transfer and maintenance, are derived from special education and behavioural psychology, and are critical to ensuring learning intervention makes a difference that is relevant and that lasts.

Sometimes ILOs are explicitly written with a specific type of assessment in mind, usually a criterion referenced test that has shown gaps that are the target of the intervention, or which provides a progression that explicitly defines the next learning outcome. For example, the Six Tasks of Place Value (SToPV) (Berman,

TABLE 10.1 Goals of learning intervention

SMART goals	SMARTI goals Pameijer (2016)	Mediated Learning (ML) goals Skuy (1997)
Specific or strategic	Specific	Conceivable
Measurable	Measurable	Believable
Attainable or Achievable	Ambitious	Achievable
Relevant	Realistic	Modifiable
Time-bound or Time-based or	Time-bound	Desirable
Tied to routines Sustainable	Inspiring	Growth facilitating

2011) assess conceptual understanding of the place value of two digit numbers. This knowledge is fundamental to further learning in mathematics. Based on cognitive research into children's development of understanding of place value, this task-based interview focuses on key concepts that need to be established. The student needs to demonstrate understanding of how numbers are broken into parts that together create the whole and that this is consistently represented in the order of written digits. As well, understanding of the role of 0 (zero) needs to be established. Three tasks that assess this understanding are shown in Table 10.2, along with levels of response that represent the learning progression within this domain of learning.

These conceptual understandings go together with skills in counting by tens, and in writing and reading multi-digit numbers, which are the basis of the other three tasks in this short assessment. Students who have established understanding of place value will provide highest level responses for all tasks. Otherwise, the student may still be constructing that understanding (some partially successful responses) or be still in an emergent stage of learning (indicated through some lowest level responses).

The evidence-based learning progression in this domain of conceptual under-standing is built into the assessment activity and summarised in the profile of levels of response. It is possible to place a student within this learning progression and

TABLE 10.2 Intended learning outcomes (**bold**) for Tasks 1, 2 and 4 within the SToPV

Part-whole representation of two digit numbers	*Unsuccessful response*	*Partially successful response*	**Highest level of response**
Task 1 Using base ten blocks to construct 52 and explaining tens and ones in reference to the blocks	The student could not make 52 using tens and one blocks (there are not enough ones to use these to complete the task)	The student constructed the number but did not provide a correct explanation.	**The student created 52 using base ten blocks and explained the tens and ones in the representation**
Task 2 With irregular grouping of counters for 26	The student refers only to the whole number, or does not know what it means at all.	The student provides an explanation referring to twenty and six, or referring to the six groupings of four and two left over.	**The student's explanation matches the two digits (26) with tens and ones**
Task 4 With 0 (zero) in the tens column (e.g., 05)	The student says the number is 50 or doesn't know what number it is.	The student states that the number is not 50 but is not sure what it is.	**The student explains that the number is five, and the zero is holding a place for the tens.**

Source: Berman, 2011.

TABLE 10.3 Matrix for analysis of factors supporting and hindering learning

Description of what the student brings to their learning or a characteristic of the learning environment	Explanation of how it is supporting learning (wrt ATRiUM)	Explanation of how it is hindering learning (wrt ATRiUM)	Evidence – how do you know this?	Generation of implications for intervention
A				
T				
R				
iU				
M				

Note
wrt   *with reference to*

then teach towards the higher-level responses that are already explicitly written intended learning outcomes. In this assessment it is possible to use other numbers to assess the same understanding incidentally or formally as is appropriate, until the student consistently demonstrates established understanding. In this example of intervention there is also embedded monitoring based on the explicit learning progression. Some packaged intervention programs provide prepared monitoring sheets that allow both student and teacher to notice growth in learning and per-formance. In other instances of intervention, it may be necessary to set up discrete processes for noticing growth and monitoring learning. Many teachers use simple checklists and observations as well as more structured tests or quizzes, as appropri-ate, to accomplish this monitoring.

Being explicit about what it is that is to be learnt can be done in a number of ways, but most importantly it needs to be aligned with the assessment used to determine whether the intended learning has been realised (that is, the baseline and outcomes assessment to be used). The matrix in Table 10.3 provides a scaffold for analysing assessment information in such a way that it is clear what is supporting and hindering learning and the implications for future intervention that flow from this understanding. This is done using ATRiUM as an organiser.

The next deliberate action builds on this one, by putting into action the pro-cesses of monitoring growth and learning. Explicitly tuning into current com-petence through the monitoring of learning extends this activity into providing opportunities for the demonstration of learning.

4. Explicitly tuning into current competence as well as providing challenge for developing competence

The fourth deliberate action of responsive teachers is to be conscious of actual competence in terms of skills and knowledge, as well as what an appropriate challenge in learning looks like. This is well defined through careful continuous assessment within the interactions. We refer to the zone of proximal development that is the basis of dynamic assessment (see Chapter 8). In this context, of responsive teaching, the ZPD is defined by current competence and supported competence and is fundamental to this deliberate action of teachers (Figure 10.4).

Based on this description of developing competence, the teacher can match teaching strategies with learning needs, affirming current competence and building on it by providing just enough challenge, and also appropriate opportunities within which learners can demonstrate supported competence. It is the student's ZPD that will change with any learning, and which constantly redefines what is to be learnt next. Within the ZPD there is constant exploration and strengthening of learning strategies that are being used to support learning. Students can be made aware of how their ZPDs are inferred and can become conscious of deliberately defining what it is they can do independently, what they can do with assistance, and how they are going to develop the next level of competence.

It is not uncommon for students to be able to do something with teacher assistance and then go away expecting to be able to do it alone. This does not always work, so it is important for teachers to be open about this experience and to frame learning developmentally, by making a distinction between what a student can do independently (*I can do this on my own*) and what can be done in collaboration (*I can do this with you*). This helps to provide a rational explanation for why learning is not always immediate, especially when the learning is focused on the development of complex conceptual or higher-order skills. It is useful for the learner to understand that it may take a few (or many) experiences of assisted competence before the knowledge or skill is internalised and becomes an independent achievement.

Supported competence (assisted achievement) is
demonstrated in a collaborative task

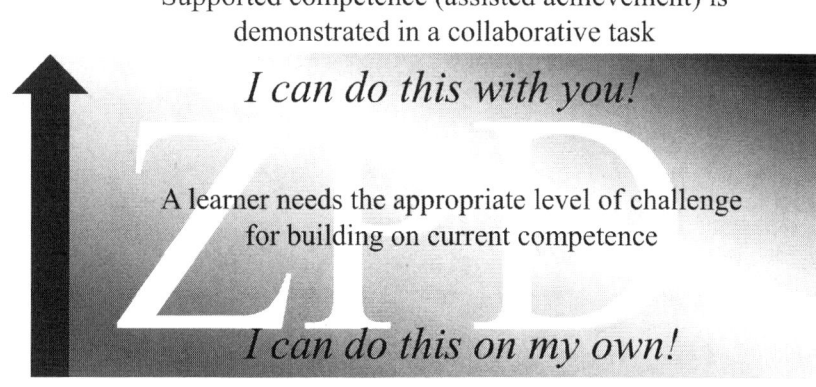

I can do this with you!

A learner needs the appropriate level of challenge
for building on current competence

I can do this on my own!

Current competence (actual achievement) is
demonstrated in an individual task

FIGURE 10.4 Zone of Proximal Development-defined current and developing competence

This focus on tuning into developing competence and learning as well as potential learning provides a new dimension to explicit teaching. Explicit teaching is generally thought of as explicitly teaching what is to be learnt, and ensuring that parts of it are not assumed but instead checking that all component skills are established or consolidated. We stress that as well as knowing the content well enough to explicitly teach it, responsive teachers need to know their learners well in order to explicitly match teaching strategies to learning needs. Thus, explicit teaching involves not only developmental knowledge of the content, but also developmental knowledge of how a learner responds to teaching.

Such explicit teaching also depends on constant observation, noticing learning and the strategies used by the learner through all responses to teaching. While effective teachers respond appropriately to both anticipated and unanticipated responses of the learner in such a way that the learning is optimised, less effective teachers may not notice when learning opportunities or the teaching strategies need to be altered in response to the learning needs of the moment. This lack of responsiveness can result in teaching things that are already known, or expecting further practice of skills that are established. Both situations can be demotivating to learners and make learning seem boring and irrelevant. It also means the time is wasted, when it could be used for teaching and learning.

It is important to keep in mind the feedback that is being provided every time the teacher makes a contribution to the teaching–learning session. Every teaching strategy, every interaction, will be received by the learner as feedback. Often without a word being spoken learners draw conclusions about their current competence based on the facial expressions, movements or pauses of the teacher. Every action and word needs to be carefully managed so that the student gets the appropriate feedback – feedback that supports learning.

5. Interpreting and sharing meaning in the teaching and learning

This fifth deliberate action of teachers is about generating meaning, both the conceptual understanding that underpins curriculum knowledge, and cultural meaning. Together, teachers and students are making and sharing the meaning of our world.

Teachers help develop the conceptual meaning of the content of learning opportunities by providing information and descriptions, explaining patterns, summarising and interpreting concepts. Teacher use of language to explain, describe, summarise or interpret is core teaching. In a classroom discussion or informal interactions in a class, the language will be selected to meet the group and individual learning needs as perceived by the teacher. In an individual learning intervention session, instead of using a wide range of levels of language as needed for a group, it is possible to more easily shape language to meet one learner's comprehension needs.

However, this can be problematic and needs to be carefully evaluated. It is possible to assume a particular level of language is appropriate, when in fact it is restricting and limiting. Effective learning intervention teachers need to constantly extend the level of language and test whether it is appropriate, providing higher levels whenever they might be relevant and pulling back if they do not work. This skill of constantly testing the understanding of the learner and providing the most appropriate level of language for instruction is important to effective learning intervention interactions.

Questioning is often presented as a separate skill for teachers. However, we include consideration of questioning in conjunction with guided and direct statements. Questions turn responsibility for meaning over to the student, and ask for their explanations, descriptions, summaries and interpretations. Questioning is used to check learning and to give opportunities for learners to voice their thinking, while serving as an opportunity for teachers to model thinking. A useful way to think about questioning embedded in intervention interactions is along the continuum of directness.

Within questioning there is also a dimension of directness that needs to be used flexibly and responsively, from open questions to increasingly direct, focused questions. A fully open question is useful at times, while a partially open one, or a directly explicit question, may be more appropriate at other times. The expression of teacher expertise lies in increasing and reducing support as interactions progress, providing the most appropriate level of support at any time that will move the learning on, and providing questions that the student can respond to successfully and meaningfully. Questions should not be used as tests, or hurdles to jump, but instead as techniques to successfully share and extend meaning making.

During any set of interactions it is often appropriate to recall recently used ideas or actions, and link them to what is being focused on at the time. This is in addition to considerations of prior learning that may have happened in designing the activities or in setting expectations for the session. It is reflected in this script: "Remember when we practised the use of …, now we are going to use those in problems." Using such strategies allows the student to be shown explicitly how experiences are linked.

Connecting knowledge, actions and ideas is a vitally important part of learning, and thus of teaching. The SOLO taxonomy assists in making sense of this strategy to assist in making connections or relations. SOLO clearly shows the progression from building a bank of knowledge (quantity of knowledge) and then making relations (quality of understanding). Some learners are very quick to see connections, while many of the learners with whom learning intervention teachers work find this difficult, or make connections in different ways that do not necessarily align with the connections anticipated by the curriculum or their teachers. Explicitly noticing, talking about and emphasising connections is a central part of learning intervention.

The second crucial aspect of meaning making in teaching and learning has been explored through the lenses of culture, with the understanding that teachers need to make connections with students within the context within which they are teaching (Gay, 2013). Culturally responsive teaching (Gay, 2010), culturally relevant pedagogy (Ladson-Billings, 1995, 2014), culturally sustaining pedagogy (Paris, 2012) and culturally responsive special education practice (Macfarlane & Macfarlane, 2013) emphasise this dimension of meaning. This aspect of learning is especially important for students who are not of the culture of the system within which they are attending school, particularly when they are involuntary minorities, including Indigenous students in historically colonised countries.

Effective individualised teaching creatively uses different ideas or 'ways in' to teaching when it is clear the current approach is not as effective as anticipated. This is particularly important when dealing with the development of conceptual understanding and higher-order thinking when it may take considerable effort on the part of the learner to grasp a construct. Some intervention programs have readily prepared pathways to particular learning, based on what works for many learners. However, these pathways may not work for all students, so a teacher needs to be creative in trying alternative ways to reach the same outcome. Metaphors are often used in this situation, drawing on familiar ideas and contexts to introduce the power of new ideas. Generating multiple ideas through brainstorming and then evaluation and elimination is another way to reach a particular idea. Teachers sometimes provide a really wrong or silly idea or solution as a contrast to the intended idea. Learners then discount that idea and have a basis from which to generate other more reasonable ideas to be considered. All of these strategies are drawn on as appropriate to enhance meaning.

In the context of individualised instruction, aligning appropriate representations with what is known about a particular learner is easier in individual intervention than for a class. It may be necessary to have a few different representations available initially and then to use the preferred ones. But it is also important to extend a student's ability to engage with teaching strategies particularly those more readily available in the classroom. This is also an issue when one particular representation of an idea does not seem to be accessible and an alternative needs to be tried. This happens often when something is being explained but does not seem to be understood. To complement the explanation (linguistic representation) effective teachers may make on-the-spot changes to representation by drawing sketches, arranging materials on the table or acting out ideas. These complement the linguistic representation and can be used as alternatives or to scaffold access to the linguistic representation, and then are faded as they are no longer needed.

It is also important to ensure any printed materials are the most accessible for the focus learner. This includes aspects such as font type and size, space between lines and words, the glossiness of paper, amount of information on the paper, lighting and distance from reader. Access to video information may be enhanced with captions and written information may need to be read by someone else, either onto audio files or by the teacher during the session.

The focus of this deliberate action of responsive teachers is the learning of knowledge and skills that have meaning in a student's life at the moment. This is extended to include meaning in the future and across relevant and potentially relevant contexts in the next deliberate action for teachers.

6. Highlighting the relevance of the learning for other times and in other situations (particularly for learning in the classroom)

The sixth deliberate action of responsive teachers extends the notion of meaning, with a focus on transfer of learning to other contexts. Within any individual intervention, it is important to constantly work towards the transfer of skills and knowledge into other learning situations, and to be explicit and transparent about that process. Being aware of the context within which particular skills or knowledge are to be used will guide this process. This is also a topic to be touched on often in interactions, since the aim of intervention is to explicitly teach strategies for transfer.

All learning needs to be linked to real life, away from the artificial setting within which it may best be taught. This needs to happen from the beginning of the intervention and continuing throughout. Transfer of skills into context is part of Stage 2 of the five stages of expertise in Dreyfus's model (Figure 9.1). This placement of context so early in skills development (advanced beginner) emphasises the importance of the built-in transfer of learning to support subsequent competence (Stage 3) and the planful use of skills, extending to increasingly nuanced situational discriminations with proficiency (Stage 4) and expertise (Stage 5). Similarly, considering knowledge transfer within SOLO learning cycles (see Chapter 9), confirms that it is essential to move from quantity of knowledge (multistructural) to linking knowledge to context and to other knowledge as soon as possible to make it useful (relational).

Using opportunities to focus on transfer should be an explicit part of teaching interactions that will vary in terms of intensity depending on the needs of the student at the time. Seeking the student's perceptions of how current learning links to what is already known helps set up an expectation that this learning is connected to other contexts. A more direct strategy takes the form of careful guiding to similar tasks or different contexts that can explicitly extend the learning within the session, and the provision of tasks or contexts designed for supported transfer and guided practice. This focus on transfer links with the notion of maintenance to represent sustainable learning that can be drawn upon as appropriate throughout life.

7. Developing consciousness and self-regulation of thinking and behaviour in learning

An underpinning goal of any teaching is to increase student consciousness of their own learning and to develop their nuanced self-management of thinking and behaviour so that learning is most effective and sustained. The final deliberate action of teachers is therefore to do with being aware of the learning and teaching as it happens so that the student can be encouraged to become increasingly self-regulated. This intention is explicitly embedded in responsive teaching for sustainable learning that focuses on the development of ATRiUM capabilities, one of which is managing self (M). Although knowing that you need assistance is central to managing self (M), seeking and accepting help are also skills within the capability of relating to others (R). Part of an intervention may need to focus on developing these skills so that the learner becomes more self-sufficient and able to contribute to the interactions in ways that assist the teacher to know how best to teach at any time.

This final action of teachers draws on all the others. It depends on setting expectations about the intention of the intervention, having a safe relationship within which the student is comfortable to share the ups and downs of learning, knowing the learning goals and being involved in noticing learning, and also noticing what it was about the teaching and use of learning strategies that supported learning, and what factors hindered learning. Some dimensions related to this development of self-management include self-regulation, planning, persistence, confidence, self-concept, self-efficacy and self-esteem, metacognition, and emotion and/or mood regulation (see Figure 7.2). Each of these constructs has a significant research evidence base that can inform teaching strategies.

Reflecting on learning and the evaluation of thinking and behaviour can be built into teaching–learning interactions at whatever intensity or directness is appropriate. As the aim of teaching is to pass responsibility to the learner, it is important to provide room for that responsibility to be taken up, but also to model and give the direction for this thinking task as needed. As a result teachers may use low intensity interactions to invite students to take responsibility for reflection and evaluation, such as: *Tell me about your thinking as you did that.*

Many students are not used to sharing their thinking and so may need some more encouragement and scaffolding. A teacher can model this process, and then ask the student to copy, or can use more direct or explicit questions, such as: *Why did you use six blocks for this number?* It is also appropriate to elaborate on partial reflections or evaluations, and thus provide a real life model of thinking out loud for a learner. For example, when a single word response is provided the teacher can extend it to become a whole phrase or sentence, so that the response describes more explicitly the thinking that has happened.

The focus of any individualised instruction is the learner, as it is the learner who is to have learning needs met and to be transformed. It is important for teachers to ensure their own needs are not driving the interactions, particularly in terms of needing to be *an expert*. Professional teachers need to ensure that these personal needs are not in play during intervention sessions, and that the primary purpose of passing responsibility for learning to the learner remains paramount. All of the previous deliberate actions of teachers lead to this one, as they have cumulatively revealed thinking and behaviour that has contributed to learning, and have strengthened aspects that have supported learning and reduced those that have hindered learning.

Summary

In this chapter we have considered the activity of teachers in mediating learning opportunities to activate learning and to support the development of capabilities for continued learning. We have used the context of a single teacher–student set of interactions around a learning opportunity – what happens in individual intervention sessions – in order to simplify the discussion. Focusing closely on one set of teacher–student interactions is an important opportunity for unpacking the complexity of learning intervention and educational casework. However, it is useful to then consider these insights and skills in the context of multiple learners. More complex sets of interactions are not the same as just adding on. Instead, with each additional learner and any other mediators, a different dynamic altogether is generated, within which learning intervention professionals need to make sense of what is supporting learning. Learning intervention needs to happen within the ZPD. Being able to target the teaching to be in the ZPD is one of the most difficult aspects of teaching: it depends on a teacher's knowledge of each student as a learner as well as of the domain of curriculum and the ATRiUM capabilities that are supporting and hindering learning.

References

Berman, J. (2011). SToPV: A five-minute assessment of place value. *Australian Primary Mathematics Classroom, 16*(4), 24–28.

Feuerstein, R. & Feuerstein, S. (1991). Mediated learning experience: A theoretical review. In Feuerstein, R., Klein, P., & Tannenbaum, A. (Eds.), *Mediated learning experience (MLE): Theoretical, psychosocial and learning implications.* London: Freund, 3–5.

Feuerstein, R. & Rand, Y. (1974). Mediated learning experiences: An outline of the proximal etiology for differential development of cognitive functions. *International Understanding, 9/10*, 7–37.

Fisher, D. & Frey, N. (2008). *Better learning through structured teaching: A framework for the gradual release of responsibility.* Alexandria, VA: Association for Supervision and Curriculum Development.

Gay, G. (2010). *Culturally responsive teaching: Theory, research, and practice.* New York, NY: Teachers College Press.

Gay, G. (2013). Teaching to and through cultural diversity. *Curriculum Inquiry, 43*, 48–70. doi:10.1111/curi.12002

Hattie, J. (2009). *Visible learning: A synthesis of over 800 meta-analyses relating to achievement.* Abingdon: Routledge.

Hattie, J. (2011). *Visible learning for teachers: Maximising impact on learning.* London: Routledge.

Hattie, J. (2015). The applicability of Visible Learning to higher education. *Scholarship of Teaching and Learning in Psychology, 1*(1), 79–91.

Hattie, J. (2016). Shifting away from distractions to improve Australia's schools: Time for a reboot. Jack Keating Memorial Lecture, University of Melbourne, June.

Hattie, J. (2017). What works best in higher education. Keynote address, University of Melbourne Teaching and Learning Conference, May.

Hattie, J. & Yates, G. (2014). *Visible learning and the science of how we learn.* Abingdon: Routledge.

Jung, L. (2007). Writing SMART objectives and strategies that fit the ROUTINE. *Teaching Exceptional Children, 39*(4), 54–58.

Ladson-Billings, G. (1995). But that's just good teaching! The case for culturally relevant pedagogy. *Theory into Practice, 43,* 159–165. doi:10.1080/ 00405849509543675

Ladson-Billings, G. (2014). Culturally relevant pedagogy 2.0: a.k.a. the remix. *Harvard Educational Review, 84,* 74–84.

Lidz, C. (2002). Mediated learning experience (MLE) as a basis for an alternative approach to assessment. *School Psychology International, 23*(1), 68–84.

Liem, G. & Martin, A. (2013). Direct instruction. In Hattie, J. & Anderman, E. (Eds.), *International guide to student achievement.* New York, NY: Routledge, 366–368.

Macfarlane, S. & Macfarlane, A. (2013). Culturally responsive evidence-based special education practice: Whaia ki te ara tika. *Waikato Journal of Education Te Hautaka Mātauranga o Waikato, 18*(2), 65–78.

McWilliam, R., Casey, A., & Sims, J. (2009). The routines-based interview: A method for gathering information and for assessing needs. *Infants and Young Children, 22*(3), 224–233.

Mitchell, D. (2014). *What really works in special and inclusive education: Using evidence-based teaching strategies* (2nd ed.). London: Routledge.

Pameijer, N. (2016). *Assessment for intervention: A practice-based model.* Keynote address, International School Psychology Association Conference, Amsterdam, July.

Paris, D. (2012). Culturally sustaining pedagogy: A needed change in stance, terminology, and practice. *Educational Researcher, 41,* 93–97. doi:10.3102/00131 89X12441244

Skuy, M. (1997). *Mediated learning in and out of the classroom.* Moorabin, VIC: Hawker Brownlow.

11
EVALUATION OF LEARNING INTERVENTION

After implementing any learning intervention there needs to be a careful evaluative phase that is based on the evidence collected during the intervention. This phase has three elements. The first element is a response to the final question of the Educational Casework Process – How did the intervention support the student's learning? The second element comprises evaluative questions focusing on the implementation of the intervention. These questions aim to specifically understand what factors within the implementation supported or impeded the effects of the intervention. This information is crucial for designing future intervention for particular students, as well as for building professional knowledge that will be used in other educational casework opportunities. The third element is a review of the practice of the learning intervention professional, a focus that is imperative for building capacity for future intervention at all layers. This chapter is thus an opportunity to draw on hindsight, by looking back at decisions made and practising professional reflection in response to the questions:

- How effective was the intervention for this student's learning? What is the next step?
- What implementation factors (competence, organisation and leadership) supported or impeded the effect of the intervention?
- How did my practice as a learning intervention professional support the intervention?

Effectiveness of the intervention

Response to the question about the effectiveness of the intervention for student learning is more than a simple description of outcomes, whether intended or unintended, and the factors that supported and hindered learning (see Chapter 6).

Considered more deeply, this evaluative focus draws on evidence about responsiveness to intervention in order to support decisions about whether a continuation of this type of intervention is appropriate. Essentially this is the difference between what the student brought to the educational casework and what they have since achieved. In simple terms, it is the difference between what was known and what could be done and what is now known and can be done, and why this change has happened.

In many cases, the next step in casework for a student will be to take intervention-related information into account in inclusive classroom programming by way of Steps 3 and 4 of the Responsive Teaching Framework. These steps define what students bring as learners and what needs to be taught now. These questions are particularly appropriate when there has been a short-term intervention designed to fill gaps in a student's knowledge or skills development, or to accelerate learning so that the student is better able to engage with class learning opportunities (Layer 2). If the intervention is part of longer-term instructional strategy (Layer 3), then the questions will be slightly different with a focus on how to best support this student in the next phase of learning, or within the next topic in the class program. For example, if the student's learning needs mean that there is a need to provide more opportunity to practise vocabulary for each topic, then this will be continued but may be adapted based on the evaluation of the student's previous vocabulary learning.

In the Educational Casework Process, we draw on scientific research to support case analysis and design of intervention, and we again return to these sources as we evaluate the effect of the intervention and its implementation. Additionally, it is necessary to consider how the outcomes align with the published evidence, and what might have contributed to any differences.

Key implementation factors

Intervention depends on multiple factors that separately and together can influence the effect and the integrity of the intervention. It is vital for learning intervention professionals to be conscious of these factors and to take time to determine how they have supported or hindered learning. Integrity of intervention is about how well an evidence-based set of learning opportunities and teaching strategies have been implemented, in reference to previous research.

Evidence supporting a particular program is not enough for us to be sure it will work in different contexts and with different learners. We also need evidence about the way the program was implemented in the field (Kelly & Perkins, 2012) in order to better understand how to take an evidence-based intervention and implement it for other students. The field of *implementation science* has a focus on making programs and interventions effective in real-world contexts. Distinctions have been drawn between a specific intervention that aims to make change for learners, and its implementation, that is, the activity of carrying out the intervention in systemic contexts (Fixsen, Naoom, Blasé, Friedman, & Wallace, 2005; Dunst, Trivett & Raab, 2013; Kelly, 2012). Such focus on implementation has implications for all educational initiatives in terms of their promotion, prevention, early intervention and fidelity (Fixsen, Blasé, Naoom, & Wallace, 2009). The core components, or implementation drivers (Bertram, Blasé, & Fixsen, 2015), of implementation science relate to issues of competence, organisation and leadership. By considering these dimensions alongside the Educational Casework Process, we highlight aspects of intervention implementation that need to be considered in evaluation as well as supported throughout intervention.

The competence of all involved in learning intervention is vital to the effectiveness of intervention. We have stressed this dimension many times. Specifically, foundational competence of learning intervention professionals lies in their assessment of student learning needs, sourcing evidence to support the design of learning opportunities, and the selection of teaching strategies that will best meet specified needs. As well, the competence of the people providing and mediating the learning opportunities, and those who are responsible for supervisory support and monitoring of effect, is vital. Finally, there is also a need for competence in evaluating the intervention in order to inform future intervention.

Organisation supports many aspects of the intervention and is pertinent to scoping and accessing evidence to support decision-making. It involves organising the assessment (from preliminary to outcomes), organising the learning opportunities (including design, arrangement, intensity and resourcing) and the mediation (or teaching), constructing feedback and reports, and structuring the evaluation.

Leadership in this model directly refers to school and education system leadership that supports larger-scale intervention. The essence of this support is school leadership that values and supports learning intervention. As well, in the context of educational casework, leadership is more closely positioned within the intervention activity. Responsive classroom teachers and educational casework professionals need to share leadership responsibility as appropriate during any learning intervention. Some more detailed reflective questions about key implementation factors are included in Chapter 12.

Documenting learning intervention

Many education systems and schools have structures and expectations around documentation of learning intervention for some of their students. Usually these documents are developed to meet administrative and accountability requirements of systems and are reviewed and rewritten regularly in light of planning and review meetings. There are many different names for these in education systems including individual education plans (IEPs), individual learning plans (ILPs), individual intervention plans (IIPs) and personalised learning plans (PLPs). In keeping with the language used in this book, we term these educational casework plans (ECPs). This individual plan complements Inclusive Class Programs (ICPs) (Graham, Berman & Bellert, 2002) that a class teacher develops and maintains.

Written plans make the processes of planning evident; they are punctuation marks which try to capture the process at different points of time, documenting the decision-making that has occurred and outlining expectations of the people involved. Such written documents explicitly define the shared understanding that has been developed by all involved. They contain information about the scope of the intervention, that is, the focus, contexts, timing, people, place and space for the intervention. They also include the assessment used throughout the intervention; the specific learning opportunities and their arrangement, intensity and resourcing; and any specific teaching strategies. The plan also makes evident the constructive alignment (Biggs & Tang, 2011) that is necessary in learning intervention, between the intended learning outcomes and the activity that is being put in place to teach towards, and to assess, those intended learning outcomes. Reporting and evaluation are also key issues to be noted.

When working in educational casework for learning intervention it is important to be aware of the expectations of systems and schools in terms of documenting practice. This is part of Step 1 of the Educational Casework Process that refers to frameworks within which the professional activity is to be carried out.

Whatever the context, the following key questions need to be asked:

1   What documentation is required? What is the purpose of the documentation? Who will have access to it?
2   What is to be included in it? Is there a specific structure?
3   Who will contribute to compiling it?
4   How will the student and family be involved?
5   What is the time frame for reviewing the documentation? How does this happen?

Effectiveness of my own practice

Reflective practitioners are constantly asking themselves questions about their own practice, how it supported learning intervention and how it needs to be strengthened further. We need to understand how competence, organisation and leadership of learning intervention professionals support the intervention and what next steps in professional development may be necessary. Consideration of this question links to the second step of the Educational Casework Process, which concerns what each professional brings to their practice.

Within this second step of practice, there are reflective questions about cultural and professional competence that can be used as guides for reflection. There are also prompts to consider relevant developmental and educational knowledge and the limits of knowledge and extent of competence. In the remainder of this chapter, we provide some reflections on three aspects of reflective practice itself, formal requirements, ethics and beliefs.

Formal requirements for reflection

Reflective practice involves professionals "routinely evaluat[ing] their own knowledge, skills and practice and us[ing] this for the ongoing professional development of themselves and others" (DEWA, 2015, p.11). For learning intervention professionals such reflection leads to continued learning. Reflective practice is made explicit in professional frameworks for learning intervention professionals in various ways. An example of what is involved in reflective practice taken from the Core Competencies for psychologists in Aotearoa New Zealand is provided in Figure 11.1.

In psychology and in education much reflection is carried out within supervisory relationships, and is complemented by individual personal reflection activities that respond not only to inherent sustainable learning and personal growth factors, but also to professional registration and system accountability requirements. In most countries there are professional standards for those working in learning intervention against which professional competence is checked. In the UK and the US there are standards specifically for special educators, but this is not yet the case in Australia (Dempsey & Dally, 2014) or New Zealand. The set of Australian Professional Standards for Teachers (AITSL, 2011) provides a systemic reference for all teachers across all career stages, however. Although only three of the AITSL standards are highlighted as being specific to teachers of students with disabilities in the Victorian *Special Needs Plan* (Victoria Education and Training, 2016), every standard is relevant in some way for learning intervention teachers and for learning intervention practice.

REFLECTIVE PRACTICE

This set of competencies covers the steps involved in the attainment and integration of information regarding one's practice. It includes critical and constructive self-reflection and seeking external review of one's practice (including supervision). Reflective practice and professional development in psychology is viewed as a continuous process of accurate self-assessment, understanding the skills necessary to be a psychologist and undertaking activities for professional development. This is often done in consultation with a supervisor. The psychologist will be able to demonstrate:

Knowledge	Skill
Understanding of their personal strengths and weaknesses, patterns of behaviour, emotional and cognitive biases, motivation, beliefs and values and how these may impact on clients and professional functioning.	• Accurate reflection on and evaluation of their own practice (skills, knowledge and bias). • Management of the impact of personal characteristics on professional activities. • Recognition of and practice only within the limits of their professional competence.
Understanding of limitations and boundaries of their competence.	• Planning for, establishment, prioritisation, implementation, and evaluation of professional development plans based on critical self-evaluation and critical feedback.
Knowledge of the need for professional development and how to identify areas for their own professional development.	• Articulation of clear learning objectives. • Effective use of supervision and constructive use of feedback.
Knowledge of potential occupational risk factors	• Integration of learning. • Effective self-care.

FIGURE 11.1   Reflective practice competency for psychologists

Source: New Zealand Psychologists Board, 2015, p.12.

Ethical practice

In learning intervention practice we aim to change outcomes for our students. There are many ethical issues around this type of involvement in others' lives that we need to consider and respond to carefully. It is not possible to deal with ethics at the beginning of casework and then not think about these kinds of issues again. Instead, the ongoing consideration of ethics is core to reflective practice. Specifically, guides for ethical practice have been developed that are integral to the work of learning intervention professionals (see, for example, Victorian teaching profession code of conduct, VIT, 2015). Codes of conduct and ethical behaviour are culturally reflective and therefore need to be considered within cultural contexts. To go some way towards aligning professional codes with Indigenous culture, the New Zealand Psychological Society has produced Codes in both English and Te Reo Māori (New Zealand Psychological Society, 2012). Since it is not meaningful to have direct literal translation, it is important to have cultural mentors interpret the sense (kaupapa) of these guidelines for ethical practice.

A focus on ethics reminds us of the purpose of all learning intervention and the need to ensure all our practice is supportive of the self-determination of all students. Ethics permeate everything we do, as individuals, as groups of professionals and as contributors to systems. We need to ponder ethical issues as they arise and ask whether decisions were appropriate and continue to be appropriate, or whether changes need to be made to protect the integrity of learners and families, or teachers, or the intervention process itself.

Beliefs and attitudes

A dimension of reflective practice, and of knowing yourself as a learning intervention professional, is related to personal conceptual understanding and attitudes about such big issues as inclusion and special education. Ethical issues can arise when learning intervention professionals have particular opinions about inclusion that are not necessarily the same as those of the families and teachers with whom they are working, nor aligned with the spirit of statements like the *Salamanca Statement and Framework for Action on Special Needs Education* (UNESCO, 1994) or the Melbourne Declaration (Dawkins, 2008). A developmental progression in this domain of professional practice has been articulated as moving from a "mere acceptance of diversity" to a "commitment to ethical decision-making and quality inclusive education" (Bentley-Williams and Morgan, 2013, p.173). Professionals in learning intervention are expected to hold positions at the higher end of this progression. However, this can be complicated. For example, professionals in segregated special education facilities will be influenced by that situation, by their experiences of intervening in that context and by the attitudes and beliefs of families with whom they work. Conscious understanding of these influences is necessary in such situations.

Even the definition of 'inclusion' can be problematic. It is vital that each professional has a clear understanding of the notion that is more than "to teach *all* students in *one* class" (Gordon, 2013, p.754). Many education systems and schools still operationalise inclusive education this way as a simple placement issue. We have considered this simplistic interpretation of inclusion earlier in this book. It is important for all professionals to explore what this construct means for them in terms of theory and practice so that conversations with families and schools are well founded. It can be useful to consider how, for example, issues around inclusion, learning intervention and educational casework can be explained to families and colleagues as a way to clarify and reflect on complex issues. It is important for all of us to understand what we believe in this domain, as beliefs influence decision-making and how we engage with our students, their families and other colleagues and professionals as we navigate the challenges of educational casework.

Within the steps of educational casework, professional activity generates many contexts for considering and evaluating professional competence, organisation and leadership. Some possible reflective questions that can be used individually or collaboratively include: How well did we scope this learning intervention? How well did I organise and implement the assessment accompanying each phase of this process? How well did we include the family and student in decision-making? How well did we access and interpret the appropriate research to support the intervention?

Many opportunities to reflect will be related to collaborative partnerships, particularly the partnership between classroom teachers and educational casework professionals, and should be considered together as well as separately. Reflective practice is not necessarily a solitary process. Many of us find it much better to reflect in collaboration with others through processes of supervision or mentoring. Individuals need to consider how they learn, and reflect, best. Most of us have some sort of supervisory relationship within which some reflective practice occurs. For some lucky practitioners an unconditionally positive supportive relationship provides all they need to plan and engage with opportunities for professional growth. Others may need to seek out mentors who can support their opportunities for reflection and professional growth.

Summary

In this chapter we have briefly explored some key dimensions of evaluation that are expected in learning intervention. It is a professional responsibility to ensure that practice builds on evidence generated within intervention, to understand what it tells about how best to intervene for particular students, to understand how the particular intervention may work for others and to recognise how continuing professional development builds the capacity of learning intervention professionals. Core components of intervention implementation derived from implementation science have been presented as ways of thinking about what makes intervention effective. These are to do with the competence of the people involved, as well as with organisation and leadership for effective learning intervention. Evaluation of our own practice is also important, with issues related to ethical practice to be considered, since all learning intervention aims to make a difference in people's lives and must be done sensitively and ethically. As well, the importance of attitudes and beliefs about foundational ideas such as inclusion has been positioned as fundamental to effective reflective practice.

References

Australian Institute for Teaching and School Leadership (AITSL) (2011). *Australian Professional Standards for Teachers.* Melbourne, VIC: AITSL. https://www.aitsl.edu.au/docs/default-source/apst-resources/australian_professional_standard_for_teachers_final.pdf

Bentley-Williams, R. & Morgan, J. (2013). Inclusive education: Pre-service teachers' reflexive learning on diversity and their challenging role. *Asia Pacific Journal of Teacher Education, 41*(2), 173–185.

Bertram, R., Blasé, K., & Fixsen, D. (2015). Improving programs and outcomes: Implementation frameworks and organisation change. *Research on Social Work Practice, 25*(4), 477–487.

Biggs, J. & Tang, C. (2011). *Teaching for quality learning at university* (4th ed.). Maidenhead: McGraw Hill.

Dawkins, P. (2008). *Melbourne declaration on educational goals for young Australians.* Melbourne, VIC: Ministerial Council on Education, Employment, Training and Youth Affairs.

Dempsey, I. & Dally, K. (2014). Professional standards for Australian special education teachers. *Australasian Journal of Special Education, 38*(1), 1–13.

Department of Education, Western Australia (DEWA) (2015). *Competency framework for school psychologists.* East Perth: DEWA.

Dunst, C., Trivett, C., & Raab, M. (2013). An implementation science framework for conceptualizing and operationalizing fidelity in early childhood intervention studies. *Journal of Early Intervention, 35*(2), 85–101.

Fixsen, D., Blasé, K., Naoom, S., & Wallace, F. (2009). Core implementation components, *Research on Social Work Practice, 19*(5), 531–540.

Fixsen, D., Naoom, S., Blasé, K., Friedman, R., & Wallace, F. (2005). *Implementation research: A synthesis of the literature.* Tampa, FL: University of South Florida, Louis de la Parte Florida Mental Health Institute, National Implementation Research Network (FMHI Publication #231).

Gordon, J. (2013). Is inclusive education a human right? *Journal of Law, Medicine and Ethics*, Winter, 754–767.

Graham, L., Berman, J., & Bellert, A. (2002). Practical literacy programming for students with disabilities: Making IEPs work in the classroom. In Gordon, B. (Ed.), *Practical literacy programming.* Sydney, NSW: Primary English Teachers Association (PETA), 121–135.

Kelly, B. (2012). Implementation science for psychology in education. In Kelly, B. & Perkins, D. (Eds.), *Handbook of implementation science for psychology in education.* Cambridge: Cambridge University Press, 3–12.

Kelly, B. & Perkins, D. (Eds.) (2012). *Handbook of implementation science for psychology in education.* Cambridge: Cambridge University Press.

New Zealand Psychological Society (2012). Code of ethics for psychologists working in Aotearoa New Zealand, Te Tikanga Matatika. Prepared by the Code of Ethics Review Group, a joint working party of the New Zealand Psychological Society, the New Zealand College of Clinical Psychologists and the New Zealand Psychologists Board, Wellington.

New Zealand Psychologists Board Te Poari Kaimātai Hinengaro o Aotearoa (NZPB) (2015). Core competencies for the practice of psychology in Aotearoa New Zealand, www. psychologistsboard.org.nz/cms_show_download.php?id=411

United Nations Educational, Scientific and Cultural Organisation (UNESCO) (1994). *The Salamanca Statement on principles, policy and practice in special needs education.* Paris: UNESCO.

Victoria Education and Training (2016). *Special needs plan,* www.education.vic.gov.au/about/department/Pages/specialneeds.aspx?Redirect=1

Victorian Institute of Teaching (VIT) (2015). *The Victorian teaching profession code of conduct.* Melbourne: VIT.

12

FRAMEWORKS FOR REFLECTIVE EVIDENCE-BASED PRACTICE IN LEARNING INTERVENTION

In this book we have examined the processes of educational decision-making for professionals charged with the responsibility of intervening in the learning of individual students who experience difficulties. A number of frameworks related to learning intervention have been presented to support practice. These frameworks are intended to make explicit the thinking and decision-making that is necessarily inherent in much learning intervention, and to provide reference points for consideration of future actions and for later evaluation. The questions they contain are the basis of the Educational Casework Process. Together with those in the Responsive Teaching Framework they act as prompts for reflection during and after any learning intervention cycle. Professionals can use these questions to structure personal reflection as well as in supervision relationships. The questions can also support planning for professional learning, and act as a framework for gathering evidence for accountability purposes, such as teacher or other professional registration requirements. In this final chapter, we present a collation of the frameworks so that they are easily accessible for use in practice, that is, to specifically scaffold the process of learning intervention through evidence-based educational casework.

The Educational Casework Process

The Educational Casework Process, derived from the Responsive Teaching Framework, is aligned with the work of learning intervention teachers and other educational professionals, such as educational psychologists, speech pathologists and occupational therapists. Both educational casework and responsive teaching go through the same phases of planning, intervening and evaluating, but the relevant steps are framed differently to account for the different perspectives needed. The eight key guiding questions for the Educational Casework Process, which clearly summarise the eight steps within casework, have been used to structure this book.

1　What frameworks do I need to consider?
2　What do I bring as a teacher or learning intervention professional?
3　What do we already know and what do we need to find out about this student's learning and development?
4　What are the priorities and parameters (scope) of the intervention?
5　How do we intervene?
6　What did this student learn?
7　What reporting and feedback support this student's learning?
8　How did the intervention support the student's learning?

Within each of these steps there will be further fine-grained questions to prompt practice that focus on different aspects of the casework, and there are many of these embedded within this book. In this final chapter we have highlighted some of these, as scaffolds for professional practice in learning intervention. In particular we focus on scoping, evidence-based practice, assessment embedded within casework, planning learning opportunities and teaching strategies, and evaluating learning intervention. To finish off we focus on the particular situation of professional education for learning intervention professionals and provide some scripts for engaging with learners about what learning intervention is, and how it will happen.

Scoping learning intervention

Scoping is about determining the priorities and parameters of the intervention. It is guided by the following questions from Chapter 4.

1　How was this learning intervention instigated? What sort of reporting will be required?
2　What is the focus of the learning intervention in reference to curriculum and the ATRiUM capabilities?
3　What is the context within which the learning will be applied?
4　What is the time frame for the intervention?
5　What people are involved in the intervention (professionals, teaching assistants, family and other students, professional education student)? What is the current learning group?
6　What is the learning environment within which the intervention is to be implemented?
7　What layers of learning intervention are appropriate? How will these be connected to classroom teaching?
8　What factors will support and hinder intervention implementation?

Accessing evidence for learning intervention

Evidence is used throughout educational casework, and it may come from a range of sources, not just from scientific research evidence. In this book we have identified four strands of evidence that need to be brought together to underpin decisions at each step of educational casework. We are considering what intervention towards the intended learning is evidenced in scientific literature, in professional experience (own and colleagues) and from family and student perspectives, and how these four bodies of evidence be brought together into effective learning intervention. Each of these is discussed in Chapter 5, and they are summed up in the guiding questions:

- What is the evidence from scientific research about the effectiveness of particular learning opportunities or teaching strategies?
- What evidence from professional practice do I bring in relation to this student's learning needs and the focus of intervention?
- What is the evidence from the student and family about response to previous intervention, and current issues that will affect intervention? How can these three bodies of evidence be brought together to underpin learning opportunities and teaching strategies?
- What evidence do I need to gather as the intervention is implemented?

Planning assessment for learning intervention

It is important to plan assessment carefully in order to gather the appropriate information needed to make informed decisions about learning intervention. We have considered the purposes of assessment and the content of assessment as foundational to decisions about how to do assessment. Specifically, assessment strategies, tools and interpretation processes need to be carefully selected in order to gather the most valid and useful information on which to base intervention. We have used two key dimensions, the purpose of the assessment and the content of the assessment, against which any decisions about how to do the assessment is referenced. Table 12.1 sums up the considerations in Chapters 6, 7 and 8, and provides a scaffold for practice.

Planning learning opportunities and teaching strategies

The general principle for intervention embedded in this book is to start with the class program, then to think about adjustments and then consider alternatives outside the class program. Of course, any long-term supports, such as assistive technology, and any specific skill development required by the student need to be considered from the outset. Pulling together these two perspectives will result in learning intervention that is positioned within the most appropriate layers of support. The following key questions, discussed in Chapters 9 and 10, summarise this crucial step in learning intervention.

- What learning opportunities (tasks, instruction and materials) are appropriate?
- What arrangement and intensity of learning opportunities are appropriate?
- Who should mediate the learning opportunities?
- What layers of learning intervention are appropriate?
- What should be the size and make-up of the learning group?
- How are these learning opportunities to be resourced?

TABLE 12.1 Assessment planning in educational casework

WHY (Purpose)	WHAT (Content)	HOW (Approach and strategies)
Preliminary	*What do we already know and what do we need to find out?*	
3	Depends on the nature of the referral and the questions being asked. Development and learning and the factors that could be hindering and supporting that development and learning.	Gathering of existing assessment information in records and reports from home, school and from other outside agencies.
4	1. Curriculum referenced 2. Capabilities referenced (the dimensions of human functioning; ATRiUM)	Informal and formal assessment including standardised, normative and criterion referenced assessment by multiple disciplines (educators, psychologists, speech pathologists, paediatricians, physiotherapists, occupational therapists).
	Learning environment referenced (including teaching)	
Baseline	*What is the starting measure of learning in the focus area (actual achievement)?*	
5	The knowledge or skills that are the focus of the intervention.	Criterion referenced (knowledge and skills).
	Demonstration under conditions defined in intervention, may include generalisation and transfer, if that is a dimension that needs to be included	Can be isolated knowledge and skills or embedded in other tasks.
Monitoring	*What is the response to teaching as it is happening (actual and assisted achievement) and factors supporting and hindering learning?*	
5	As for baseline.	Some form of collecting measures of learning on multiple occasions during intervention. Often checklists that are completed as a session is in progress, or at the beginning or end of each session, or after the session based on observation during the session.
		Can be teacher and/or student managed.
		Incidental observation or observational checklist, teacher report or student self-report.

(*Continued*)

TABLE 12.1 (Continued)

WHY (Purpose)	WHAT (Content)	HOW (Approach and strategies)
Outcomes 6	*What did the student learn?* • the intended learning outcomes (actual and assisted achievement); • any unintended learning outcomes; and, • factors that supported and hindered learning? As for baseline.	Often a re-administration of the baseline assessment. Needs to be sensitive enough to measure change in the time period of the intervention. Opportunity to demonstrate learning in classroom or other setting, and to do this again at a later time. Incidental observation or observational checklist, teacher report or student self-report.
Feedback and reporting 7	*What feedback and reporting support this student's learning?* As for outcomes.	Sharing of gathered evidence of learning (intended and otherwise), perceptions of growth and development, sense of achievement.
Evaluating 8	*How did the intervention support this student's learning?* Difference between baseline and outcomes assessment, evidence of transfer across contexts and maintenance over time. Factors that supported and hindered implementation	Analysis of gathered evidence.

Evaluating intervention implementation

It is important that the processes of educational casework, including planning, assessment, evaluation and documentation do not take over from the processes of intervention, although they are what supports effective sustainable learning. A balance between implementation and intervention is required, but the reason we are doing learning intervention is to support accelerated learning for students, and this must remain the primary direction for all activity.

* How effective was the intervention for this student's learning? What is the next step?
* What implementation factors (competence, organisation and leadership) supported or impeded the effect of the intervention?
* How did my practice as a learning intervention professional support the intervention?

The first question is based on the built-in assessment that will determine the student growth during the intervention, from pre- to post-measures. Evaluation in terms of whether the investment in more intensive or expensive intervention has resulted in accelerated learning, or whether leaving the student to engage in the usual would have been just as effective. Further examination of this question is outside the scope of this book, but can be managed through careful planning, implementation and analysis of assessment (see Chapters 6, 7 and 8).

The second question is about core components of implementation and is further examined through the following sets of questions that have been adapted from Blasé, Van Dyke, Fixsen and Bailey (2012) to align with the frameworks and language in this book.

Evaluating competence

- How will the recruitment and selection processes increase the likelihood that the evidence-based practice will be implemented well?
- How does selection compensate for the limitations of training, coaching and data-driven feedback (performance assessment)?
- What training specific to this intervention is required?
- What coaching (observation, feedback and support) is required to ensure specific knowledge and skills are applied?
- How effective is the application of this knowledge and these skills?
- How well is assessment information used to assist staff to improve effectiveness using the intervention practices?
- How well is competence supported by funding, policy and resources?

Evaluating organisation

- How well is evidence of process fidelity and outcomes used to support implementation?
- How well do school administrators support learning intervention staff?
- How does the system support intervention through funding priorities, policies and enacting of legal responsibilities?

Evaluating leadership

- How does technical leadership (processes for ensuring competence and organisation) support implementation?
- How does adaptive leadership (challenging current processes, and facilitating professional learning) support implementation?
- How do these two types of leadership integrate and mutually compensate to support implementation?

Evaluating professional and ethical practice

The focus on evaluation of professional and ethical practice within educational casework is guided by the second step of the Educational Casework Process, ECP

2: What do I bring as a learning intervention professional? and elaborated on in the following questions:

- What cultural competence, professional competence and assumptions about case or context do I bring to this casework?
- Why are we doing this casework? What is the appropriate extent of involvement? What ethical dimensions are to be considered?
- What do I know about this domain of development and learning (this condition, disability, syndrome)? What assumptions are inherent in my knowledge and previous professional experience? What do I understand about what supports and hinders learning for this domain of development and learning? What else do I need to research?

In terms of ethical practice we can also consider:

- How well did we scope this learning intervention?
- How well did we organise and implement the assessment accompanying each phase of this process?
- How well did we include the family and student in decision-making?
- How well did we access and interpret the appropriate research to support the intervention?

The logical consequence of this type of reflective and ethical practice is determination of where next for the learning intervention professional, in particular, what further professional learning is appropriate at this time. There will never be a time when professionals know all there is to know about any particular domain of development, learning or teaching and thus can stop learning themselves. Instead, sustainable professional learning within practice is essential and needs to be guided by responses to the questions above.

Intervention as part of professional education

Many professional education programs in learning intervention involve a specified number of days of supervised practice that are required for recognition that leads to qualifications in special and inclusive education and in allied health professions. Those completing professional learning degrees are often already experienced teachers who may be asked to carry out a short, targeted intervention in order to advance their own learning and to demonstrate competence. They may have to submit evidence of that intervention and of reflective practice around it for assessment. Therein lies the real purpose of such an intervention, which needs to be taken into account from the beginning. Such a learning opportunity for teachers is invaluable; much can be learnt from focusing exclusively on one learner for a short period, and on what the professional does most effectively in teaching.

Talking with students within learning intervention

If you are asking a student to work with you as part of a professional learning experience, then that is how the intervention should be framed for both of you, and for the student's family and teachers. In this case, the school student's learning needs are important but not the priority; the teacher's learning needs are the priority. However, ethically it is imperative that the student gets something out of this experience as well, and that the opportunity to provide effective intervention exclusively for a student is positive for all. Such a context shapes the purpose of learning intervention differently to other occasions of learning intervention. This section provides some guidance for those involved in professional practicum situations, remembering that such intervention is always just one layer of intervention and that any individual intervention needs to be considered in relation to what is happening for that learner in the classroom.

In light of this, it is important to carefully consider the framing of short term intervention practice and the selection of a learner with whom to work. To do this we have returned to the Responsive Teaching Framework for structure, and aligned it with the deliberate actions of responsive teachers (DARTs) (Chapter 10). We have also provided questions to guide the conversations that will explicitly frame the learning intervention as effectively as possible in Table 12.2.

A couple of situations need to be explicitly articulated as part of establishing the partnership for intervention of professional and student, specifically when carrying out assessment and short-term intervention for the purposes of professional learning. The following are two example scripts: the first aims to set expectations about the intention of the intervention and of sharing responsibility, and the second is for explaining assessment, particularly when it is formal testing.

> I am a teacher who is studying further to get better at teaching. I need to practise my teaching as part of that study and hope you will be able to assist in that process. It will involve [number] sessions of [number] minutes, within which we will focus on [curriculum content]. We will start by working out what you can do and what we will aim to learn in these sessions. Then we will see how the teaching has helped; I will give you feedback on your learning and you can give me feedback on my teaching. I would be interested in knowing what tasks you enjoyed and how they helped your learning, and what tasks you didn't like, and why. I would also be keen to hear any suggestions about how teaching can be made better for you.

> I am a teacher/school psychologist/speech language therapist (some elaboration) learning more about how to use assessment that helps me understand how people are learning (or developing, or feeling, or ...).

Explain what the particular session is going to involve. Most assessment strategies have a prepared script for this but if not write something at the appropriate age

TABLE 12.2 Prompt questions for the deliberate actions of responsive teachers (DARTs)

Adapted RTF questions for explicit shared responsibility in intervention	Deliberate actions of responsive teachers (DARTs)	Prompt questions for conversations about the intervention
1. What is this intervention?	Set expectations about intention of the intervention and of sharing responsibility (DARTs 1 and 2).	Why are we working together? For how long? How many sessions? Who is involved and will know about it?
2. What do I bring as a teacher/tutor/therapist?	Establish expectations of sharing responsibility and meaning (DARTs 2, 5).	Who am I? What do I bring as a teacher/tutor?
3. What do you bring as a learner?		Who are you? And what do you bring as a learner?
4. What do you need to learn now?	Defining current competence and goals for learning, and relevance of learning for other times and situations (DARTs 3, 4 6 and 7).	What can you do now? And what will you be learning?
5. How will we do this?	Explain learning activities and frame the need for noticing learning during and after (DARTs 3, 4 and 7).	What learning activities will we engage in? How will we know what you have learnt?
6. What did you learn? What helped you to learn? What got in the way? What next?	Explicitly define new competence (knowledge and skills) and what supported and hindered learning (DARTs 4, 5, 6 and 7).	What did you learn? What can you do on your own, and what can you do with assistance? What does this tell us about what you are ready to learn next? What supported your learning? How can my teaching support future learning for you?

level for the student. Describe some of the types of activities that will be included and set expectations of the range of difficulty and challenge. For example:

Some of what we are going to do will be easy and some will be hard.

Beginning scripts such as these are just that – the beginning – and they need to be adapted to suit the particular learning intervention relationship and context. With experience, such explanations to learners can be shaped to be most meaningful and realistic. This is an important foundation for the following intervention, particularly for students who have been experiencing difficulties and therefore may be somewhat sceptical about the possibilities of an intervention, and about their own learning. Sensitivity to these aspects of a learner's experience can support what is said so that it provides a solid foundation for the partnership between the learning intervention professional and the, often reluctant, student.

Bringing it all together into learning intervention

All intervention at school contributes to how well a learner continues to learn into the future. It is always important to remember that life experiences contribute to the development of all of us and that those at school have profound effects on the rest of our lives. For learners who experience significant learning difficulties or disabilities, their experiences with teachers are vital in building self-belief and possibilities for the future. Just about everybody is able to name a teacher who made a difference, who sparked a lifelong passion for a subject, or helped develop a belief in the self as a learner or an actor or a mathematician or a creative designer or a nurturer. However, the life experiences of learners who experience difficulties are also peppered with stories of how teachers did not have enough time for them, or found them disruptive.

While schools are judged by how well they do in national and state-based assessments and how many students go on to prestigious universities, the sidelining and exclusion of learners with different learning pathways will continue. For most high-flying learners, any school and any teacher would have managed decent outcomes, setting students up for tertiary education and opportunities in their professional lives. Instead of using the high achievers as a measure of excellence in education, we can look at this differently, by judging schools on the growth they have generated, particularly for students who experience difficulties learning for any reason.

Hattie's (2015) push for a year's growth for a year's teaching encourages us to think about responsive teaching and educational casework through the notion of accelerated learning. Learning intervention at Layers 2 and 3, involving small group or individual intervention, thus has to aim to accelerate growth through intensive learning opportunities and individually responsive teaching strategies. Sustainability of learning that is instigated or accelerated through learning intervention is considered in terms of how that accelerated learning is evident in the classroom. Learning intervention will be most effective when planned and implemented by intentionally responsive teachers and learning intervention professionals who gather evidence to support their educational decision-making, who design intervention that is most appropriate at the time and who evaluate it sensibly so that each student's learning is optimised. Whether learning intervention is needed to fill gaps that have been missed through lack of opportunity to learn, whether there has been inappropriate teaching or whether dimensions of a student's life and development interfere with learning, it is always the same process of using appropriate assessment to make sense of what is supporting and hindering learning, and then responding with the most appropriate evidence-based learning opportunities and teaching strategies to accelerate learning at the time.

Summary

In this final chapter we have provided sets of professionally reflective questions and frameworks drawn from the previous chapters, to guide effective practice in learning intervention. Additionally, these frameworks can be used for guiding professional reflection and the evaluation of practice. They can also assist in checking the continual development of competence for both students and teachers that is sustainable learning. These frameworks are scaffolds and, as such, are designed to make practice explicit, but also to fade over time, so that as competence grows, reliance on them will be reduced as much of the framework is internalised, and each practitioner becomes their own unique learning intervention professional.

References

Blasé, K., Van Dyke, M., Fixsen, D., & Bailey, F. (2012). Implementation science: Key concepts, themes and evidence for practitioners of educational psychology. In Kelly, B. & Perkins, D. (Eds.), *Handbook of implementation science for psychology in education.* Cambridge: Cambridge University Press, 13–34.
Hattie, J. (2015). *What doesn't work in education: The politics of distraction.* London: Pearson.

INDEX